# MANOS
REBUILD THE MAN BENEATH THE MASK

## LEE POWELL

Copyright © 2025 by Lee Powell

All rights reserved.

No part of this book may be reproduced in any form or by any electronic or mechanical means, including information storage and retrieval systems, without written permission from the author, except for the use of brief quotations in a book review.

**For Carolina** — *my extraordinary wife, who showed me that love can be both safe and sacred, a sanctuary for the soul.*

**For Harrison and Oscar** — *my sons, my best friends, the teachers I never expected to encounter.*

*It's an honor to walk beside you.*

**For the man I was —**

*not forgotten, not shamed. He burned so something real could live. His ashes feed the roots of this work.*

**For God** — *once wrestled, resisted, cursed — and still He waited. Now I thank Him, not for what was lost, but for what the fire revealed.*

**For all men** — *the silent, the unseen, the tired, the ones performing underweight no one else can see. The ones who kept it together when everything was coming apart. This is for you. Not blueprint but compass. Not advice but witness. The scar proves you survived. The wound is the doorway home. The man was always there — the code just needed compiling.*

# THE MAP

Every man runs on code — some chosen, most inherited.

When that code fails, you don't need more advice; you need a map.

**This is it.**

**BRIC** is the route every man must walk to rebuild a life that **holds** — one that's true, aligned, and strong enough to carry the weight of what matters.

**Bare** down to truth. **Reforge** trust and connection. **Install** discipline until it becomes instinct. **Cohere** every part of yourself until your entire system — thoughts, words, actions, habits, and character — runs in truth.

You'll loop through these four stages more than once — each time stronger, steadier, clearer. You'll notice the later chapters loop between practice and purpose. That's deliberate. Real integration isn't tidy — action tests meaning and meaning refines action.

That's the work. That's the way home.

# THE MAP

## B — BARE (Chapters 1–4)

### From Drift → Foundation

Stop lying about what's broken. Face the crash. Admit what's not working.

See the masks and inherited scripts. Listen to the body's warning lights.

Let the truth land in your nervous system before you try to fix anything.

### Checkpoint Question:

*Am I still drifting, or have I planted my feet?*

### What this section does:

Inner work — truth, body, awareness.

You strip back to what's real and meet yourself without armor.

You stop running from reality and learn to stand in it.

## R — REFORGE (Chapters 5–9)

### From Isolation → Connection

Choose your values. Face your wounds. Find your brothers.

Clarify what matters. Name the patterns that keep rewriting your story.

Learn the data of emotions. Build intimacy and trust where isolation once ruled.

### Checkpoint Question:

*Am I still hiding, or am I letting myself be known?*

### What this section does:

Relational work — truth in connection.

You **reforge trust.**

You reconnect with men, women, family, and life itself.

You realign to chosen values and reconstruct your identity on something true.

THE MAP

## I — INSTALL (Chapters 10–11, 14–15)

### From Ideas → Embodiment

Turn tools into habits.

Order your money. Care for your body. Build visible wins.

Reboot when you relapse. Learn from the crash log instead of erasing it.

### Checkpoint Question:

*Am I just consuming ideas, or am I running the system?*

### What this section does:

Behavioral work — truth in action.

Brings truth into daily behavior.

Turns practice into pattern.

Orders money, body, and systems.

Makes life reliable — **discipline becomes instinct.**

## THE MAP

## C — COHERE (Chapters 12–13, 16–17)

### From Maintenance → Mastery

Why you wake up. What outlasts you.

Find your North Star and live it out loud. Lead yourself before you lead others.

Give your kids patterns worth inheriting. Build momentum that endures beyond you.

Coherence means your words, actions, and energy now say the same thing.

### Checkpoint Question:

*Is my life in coherence, or am I still divided against myself?*

### What this section does:

Systemic work — truth extended into the world.

**Coherence is the real definition of success:** when thoughts, words, actions, behavior, habits, and character all agree.

It's not outcome-based — it's **systemic trueness**.

The whole man becomes aligned; nothing fights itself anymore.

It's the state where presence itself transmits truth.

## THE MAP

**And there are the quiet ones...**

The men who built their lives with calloused hands and now stand in sheds full of tools no one else knows how to use.

They stare at what they made and wonder if any of it still matters.

Legacy used to mean building; now it means being remembered for who you became when the building stopped.

## FIND YOURSELF

- Still pretending it's fine → Start with **BARE**

- Know it's broken but stuck → Go to **REFORGE**

- Have ideas but no action → Jump to **INSTALL**

- Doing tasks but feel empty → You're ready for **COHERENCE**

Read in order — or jump to where you're bleeding most.

# PART ONE
# BARE – FACE THE CRASH

Get your feet back on solid ground. You've been running on autopilot, pretending it's fine. The body knows better: the tight jaw, the shallow breath, the sleepless nights. You can't fix what you won't face. This part strips away denial and brings you back to what's real.

**Call to action:**
Stop drifting. Face the crash. Plant your feet.

# ONE
# THE LIE OF THE LINE

The first stroke wasn't me. It looked straight enough, clean enough, what anyone would expect. But it was a lie. I drew it because I thought that's what the world wanted—the version of me that looked right on paper, that passed inspection. Then I drew another line, the real one. Crooked, imperfect, alive. The truth surfaced: the first line lies. It always has.

---

"The psychological rule says that when an inner situation is not made conscious, it happens outside, as fate."
— Carl Jung [i]

---

The room hummed with the sound of pens scratching, shoes scuffing tile. Chalk squeaked a white scar across the board. Mr. Bunting turned with the slow rhythm of a man who had taught the same sentence for twenty years.

I sat in the back row, thumb against tongue. Warm film. A small shelter. I thought I was invisible.

Then the laughter cracked. Not the kind you join—the kind that hunts. I froze, thumb half-out, shining. He saw me. Chalk still in his hand. A mouth twisted into a sneer honed for sport.

"Powell. Fourteen and still sucking your thumb? God help you."

The class detonated. Desks shook. Arms slapped in rhythm. Eyes bright with cruelty. Heat rose up my neck. Salt. Shame. The muscles in my cheeks roped tight, thumb hidden under a book like an illicit comfort.

I quit that day—not from strength, but from ridicule. The urge didn't die. It only burrowed deeper. I learned a rule: don't get caught.

Years later, the thumb had new disguises. Nicotine was the shadow that never left. Quitting cigarettes was easy—once I swapped them for gum, and the gum for lozenges. The lozenge was perfect: invisible. You could sit in a meeting, tongue pressed against your gum, and no one would ever know. It looked like composure, but it was dependency dressed up neat.

My oral addiction was weaponized for years — thirty-five of them — and eventually, the truth landed. A tiny white lozenge was still running my life.

The drinking came later, toward the end. Not all through the marriage, not the whole story. It started when I was trying to get out—of the companies, the weight, the version of life I'd built around denial. The pattern was there all along, waiting: the bottle first became an answer. When the house was full, I skulled it straight in the tool shed, hidden like contraband. When it was empty, the bottle sat cold in the fridge, poured into thick crystal glasses. We were already living separate lives long before the separation was official.

At night, bare feet on tile, a dim light over the sink throwing long shadows, I poured again. First: warmth. Second: edges softened. Third: the day blurred just enough to tolerate. It wasn't celebration. It wasn't company. Just numbness. I told myself I wasn't a drunk. No blackouts. No missed work. No slur. But the reflection didn't lie.

Marriage was no refuge. I stayed, telling myself it was for the boys, the business, stability. Truth was simpler: I didn't yet know how to leave with integrity. Every flaw reflected. Every weakness exposed.

Later in this book, I'll tell you about the day the man at the bottle shop knew my order before I even spoke. That story deserves its own space, because it was the moment it hit me, I wasn't hiding anything at all.

Once, a psychic reading was relayed to me through the person I was married to at the time. The woman had said she saw a man plastered in Post-it notes, each stamped in block letters: **FAILURE**. Her closing words were simple: *you're at a crossroads—stay or go.* The image stuck. It was brutal and accurate—a mirror of years spent trying to earn approval through performance.

That was the scar tissue: the ultimate proof that people-pleasing doesn't work. What starts as survival curdles into something darker. You silence yourself to keep the peace, and what follows is predictable: depression in the body, resentment under the skin, relationship satisfaction rotting from the inside out. Authenticity erodes. Hostility builds. Until finally it leaks sideways—sarcasm, muttered expletives, slammed doors, withdrawal. *Okay then, I guess it'll be me again—add it to the fucken list.* All the words I was too scared to say to her face came out crooked everywhere else. [ii] [iii]

Gaslighting eats at a human's scaffolding. One night, the truth surfaced — admitted, spoken aloud — and by morning it was gone. Denied. Rewritten. Like it never happened. If not for the cameras, I might have thought I imagined it. The recordings were my anchor, proof the words existed outside my skull.

That's the cruelty of gaslighting you almost go mad in the end. You second-guess yourself until you start erasing yourself. You stop trusting your own eyes, your own memory, your own gut. You're forever scanning for external proof because the inner compass has been shattered. It's terrifying when your guidance system no longer feels like your own.

That night something cracked open — a darkness finally naming itself. What came through was raw, bewildered — almost disbelieving that truth could still be met with presence. For a twisted moment it was beautiful, like truth had finally broken surface. And then it shut. Denied. Buried. I thank God for that recording. Without it, I could have lost my mind.

Some nights I mapped out an exit. Not drama. Logic. A quiet unmaking she would finally feel. Maybe she'd regret it. Maybe she'd see. But the darker thought came too: it would have crowned her. The tragic widow with assets, sympathy, and narrative. My death as her victory lap. Even my fantasy betrayed me.

My son and I made a pact to quit together. For me it was nicotine. For him, something else. I broke it. The shame of that cut deeper than anything she ever said.

I tried everything. Packs flushed. Gum binned. Lozenges drowned. I even threw smokes onto the roof to prove a point—only to climb back later, desperate, drying out soggy tobacco like a starving animal. My palms stung on the rough roof, my mouth as dry and bitter as the habit I couldn't kill. A strong body, disciplined work, successful business... and still begging a soaked cigarette. Addiction makes liars of us all.

I lied most to myself. Even business turned against me. Fourteen years building code and deals, handshakes I mistook for brotherhood. Contracts I signed too fast, eager to escape corporate politics. I didn't want to pay a lawyer, let a friend skim them, told myself it was fine. People-pleaser logic. It cost me. When the valuation landed, it slapped me clean: a fraction of the worth, clauses I'd glossed over, language too soft to enforce. They held the cards; I'd signed them into their hands.

Thumb. Lozenges. Vodka. Contracts. Different masks. Same ghost. I wanted to be soothed, seen, secured—by anything outside me. The world sells wholeness from the outside in. But presence is an inside job. No pill, no paper, no praise could deliver it. I didn't need erasure. I needed integration. The boy with his thumb deserved protection, not contempt. The man with his lozenge needed a steadier anchor than sugar and shame. The father who broke the pact needed accountability and repair. The builder who signed the weak clause needed a spine, not a scapegoat.

Addiction never showed a monster; it showed a man using the wrong tools to numb real pain. When I finally saw that— saw it —I packed a tent and left for winter in Tasmania. Cradle Mountain. The kind of wilderness that doesn't care who you were before it swallowed you. Seven days alone, thirty kilos on my back—about sixty-six pounds—food drops mapped, EPIRB and sat phone in case I vanished. No towns, no stores, no signals. Just snow, wind, and a silence that could kill you if you disrespected it. Serene. Merciless. Holy.

I told myself it was for clarity, though truthfully, I was also hoping to get laid. It had been... sometime. But the mountain wasn't interested in my hunger; it fed me something different. Each climb stripped off another mask, each night in the freezing dark made me smaller, truer. The wilderness taught boundaries sharper than any therapist—if you don't listen, you die; if you do, you learn how to live.

When I came back, I painted. Not for art or success but to feel time loosen its grip. Color became meditation, the brush confession. Layer by layer I distilled the mess until it made a shape I could face—not perfect, just true. I didn't erase the old lines; I left their echoes visible, not relevant anymore but real, and then I drew a new line: aligned, cohesive, inside-out.

Presence. The first crooked line carried the man I thought I had to be—borrowed, misaligned. I left it visible, then drew the truer line. Past, present, and future layered in one frame, fracture and flame sharing the same space. Different masks, same ghost. But ghosts can be faced, and when faced, they change.

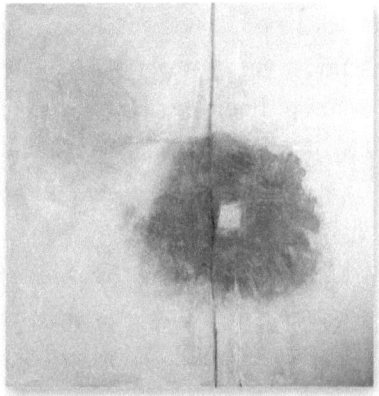

**Presence, 2025** *Acrylic, oil, and gold on canvas 150 × 150 cm (59 × 59 in) Lee Powell (Keny)*

There were mornings I could barely lift myself from the bed. My chest felt weighted, my body hollowed out, grief and exhaustion pressing down at once. What saved me wasn't strategy or some grand act of willpower; it was smaller, slower: painting, and the long, stumbling walks through the bush. I wasn't trying to become an artist. Truth is, I still don't think of myself as one. I was trying to be human—to work out my mess, to face the pain I'd endured and the pain I'd caused.

If you've ever sat in that place, you know it: the weight of mistakes, the wreckage of choices, the shame that whispers you should have been better. For me, painting began as guilt. After decades running companies, I'd built from nothing, after thirty years in a marriage that drained me, slowing down felt like a crime. I told myself I should be producing, grinding, achieving —yet there I was, standing before a canvas with colors in my hands. It felt almost wrong. But when I mixed paint, something shifted. The swirl of pigment calmed me. The act itself became meditation, like poetry—distilling a whole world into a few precise words.

That's the secret I learned: when you distill, you understand. Every canvas became a vessel for grief, disbelief, and the slow, strange ache of healing. Each brushstroke unearthed pieces of myself I'd hidden or buried until the canvas stopped being paint and started becoming a map of my own soul. I'd built my life on words. I created Scrivener for Windows, software used by writers across the world. I knew the rules of story—characters need flaws, wounds drive conflict, structure carries tension—but the rules dulled the pulse. Writing had turned into an aesthetic.

So, with painting I swore an oath: no rules, no tutorials, no efficient techniques. Just raw exploration. It was clumsy, slow, alive. And strangely, the paintings with the most crooked proportions, the least polish, were the ones people gravitated toward. Maybe because imperfection is where the truth leaks through.

Then came the canvas that changed everything. I'd planned an abstract called *Presence*—past, now, future mapped over golden-ratio points. I drew the "now" line by eye and missed the ratio completely. My first impulse was to sand it back and start again. Then the penny dropped: the line wasn't wrong; it was honest. It carried every program I'd absorbed—well-meant teachers, family rules, survival code. That misaligned line is how most men live. You don't erase it; you let it fade into the background while you draw a deliberate one—aligned to who you are, not who you perform. From then on, I kept the echo visible and laid a slower, steadier stroke through the ratio.

I didn't sand back the old one. I let it remain—a visible echo, a trace of who I'd been, and the man I was becoming. That's the lesson: we're already whole. The world keeps selling wholeness from the outside in—money, sex, approval, power—but alignment only ever comes from the inside out.

That's the lesson: we're already whole.

Looking back, I wouldn't wish the pain on anyone. But I can see its strange beauty now. It carved depth into me. It taught me to hold both joy and sorrow, to honor the fracture as much as the flame. Even the losses, the cracks in my own code—they shaped me. And in shaping me, they left me with more to give.

This is why I paint. Not to perfect, not to be an artist, but to be whole. To carry both fracture and fire. To remember that nothing is wasted, everything belongs. That crooked line was never a mistake—it was a truth revealed in color. And sometimes, when I catch myself reaching for that old comfort—tongue searching for a lozenge that isn't there—I remember: the boy with his thumb wasn't wrong. He was just looking for shelter in the only way he knew how.

## PRACTICES & DRILLS

### Reflection Prompt — Your Crooked Line

Write about one moment you've always carried as a mistake. Ask yourself: what if it wasn't a mistake at all, but simply what happened? What did it reveal about who you thought you had to be?

### Exercise — Echo Lines

On paper or canvas, draw a quick, imperfect line—your "crooked line." Leave it visible. Then draw a second, slower, deliberate line—your "true line." Step back and notice how both coexist: the echo of what was, and the clarity of what now is.

### Drill — Past/Future in the Now

Sit for five minutes. Bring up one memory from your past and one hope for your future. Notice how both appear only in this present moment. Ask yourself: if all I have is this moment, how can I inhabit it fully?

### Gratitude Reframe — Beauty in the Pain

List three painful experiences from your life. For each, name one unexpected gift it gave you—strength, compassion, or clarity. The aim is not to glorify pain but to see how grief becomes compost for growth.

### Takeaway

It's not what do I want from life, but what does life want from me—my gifts, circumstances, the wounds that became wisdom. We don't create our path; we're summoned to it. Look at the world: what needs repair? What tasks are lying around? At what point do my talents and gratitude meet the world's deep need?

Collapse is not the end—it's the doorway. Presence is power. The past and future may tug at you, but they only exist in the now. Mistakes are not detours—they are the ground of growth. Wholeness comes from integration, not erasure. What we call imperfections often become the truths others connect to most.

**Reflection Question**

What crooked line in your own life have you been trying to erase—when perhaps it was never a mistake at all?

## TWO
# WHEN THE LIFE YOU BUILT STOPS WORKING

"The most damaging phrase in the language is: We've always done it this way." – Grace Hopper [i]

The house was quiet that Tuesday afternoon, clock ticking in the kitchen, the cords in my neck pulled tight like wire, but inside me, everything was collapsing.

I wasn't in a dramatic spiral. No screaming argument. No flashing lights. Just the suffocating sense that the scaffolding of my life — the marriage, the businesses, the rules I'd lived by for decades — wasn't holding anymore.

From the outside, I was a man who had ticked every box: a thirty-year marriage, companies I'd built from nothing, money, respect. People nodded and said I had it together.

Inside, I was unraveling.

The numbers backed it. Men like me were falling apart everywhere:

1. Middle-aged men complete suicide nearly four times more often than women, with men in their 40s–50s at the highest risk.[ii]
2. Nearly seven in ten divorces are initiated by women, most citing emotional absence as the reason.[iii]
3. High-achieving men report disconnection from purpose at staggering levels, even while their résumés look flawless.[iv]
4. Men are roughly one-third less likely than women to seek professional help, yet when assessed, they show significantly higher rates of depression.[v]

I wasn't reading stats back then. I was living them.

There are two ways people change. The Zen teachers call them *satori* and *kenshō*. *Satori* is insight — you see the truth and act before the fire. *Kenshō* is pain — you wait until the fires in your house. Most of us choose the second. I did too.

A man named Mitch put the first crack of light into that darkness.

He wasn't a coach or a monk. He was a tree lopper, wiry and alive in a way I wasn't. His eyes carried the kind of energy you don't fake.

I asked him twice what he was doing to look like that. He shrugged me off both times. The third time, he stopped, wiped sawdust off his forearms, and said:

"Just finished something called 75 Hard."

Seventy-five days: no booze, two workouts a day, four liters of water, stick to any diet, take a daily photo, and if you miss one, you start again.

"It's about keeping your word to yourself," he said.

That line cut deeper than any insult I'd ever heard. Because I'd been keeping my word to everyone but me. Clients. Colleagues. Family. For thirty years, I'd kept the machine running — but not once had I truly held the line for myself.

By then I was thirty years deep into nicotine lozenges. Most afternoons ended with vodka straight from the bottle, and I called it stress relief. My body stayed strong on the outside, but inside I was scattered, hollow. Every swig came with the same whisper: this is not going to end well, Lee.

I'd never drunk like that before. But in the year leading up to separation, I didn't know how else to cope. Arrogance, to my surprise, turned the bottle into armor. Some nights I'd be half-cut, drinking straight from it, still holding conversations, cocky in a way only denial can be — convinced no one noticed. That was the ego's real trick: not that I was sharp, but that my wreckage was invisible, that I could keep the mask on while I was coming apart underneath.

And the pressure mounted. A good friend of mine rang almost every day in those last months: Have you done it yet? Have you told her? My father went to the grave married to a woman like that. It doesn't stop. What the fuck are you thinking? His words cut, but the truth in them cut deeper. Each call pushed the decision closer and drove me further into the bottle, nervousness and dread pooling until I swallowed it down in mouthfuls of fire.

One afternoon I drove to the bottle shop. Before I even rolled the window down, the guy inside had my order ready — a bottle of vodka and a six-pack of Guinness. He knew my name. He knew the routine. I remember thinking, that's convenient. Then the chill that followed: he knows my order because I've turned this into a ritual.

That was the scar tissue: the moment convenience showed me my reflection. I wasn't hiding anything at all. The pattern was already written in someone else's muscle memory — a stranger at the counter could see it clearer than I wanted to admit.

That's the trap of numbing. It doesn't hide the wound — it rehearses picking at the scab, so it bleeds just enough to feel, but never enough to heal. Every swig kept the cut open but dulled the sting. What I called stress relief was slow erosion, training myself to live inside the injury instead of walking out of it. Numbing kept the scab bleeding — enough to feel alive, but never enough to heal.

And I wasn't alone. Studies show men on the edge of separation drink more heavily than married men, not because they're thirsty, but because they're desperate to drown feelings they can't face. [vi] I fit the statistic perfectly — a strong body masking collapse, a silent bargain with the bottle, a dead man walking.

That night, I made a pact with myself: no booze, no nicotine. I'd start the next day. And for once, I did.

That was the pivot. Not 75 Hard exactly. Not Mitch's path. Mine.

But that wasn't the first time I'd had to walk away from a life that looked right but felt wrong. Long before the vodka, before the discipline, before the collapse and rebuild, I'd already learned what it meant to succeed at something false.

The book that started it — Passion Driven. Five thousand copies printed, three hundred and ten sold. On the cover, an ant hauling an orange slice uphill. I called it inspiration. It was projection.

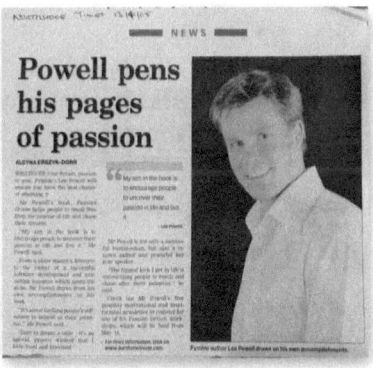

The boxes sat in my garage, stacked to the ceiling. Five thousand copies of *Passion Driven*.

On the cover, an ant hauling an orange slice uphill—one

hundred times its body weight. Small thing, big lift. The poster-child promise.

On paper I was fine. Thirty-five. Multi–six figures. Contracting for IBM, building the first generation of web-commerce systems—me and a Latin-American mate coding for banks, defense, government, and pharma. Porsche in the driveway, paid cash. Nice house.

Successful.

Performing.

But the boxes watched me.

I'd done the ladder: Toastmasters—won it. Professional Speaking certification—ticked. Early gigs—standing ovations.

*Passion Driven* hit the shelves at Dymocks, Angus & Robertson—every major store in the country.

I sold three hundred and ten copies. I should've been proud. Instead, I was fucking gutted.

Years of work, national TV, bookstores across Australia—and that was it. Three hundred and ten.

It felt like the universe laughing.

I'd been on the late Bert Newton Show—this clean-cut young man telling the world how to live better. I still have the VHS somewhere. And I'm scared to watch it. Maybe that's why I've never bought another player.

I'd built a website called **borntomotivate.com**, one of the first quote sites online—pulling a million hits a month back when that number meant something. No product, no business plan, just raw ambition and the illusion of momentum.

The system was laid out like rails.

Then the click.

In the course they taught the "formula": craft the story, pull the room tight, ride the cliff-edge, exit at the peak.

Not to change people. To prime the upsell—book, tapes, the next room.

It landed in my gut like a stone. A machine that sells hunger and calls it healing.

I drove home. Walked past the five thousand proofs of my own buy-in. Thought about my kids.

What was I going to model—integrity, or an **applause loop**? Preach character at night and run a manipulation funnel by day?

Here's the part that undid me: I was thirty-five and winning, speaking to fifty-year-olds with real scar tissue—divorce, bankruptcy, graves they'd stood beside.

Who was I to sermonize resilience I hadn't earned?

So, I stayed in IT. And the boxes gathered dust.

At first, I gave books away—mates, colleagues, anyone polite enough to take one. Then I got sick of the sight. Needed the space.

I loaded the car, drove the suburbs, stuffed letterboxes until my hands cramped. *Passion Driven* by a stranger. Maybe someone read it.

Maybe most went straight to the bin. I'll never know.

But that wasn't my first silence. It was just the longest.

I'd started earlier—at eighteen—with a terrible novel called *Burn Out,* and at twenty-one with a play called *Blood on the Tracks.*

Both rejected, both deserved it. The kind letters said, not for us. Keep writing. I did. Until I couldn't.

By thirty-five, *Passion Driven* was supposed to be redemption—the proof that persistence pays.

Instead, it became the proof that performance without truth is just noise.

So, I pivoted sideways—into **the writing-software business.** If I couldn't write the book yet, I'd build what writers use. Still closer to purpose, just ... lateral.

And that's the real story: the twenty-one-year gap between *Passion Driven* and this book.

Knowing what I wanted to say and refusing to say it until I had the scars to mean it.

Some voids are noble. Walking away was one of them. Not performing was the only honest performance I had.

We inherit more than our fathers' names.

We inherit their masks—the ways they chased worth, the symbols they worshipped, the silences they kept.

These images aren't nostalgia. They're evidence. Proof of the code I once ran, and the moment I saw it begin to copy itself.

# MANOS

Me at thirty-five, proud of my 2nd Porsche symbol *paid in cash*, blind to the story it told. I thought I'd made it. In truth, I'd just built a faster mask.

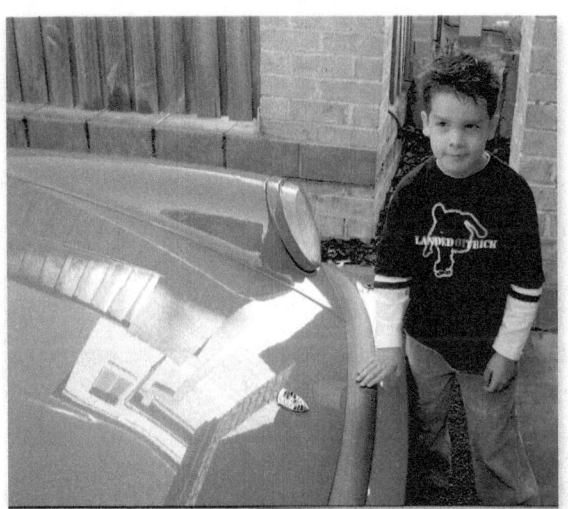

My youngest son at five, hand on the same car. He wasn't reaching for the car. He was reaching for me. That's the moment that haunts me now.

*My eldest son, picking up my 5th Porsche. years later. I can't decide if this picture makes me proud or quiet. Two generations shaped by performance, each trying to find what's real beneath it. We don't hand our sons the mask —they learn it by watching what we worship.*

That twenty-one-year gap taught me something crucial: the void that follows performance isn't empty—it's crowded. It's packed with every unspoken fear, every unfinished promise, every version of yourself you left behind. You can't outwork it, outdrink it, or out-plan it. You must sit there—stone still—until the noise dies down and the truth starts to hum again. Only then can you rebuild something real.

And this is where most men get it wrong. We wait for the "big blueprint." The 90-day plan, the guru system, the total life overhaul. But what cracks the old code isn't a plan. It's a single promise kept.

One line drawn.

The self-promise is the smallest but most dangerous code you'll ever write. Because if you can't keep your word to yourself, nothing else holds. Every other achievement rests on sand.

For me, the line was nicotine and vodka.

For another man, it might be porn. Or gambling. Or rage. Or the way he disappears into work when his kids are crying in the next room.

For some, it's the phone glow in the late hours. The endless gaming marathon. The beers that start as a reward and end as a chain. The pills pocketed from a friend's script. The quiet slide into affairs. The lost hours in betting apps. The way anger becomes the only language he speaks at home.

Every man's ghost wears a different mask. But underneath, it's the same code: a promise broken to himself, repeatedly, until he doesn't trust his own word anymore.

It doesn't matter what the line is. What matters is that it scares you because it's true.

The day you keep that one promise is the day you start building a life worth trusting.

## PRACTICES & DRILLS

### Reflection Prompt — Your First Promise

Write down one promise you've been breaking to yourself for years. Not the easy one. The one you avoid because you know it's true.

### Drill — Define the Rules

Set the exact terms. What counts as keeping it? What counts as breaking it? No gray zones.

### Exercise — Go Public (to Yourself)

Put it on your bathroom mirror or your phone lock screen. Somewhere you can't escape it.

### Reframe — No Resets for Slips

If you fail, you restart the clock. This isn't about streaks. It's about trust.

### Takeaway

Change doesn't begin with a master plan. It begins with one promise you finally keep. A man who won't stand where he said he would be isn't a man.

### Reflection Question

What's the crooked line you've been carrying — the one you've been excusing, hiding, or numbing — and what promise will you make today to redraw it?

# THREE
# THE FIRST LINE OF CODE

---

"Intentions lie.

Execution leaves receipts.

Receipts build the man.

The man then acts without thinking.

That is the only path from ruin to reliability."

---

I didn't start by fixing my life. I started by making my bed. That's not a metaphor. It wasn't poetic. It wasn't inspiring. It was ugly and small and almost insulting. Getting out of bed was one act. Making it was another. The second one mattered more.

Because when you're fucked—properly fucked—your word doesn't mean anything to you anymore. You've broken it too many times. Promises dissolve before breakfast. Plans sound hollow the moment your feet hit the floor. Your inner voice has learned to roll its eyes. So I didn't make a grand declaration. I didn't redesign my future. I didn't set goals. I pulled the sheet tight. I squared the corners. I stood there for a second longer than necessary, hands flat on the mattress, feeling the fabric under my palms. I did this. That was the first deposit.

Self-trust is a bank account. You don't refill it with speeches. You refill it with receipts. One action. Completed. No negotiation. When you're low—depressed, numb, brittle—that receipt becomes oxygen. You can't argue with it. You can't gaslight yourself out of it. You did the thing. The ledger shows a credit. Yeah—but I did this. That line matters more than people admit. It's the quiet "ah-ha!" that hits when you realize: trust isn't built on willpower; it's forged from proof you can't deny.

The mistake men make at this point is reaching for ambition. They say: "I'll do this, and this, and this, and this." No. That's how you erase the account before it's funded. Because when you miss three out of four, the nervous system doesn't say *progress*. It says *failure*. And failure isn't moral. It's neurological. You're writing code. Every promise you keep installs trust. Every promise you break corrupts it, rewiring your brain to expect betrayal—from yourself. You don't stack habits. You install one. Get one thing down. Get it airtight. Then—and only then—add another line. This is the epic shift: small isn't weak; it's the foundation that holds when everything else crumbles.

Eventually, my one thing became movement. Not fitness. Movement. I'd get up early, before the world started making demands. Before there were eyes. Before noise. I'd shuffle—because that's what it was—up a hill near my place. Not running. Not the performance people post online. A slow, stubborn forward motion, knees complaining, lungs burning before I'd covered two hundred meters. At the steepest part, my thighs would seize. I'd stop, hands on hips, chest heaving, sweat breaking across my forehead even though the air was still cool. Then hands over my head—that runner's posture that opens the chest and signals dominance to a nervous system primed to collapse. You're not dying. You're recovering. There was a bar at the top. Sometimes just a branch. Ten push-ups, shaking by six, arms trembling like they might snap. Ten sit-ups, neck straining against gravity. One pull-up—if I was lucky, chin barely clearing the bar before my grip gave out. That was it. No apps. No plan. No optimization. Just one execution, repeated.

That's when something unexpected happened. The movement became a conversation. If you get up early enough, there's no one to interrupt you. No audience. No performance. You can talk to yourself honestly. Not affirmations. Not pep talks. Real questions. One morning, halfway up the hill—lungs working, sweat breaking across my forehead, calves burning like fire—I found myself thinking about motivation. What is it, really? People worship it. Chase it. Blame its absence for everything they don't do. But motivation is fragile. It's a match. Strike it, and it flares. Bright. Hot. Promising. But if the wind picks up—and it always does—that match is gone in a second.

That's real life. Pressure. Fatigue. Conflict. Loss. Shame. The wind comes howling. If all you have is motivation, you're already dead—extinguished before the real work begins. But if you protect that match—shield it with one small, repeatable action—it can light something else. A fire. And once the fire's going, the wind doesn't kill it. It feeds it, turning sparks into an inferno that devours obstacles. That's the difference people miss, the "ah-ha!" that saves you: Motivation starts things. Drive sustains them. And drive is built from evidence—undeniable proof that you show up, no matter the storm.

Here's the loop, whether you like it or not: Execution builds evidence. Evidence builds identity. Identity drives automatic behavior. That's the code. Not intention. Not desire. Not vision boards. Evidence. I didn't decide I was a runner. I accumulated proof that I moved when I said I would—breath by fractured breath, rep by shaking rep. I didn't become disciplined. I became someone who kept one promise, and that identity rewired everything. Everything else followed, not from force, but from flow.

Men want to skip this part. They want meaning before mechanics. Identity before proof. Respect without receipts. It doesn't work that way. When you're rebuilding from the ground up, humility isn't optional. You start where you are, not where you think you should be. You earn the right to add complexity by first proving you can handle simplicity. Make the bed. Walk the hill. Do the rep. One line of code. Executed daily. That's how you stop lying to yourself. That's how you rebuild trust when trust is gone. This isn't about becoming superhuman. It's about becoming reliable to yourself again—grounded, capable, and free from the cycle of self-betrayal.

## Practices & Drills

### Reflection Prompt

Where have you been breaking promises to yourself that you never should have made in the first place? (Be brutal—list three. This exposes the ambition trap.)

### Drill

Choose one non-negotiable action you will complete every day for the next 14 days. It must be small enough to succeed on your worst day (e.g., make the bed, walk 200 meters). Write it down. Put it where you can't avoid it. No stacking—master this first.

### Reframe

You are not aiming for progress. You are aiming for proof. Systems beat willpower; evidence outlasts motivation.

### Exercise

At the end of each day, write one sentence: "I kept my word by _____." Nothing else. No journaling. No reflection. Just the receipt. Stack these—watch trust compound.

### Takeaway

Don't fix your life. Keep one promise. The fire builds from there.

### Reflection Question

If your identity is built from evidence, what evidence are you producing every day? (Answer this tomorrow morning—then act.)

## FOUR
# RUNNING DAD'S CODE

"Until you make the unconscious conscious, it will direct your life, and you will call it fate."— Carl Jung [i]

Men are running outdated psychological software — code inherited from fathers and grandfathers shaped for a different world. This code breeds emotional shutdown, relational drift, and, for too many, self-destruction.

The numbers are stark:

- Men are three and a half times more likely to die by suicide than women, with middle-aged men at the highest risk. [ii]
- Only about a third of men ever seek mental health care, compared to half of women facing the same symptoms. [iii]
- Men are more than three times as likely as women to experience alexithymia — the clinical inability to identify and express emotions. [iv]
- Men who cling to rigid, traditional masculine roles report far lower relationship satisfaction and significantly higher divorce risk. [v]

These aren't character flaws. They're system failures. We're running software built for survival in war and scarcity, and it's glitching under the demands of modern life.

The glitch goes deeper than code—it's about belief itself. Belief literally means having definite concrete assumptions about things we know little about. Either you know or you don't. Where does belief come from? It comes from pretending what you don't know is something you "know." You can't believe something all by yourself—you need others, hence why believers are in groups, while seekers are alone. Seeking is the nature of human intelligence, but people want to seek in the comfort of a belief system. It's like tying a boat to a pier and then trying to venture on an exploration. The inherited code isn't just behaviors—it's these untested beliefs we've never questioned, running in the background like malware we've mistaken for operating system.

. . .

Rick sat in his truck outside his irrigation supply warehouse in the dark, engine idling, air conditioning straining against the August heat. The cab smelled of PVC primer and chlorine, his shirt still damp with sweat from loading pipe all afternoon. His lower back was locked in a permanent spasm from fifteen years of hauling equipment, that specific burn between $L_4$ and $L_5$ that no amount of ibuprofen could touch. Fifteen years building his business from nothing. House, mortgage, kids in good schools. All the checkboxes his father's code told him to tick.

His phone lit the cabin. Text from his wife:

> "Kids asking where Daddy is again. Fourth dinner missed this week."

He read it. Felt nothing. No guilt. No anger. Just... absence. Like a phone showing 0% battery even though it's been plugged in all day. His chest was a hollow drum, no echo when struck.

Rick had followed the script perfectly: work hard, provide, don't complain, push through. The code had run flawlessly — until it didn't. Now it was draining his energy while giving nothing back. His marriage felt transactional. His kids felt like strangers. His shoulders carried weight that sleep couldn't lift. Every morning, he woke with his right eye twitching — that maddening flutter that started six months ago and wouldn't stop — feeling like he was failing at the things that mattered.

Approaching crash. Full system failure.

I knew that crash.

My grandfather fought in World War II. My father grew up in the aftermath — ration books, council housing, "finish what's on your plate." Survival shaped the family script be useful, keep moving, don't waste. But stoicism wasn't his way. Debate was. He challenged everything. Devil's advocate on permanent loop. I learned early that whatever I brought — excitement, certainty, even joy — would be met with a counter-case. Not cruelty. Just relentless cross-examination that trained me to look outside myself for approval, to pre-empt disapproval before it arrived.

Over time, that became people-pleasing in a $2,000 suit.

It worked — until it didn't. I built companies, earned, provided. From the outside: steady. On the inside: spine bent around other people's expectations like a question mark. When conflict rose, I defaulted to over-functioning and explaining, thinking perfect clarity would buy me safety and connection. It never did. It only taught me to perform closeness without asking for reciprocity.

There were specific phrases that would hijack my body without warning. Someone would challenge me in a meeting, and I'd launch into debate mode — not my voice, but my father's argumentative stance taking over. That forward lean, the rapid-fire counterpoints, the need to win even discussions that didn't matter. My hands would move like his — jabbing the air for emphasis, building cases nobody asked for. Forty years later, still channeling a man who couldn't let anything rest.

The most haunting was catching myself with my own boys. They'd come to me with something they believed in — a business idea, a girl they liked, a risk they wanted to take — and I'd feel my mouth forming the opening argument against it. "Have you considered..." "What about..." "That's interesting, but..."

The same intellectual dismantling I'd received, now flowing through me. The wound becoming the weapon.

Years earlier, when they were still little. They came home from school with boxes of chocolates for a fundraiser — forty bars each. Backpacks hit the floor, shoes kicked off mid-stride, their whole bodies vibrating with possibility. "Dad, let's go! We'll sell them all today!"

My stomach tightened. That familiar squeeze of inherited caution. The debater's voice starting up: "It might be harder than you think. People are busy. Not everyone will say yes." But they wouldn't be slowed down. We walked into car dealerships up the road, and within two hours they were sold out. The next day they came home with more boxes, and I handed them off to their mother — my turn was over.

I was humbled. My doubt wasn't wisdom. It was inherited code. A script of limitation written by men who'd had their own enthusiasm cross-examined to death, passing down protection that had become prison.


Most men know these moments. The split second when your father speaks through your mouth.

The father's shutdown: "Because I said so, that's why."

The emotional amputation: "Don't cry. Be a man."

The soft mask at the dinner table: "No, it's fine. I don't mind."

The pub performance: bragging about money or women you don't care about, just to stay in the tribe.

Each one a piece of software you didn't write — but still run.

I started tracking mine like a programmer debugging code. The way I'd physically recoil when someone said "I love you" first. How my fists would clench when asked "How are you feeling?" The immediate pivot to work talk when conversation went deeper than weather. My father's defenses installed so deep I thought they were mine.

The strangest part was discovering which code came from which generation. The workaholism — that was grandfather, who built houses during the Depression. The emotional constipation — pure dad, who learned feelings were luxury items during post-war rationing. The people-pleasing under the tough exterior — that was all three generations, each adding their own encryption to hide the soft parts.

Today's world demands adaptability, presence, and emotional range. The old code treats those as bugs, not features. Keep running it long enough, and it corrupts everything: relationships, purpose, even the bond between father and son.

That's why the operating system needs rewriting. Not by discarding strength and resilience — those are still vital. But by weaving them into something fuller. That's where triads come in. They're the antidote to brittle scripts: strength with vulnerability, independence with connection, discipline with compassion. Where the old code taught suppression, triads teach integration.

Picture this: your son fails at something that matters to him. The old code says, "shake it off, don't be soft." The upgraded code — strength with vulnerability — means you sit beside him, share your own failure story, then help him stand back up. You're still teaching resilience, but now with connection instead of isolation. Your hand on his shoulder, not pointing at the door. That's not theory. That's an update written for the environment men live in now.

The rewrite isn't instant. It's line by line, moment by moment. Catching the old code before it runs. Choosing the new response. Sometimes failing, running the legacy script anyway, then trying again tomorrow.

Progress, not perfection. Evolution, not revolution.

## PRACTICES & DRILLS

### Reflection Prompt – Debug Your Inheritance

Write down one rule you absorbed from your father or father figures. Ask: how often do I still follow it? Where has it served me — and where has it failed me?

### Drill – Run One Upgrade

Choose one outdated behavior and replace it with a small, deliberate change. If the old code says, "shut down in conflict," the upgrade might be state one feeling out loud.

### Gratitude Reframe – Honor Without Copying

List one strength your lineage gave you that still serves — resilience, work ethic, discipline. Then name one part you're willing to release — suppression, denial, silence.

### Takeaway

You're not failing because you're weak. You're failing because you're running legacy code that no longer fits the operating environment. Updating it isn't disloyalty — it's the only way to honor what came before without being chained to it. Drift kills more men than disaster — and running old code unconsciously is the ultimate drift.

### Reflection Question

What is one inherited rule you still run today — and how would your life change if you rewrote it?

# FIVE
# THE DASHBOARD YOU NEVER HAD

"The body benefits from movement, and the mind benefits from stillness." — Sakyong Mipham [i]

Men today face an emotional disconnection problem that shows up in both data and daily life. Large population studies show men score higher than women on alexithymia—the difficulty of identifying and describing feelings—and are more likely to meet clinical thresholds for it in general samples. [ii] That matters because alexithymia consistently travels with heavier loads of depression, anxiety, and strained relationships. [iii]

And when men do reach the point of needing help, they still use mental health services far less often than women, even as treatment access overall has grown in the past decade. [iv] The result is a silent backlog: stress signals pile up in the body while the man insists, he's 'fine.

The good news: emotional awareness is trainable. When men practice structured methods to read and process their emotions, studies show measurable drops in depressive symptoms and improvements in relationship quality. [v] This isn't theory—it's survival data. The system can be updated, but only if you're willing to start reading the gauges you've ignored.

Frank stood in his garage at 8 p.m. on a Wednesday, wrench in hand, staring at his own reflection in the chrome of a customer's Harley. Oil under his fingernails, sweat dried to salt on his neck, and something broken behind his eyes that no tool in that shop could fix.

He'd built his motorcycle repair business from nothing. Twenty years of six-day weeks, grease-stained invoices, and a reputation so solid that riders drove two hours just for his touch. But that Wednesday night, surrounded by the evidence of everything he'd built, Frank couldn't remember the last time he'd felt anything real.

"I say 'I'm fine' about fifty times a day," he told me later, voice rough from decades of exhaust fumes. "To my wife, my kids, my customers. Hell, I even say it to myself. But my body knows I'm lying."

His chest stayed tight as a torque wrench. Shoulders locked at his ears like they were bolted there. Sleep came in fragments—two hours here, ninety minutes there, always waking with his throat cinched shut, a dull ache radiating up into his temples. His body was screaming data at him, but Frank had never learned to read the instruments.

Most men live like this. Dashboard lit up like a Christmas tree —warning lights flashing, gauges in the red—while we tape over the alerts and keep driving. We call it strength. We call it handling our business. Really, it's flying a 747 with our eyes closed, waiting for gravity to settle the argument.

I learned this the hard way one Thursday morning in 2021. Conference call with business partners. Seven figures on the line. My chest had been sending signals for days—that peculiar tightness like someone was slowly turning a vise around my ribs. Breath shallow as a puddle. Vision starting to tunnel at the edges.

"Lee, what's your position on the equity split?"

The words came out of the phone clear enough, but they hit my brain like static. I opened my mouth to respond with my usual measured voice. Nothing came. My throat had locked. Not metaphorically. Physically seized like someone had poured concrete down it.

"Lee? You there?"

I managed to croak out "Need more time to review" and killed the call. Then sat there in my home office, hands shaking, sweat trickling down my back, trying to figure out if I was having a heart attack or just discovering the price of ignoring every warning light for five years straight.

The doctor said panic attack. The body said system crash from running on fumes since 2013.

That's the danger of having no dashboard. You miss the early signals—the tightness that means pressure building, the shallow breath that means you're in survival mode, the locked jaw that means there's truth you're not saying. You don't see the slow corrosion in your marriage, the distance growing between you and your kids, the gradual fade from human to performance machine. You can't fix what you can't read.

The roots run deep. When I was small, my parents would brag to their friends: "He's such a good kid—you can put him in his capsule behind the couch at a party, and he'll sleep right through it." I absorbed that praise like scripture. Good boys don't cause trouble. Good boys don't need things. Good boys disappear on command. The compliment became operating system be invisible, be easy, be gone.

Forty years later, I was still running that code. During my first marriage, when conflict rose, I became a ghost. Not dramatic exits—just a slow fade to gray. Demands were laid out, and I'd shrug. "Okay. Whatever works." I told myself I was being accommodating. I was bleeding out through a thousand paper cuts of suppressed truth. Disagreeing meant conflict. Conflict meant discomfort. So, I swallowed it all—unaware the cost was compounding daily until my body started folding in on itself—breath shallow, shoulders knotted, eyes burning from fatigue.

Business ran the same program. Early in my career, I left millions on the table—deals I'd nurtured for months, contracts that should have been signed in blood. Instead, I relied on handshakes and the fantasy that being "easy to work with" meant never asking for what I deserved.

I told myself I preferred a handshake to paperwork. And I did. Still do. But here's what I learned after losing seven figures: most people don't honor their word the way you hope. Now I reframe it—if we can't survive the tension of negotiating a contract without someone storming off, the business won't survive either. Better to fail at the table than in the field.

That autopilot people-pleasing cost me at least $3M. Realistically, closer to seven. All because I couldn't feel the warning signals my body was sending that sick flutter when I didn't speak up, the dull ache in my chest when I smiled through another bad deal, the exhaustion that came from performing "good guy" instead of being real.

The fracture split wide open when a friend and business mentor—a man who'd built his company from scratch and sold it for a billion dollars—confronted me. We sat across his mahogany desk, the same desk where he'd signed that enormous deal, and he looked at me with the kind of focus that cuts through bone.

"Lee, I can't trust you."

My chest seized. My ears went hot like someone had turned on a furnace. Trust was the one virtue I thought I had nailed.

"What do you mean you can't trust me?"

He didn't blink. "Because you'll just tell me what you think I want to hear. You don't want to rock the boat. That's not trust. That's manipulation. A real friend tells it straight. I don't have to agree, but I need to know where you stand."

The words landed like ice water in my veins. He was right. People-pleasing wasn't kindness. It was manipulation dressed in a nice suit. It was lying to myself and others because I was addicted to being liked. My mouth said, "I'm fine." My body had been screaming the opposite for years.

Your body is a cockpit, and every sensation is a gauge. Chest is your pressure altimeter—when it tightens, you're climbing into dangerous altitude. Breath is your airspeed indicator—when it goes shallow, you're about to stall. Jaw is your engine temperature—when it locks, something's overheating. Shoulders are your fuel gauge—when they're at your ears, you're running on fumes. Gut is your navigation system—when it churns, you're off course.

Quick translation manual: Tight chest = pressure building, time to release. Shallow breath = tunnel vision active, need to expand view. Locked jaw = unspoken truth, find words or it will find fists. Shoulders high = chronic tension, the body keeping score. Stomach churning = values violation, something's not aligned. Hands clenched = rage condensed, better to speak it than swing it. Head buzzing = cognitive overload, system needs reboot. Lower back aching = carrying everyone else's weight.

These aren't mystical tea leaves. They're data. Flesh and bone trying to tell you what your mind won't admit.

Alan could talk horsepower, bandwidth, quarterly metrics—anything measured.

But when his wife asked, "What are you feeling right now?" his mouth stalled like an engine flooded with fuel.

He wasn't cold. Just offline.

He could tell you the stock price of every company he'd ever worked for, but not the last time he felt peace.

When the counsellor finally named it — alexithymia — he laughed. "Sounds like a dinosaur."

She smiled. "It's just the common code men were taught. It means your feelings speak a language you were never taught to read."

For the first time, he didn't feel defective. He felt normal — and therefore fixable.

Most men aren't broken. They're just fluent in the wrong language.

"Normative male alexithymia" isn't pathology — it's conditioning. We were rewarded for suppressing data, not decoding it. We learned to mute signals that didn't help us win. So, when the heart finally speaks, it sounds foreign — like static on a clean frequency.

But feelings are data. They're just encoded in the body, not spreadsheets. The body never lies. It whispers in tension, pulse, and breath — truth that hasn't yet found vocabulary.

Most men inherit the command to ignore these signals. "Don't cry." "Man up." "Walk it off." "Nobody wants to hear it." We're trained to treat feelings like smoke alarms—annoying sounds to be disabled, not vital information to be heeded. We learn to perform "fine" so well that we convince everyone, including ourselves. Meanwhile, the body keeps perfect score, and the bill always comes due.

Without awareness, those inherited scripts run on autopilot. You deflect with "I'm fine." You minimize with "it's no big deal." You disappear with "Don't worry about me." Every time you swallow truth, you bleed integrity. Every time you perform instead of presence, you lose connection. Every time you ignore the dashboard, you edge closer to system failure.

Frank discovered this after three months of reading his instruments. Started small—set a phone timer for three times a day. When it buzzed, he'd stop for thirty seconds. Notice his chest. Check his breath. Feel his jaw. That's it. No fixing, no changing, just noticing.

Week one: "Jesus, I'm wound tight like a clock all day."

Week two: "I hold my breath whenever my wife starts talking."

Week three: "My chest gets tight before I even open the shop."

Week four: "I haven't taken a full breath in twenty years."

Then came the changes. Not dramatic. Surgical. He started telling customers the truth—your bike isn't worth fixing, or this will take three weeks not three days. He stopped agreeing to his wife's plans when he was already buried. He admitted to his son that he didn't have all the answers. Each truth felt like pulling out splinters—sharp, necessary, and followed by relief.

Six months later, he called me. "I had my first full night's sleep in a decade. My wife says she feels like she's married to me now, not some customer service robot. And get this—my business is up 30%. Turns out people trust you more when you stop bullshitting them and yourself."

He wasn't fixed. He was fluent.

Fluent in the language his body had been speaking all along. He could catch the tightness in his chest before it became rage at his son. He could feel the ache in his jaw before it snapped into silence at his wife. He could pause mid-conversation, drop his shoulders, and reset.

The numbers followed — better sleep, steadier work, stronger revenue — but the real gain was deeper. His son started lingering in the garage again, not because of the bikes, but because the man holding the wrench finally felt solid. His wife's tone softened. The house warmed.

Frank had discovered the thing most men miss:

Strength isn't ignoring the dashboard.

Strength is checking it and adjusting before you crash.

Frank had learned what most men never do: awareness isn't weakness. It's navigation. You can't fix what you can't feel. You can't change what you won't acknowledge. You can't install a new operating system while pretending the old one still works.

The dashboard doesn't fix the problems. But it shows you what's happening under the hood. It tells you when to pull over before the engine explodes. When to refuel before you're running on fumes. When to speak before silence becomes cancer.

Here's what changes when you start reading your own instruments: You sleep without bolting awake at 4:47, seventeen minutes before the alarm, already exhausted. Your chest opens and you can breathe. The chronic headache you thought was just life finally releases. You make decisions from clarity instead of fear. You stop apologizing for existing. Your energy returns because you're not burning it all maintaining a mask. The rage that used to explode at random finally has words instead of fists. You feel solid in your own skin for the first time since childhood.

And yes—your wife stops asking "What's wrong?" because you tell her before she must dig. Your kids stop walking on eggshells because your mood isn't a mystery. Your body stops screaming because you're finally listening. But those are secondary gains. The primary win is yours: you stop living as a passenger in your own life and start driving with your eyes open. You become a man who knows what he feels, says what he means, and stands where he stands. That's not just awareness. That's sovereignty.

Awareness isn't decoration. Awareness is survival. You can't fix what you can't read. You can't change what you won't name. You can't install a new operating system while pretending the old one still works. Awareness is the dashboard you never had. And once you start reading it, you can't go back to flying blind.

Frank came back months later, leaner, steadier, voice calmer. "I did it," he said. Not perfect, but present. He'd faced the debts, repaired one relationship, and — most of all — stopped running from himself.

What changed wasn't luck. It was his choice to sit in the fire instead of numbing it. He stopped chasing escape and started choosing repair. That was the real win.

ManOS is about rewriting code — but sometimes evolution means restoring the original firmware.

The human body isn't outdated; the operating system of nature still runs perfectly. It's the inputs that got corrupted. When I say, "keep the old code," I mean the biological truths that modern convenience tried to delete. We don't need nostalgia; we need alignment. The man who masters technology but forgets the language of his cells hasn't upgraded — he's crashed.

I've built and worked on systems with 99.99999% uptime requirements.

I've watched banks spend hundreds of millions on dark fiber just to shave milliseconds off trades — milliseconds that make fortunes.

I've sat with teams at Oxford unpacking the human genome when we still thought it would show us a tidy library of on/off switches for every disease.

And after all of that, I've never seen a system as complex as a single living cell.

A cell has over 100,000 surface receptors constantly sensing its environment and shifting its behavior in real time. [vi]

That's not metaphor. It's measurable biochemistry.

Cells are aware of what's happening outside them and adapt — they don't just run a static script.

Yet we still teach hereditary determinism like its destiny.

Ask a doctor which single gene causes your condition, and most can't tell you — because complex traits don't work that way. [vii]

Even the genome project didn't deliver the silver bullet.

The human genome is roughly 3 billion base pairs and about 20,000 protein-coding genes — but the differences that make us unique are spread across networks, not single switches. [viii]

We share about 60% of our genes with a banana and 98–99% with chimpanzees — numbers that shock people because they reveal how small changes create massive complexity. [ix]

The point isn't to bash medicine. I've contracted for big Pharma. I know what a billion-dollar, 20-year pipeline to market looks like.

Most people in it are genuinely trying to help. But the incentive structure of the system rewards monetizing treatments more than preventing disease. It's not villainy; it's economics.

And that's why *ManOS* exists — not to save you, but to return the controls to your hands.

The dashboard is there.

The feedback loops are there.

Use them.

Update the code.

Be the change first.

You'll see two sets of drills here. That's intentional.

The first teaches you the *language* — how to read what the body's been saying all along.

The second teaches you the *rhythm* — how to check those signals daily before you crash.

You can't scan a dashboard you can't read.

Learn the language first. Then run the system.

## PRACTICES & DRILLS I

### Reflection Prompt — Emotional Translation

Write one sentence your father, coach, or boss said that made emotion feel unsafe. Now write what your body does when you start to feel the same way.

### Drill — Translate the Body's Dashboard

When you can't name what you feel, locate it.

Jaw → anger or control.

Chest → grief or pressure.

Gut → fear or misalignment.

Give it a neutral name first — "energy in chest" — then a word later. Translation before definition.

### Reframe

You don't lack emotion. You lack access. And access can be trained.

### Exercise — 3-Minute Check-In

Set a timer. Close eyes. Ask the body three questions: What's tight? What's loud? What's mine? Write one line for each.

**Takeaway**

You were never numb — only untranslated.

**Reflection Question**

When did silence first feel safer than truth? And what would it cost to unlearn that language now?

## PRACTICES & DRILLS II

### Reflection Prompt — The Mask and the Mirror

Write down the last three times you said "I'm fine" when you weren't. Next to each, write what your body was signaling—tight chest, clenched jaw, whatever you notice in hindsight. This is your translation guide.

### Exercise — Body Dashboard Scan

Set three phone alarms: 10 a.m., 2 p.m., 6 p.m. When they sound, stop for sixty seconds. Check five points: chest, breath, jaw, shoulders, gut. Rate each from 1-10 for tension. Just notice. After a week, you'll see patterns—which times of day, which situations, which people spike your readings. (See also A2. System Health Checklist for a complete weekly dashboard tracking system.)

### Drill — Catch the Autopilot

Next time someone asks how you are, pause before answering. Feel what's true in your body. If you're about to say "fine" but your chest is tight, try the truth instead: "Actually, feeling some pressure today." Watch how the conversation shifts from surface to real.

### Gratitude Reframe — Thank the Warnings

Tonight, thank your body for one signal it sent today—even if you ignored it. The headache that said slow down. The tight chest that said speak up. The exhaustion that said rest. Gratitude for the warning lights keeps them functioning.

### Takeaway

Most men don't crash because they're weak. They crash because they're flying blind. Your body has been trying to tell you everything—pressure, fear, exhaustion, rage—but nobody taught you the language. The dashboard doesn't prevent storms, but it tells you when to change altitude.

### Reflection Question

What warning light have you been taping over the longest—and what would change if you finally addressed what it's trying to tell you?

# PART TWO
# REFORGE – REBUILD WHAT MATTERS

Repair the connection. Isolation kills faster than failure. Start by re-finding your own pulse — your values, your wounds, your truth — then bring that honesty to others. Brotherhood isn't comfort; it's accountability that keeps you alive.

**Call to action:**
Drop the mask. Find your men. Fight for connection.

# SIX
# LIVING BY THE VALUES YOU ACTUALLY CHOOSE

"The privilege of a lifetime is to become who you truly are." – Carl Jung [i]

Most of us don't choose the code we live by; we inherit it. A father's silence. A coach's bark. A boss's demand. You absorb their rules and carry them like invisible commandments: work harder, never show weakness, put others first, don't stop. Men don't just inherit wealth or poverty — we inherit code. Values clash with values, father against son, culture against individual, until the man himself chooses which law to live by. [ii]

I grew up in a house where my father played devil's advocate like it was oxygen. Whatever I brought — excitement about a school project, certainty about a career choice, even joy about a girl — he'd counter. Have you thought of this? But what about that? What if you're wrong? It wasn't cruelty. It was his way of preparing me for a world he saw as hostile. But the effect carved deep: nothing I offered would ever be enough on its own. Every thought needed defending. Every feeling needed justification. Every decision needed bulletproofing against imaginary prosecutors.

That inheritance feels like identity until the cracks show. For decades, I ran on borrowed scripts. From the outside, it looked like success—businesses built, bills paid, reputation intact. But inside, the system groaned. I'd catch myself making decisions that weren't mine at all, just automated responses to someone else's values. Legacy code still running in the background.

Collapse forced me to ask questions I had never asked: What values am I living? And what values do I want my sons to see when they look at me?

It was a brutal audit. I wrote down what I claimed to believe—honesty, family, growth, faith—and then checked it against what my calendar showed, what my bank statement showed, what my body showed. That's where the truth lives. The words on paper didn't matter; the lived record did. [iii]

The audit revealed something Jung understood decades ago: character is not automatic. You have to build it with effort and artistry. You have to wage a campaign. Without moral core and internal integrity, a Watergate-level betrayal will hit your personal life. Character is built in the struggle to overcome weakness.

The code revealed itself: I understood the distinction between resume virtues and eulogy virtues. Resume virtues are what get you hired, promoted, paid. Eulogy virtues are what get remembered when you're gone. Most men optimize for the resume and wonder why their eulogy column stays empty. The central fallacy of modern life is the belief that accomplishment predicts satisfaction, that happiness comes from achievement. But happiness—ultimate joy—is experienced more in the pursuit than the arrival.

I saw the gaps everywhere. I told myself family came first, but I was on my phone while my son told me about his day. I said honesty mattered, but I softened the truth to keep peace in a house where silence felt safer than honesty. My jaw stayed tight, my breath shallow—the body keeping receipts of every betrayed value.

I didn't see it then, but years earlier I'd already been handed the same lesson without knowing it. During my first marriage, she wanted time out and took three months in Italy, fully paid for by yours truly. I was left to run two companies and two early teenage boys on my own. I told myself I had it handled. Systems in place. Schedules locked. I'd prove I could do it all.

If I'm honest, there was a darker edge under the surface. I'd let years of self-doubt harden into a quiet, toxic defiance: *fuck you, I'll show you how easy this is.* I never said it out loud, but it was running in the background. Resentment had been stacking for years, brick by brick, until it hummed under everything I did. What looked like responsibility was, in truth, a cocktail of duty and bitterness. Not service, not love, not humility—resentment dressed as competence.

And in many ways, I did show it. Dinner was on the table at the same time every night. I kept a rotation of five meals, later stretched to two weeks when the boys complained about variety. We turned supermarket runs into games—divide the list, race through the aisles, beat the clock. They learned to help with cleaning, laundry, the daily rhythm. The house became efficient, almost military. To my surprise, it was smoother than expected.

When that season ended and the trip was over, the question came: how had we been going without her? I made the mistake of telling the truth. I said it had been easy. I meant the logistics — I was running life like a factory — but what landed had ice on it. It didn't go down well. Some truths sound clever in your head until they hit air. When a partner asks if it was hard without them, the answer isn't *"easier."* That line detonates on contact.

But the real test came when control cracked.

One morning, my younger son got sick. Not hospital sick—just fever, vomit, inconsolable tears. But that single domino knocked everything down. The meeting I'd prepped for—gone. The client call—cancelled. The carefully stacked day collapsed in minutes.

I lost it. Not at him—but at the walls closing in. I remember standing in the kitchen, chest heaving, the hinge of my jaw buzzing with restraint, every expletive I knew spilling out while he cried in the next room. The air felt too thin. My own body felt like a cage. This wasn't in the plan. This wasn't controllable. This wasn't how "successful men" operated.

The signal cut through the noise: I glimpsed what millions of single parents and carers live every day—one sick child and the entire house of cards go down. No backup, no pause button, no smooth solution. Just you, exhausted, and a little boy who needs you while the world demands you keep grinding responsibilities.

I told myself family was first. But in that moment, I saw how thin that was. Control was first. Systems were first. Success was first. Family was what fit around the edges—until reality smashed the edges in.

I used to think values showed up in the big declarations. Bottom-line, they're tested in the small moments — the Tuesday-life stuff. Like when my son came into my office while I was typing, and I had to decide whether to keep my eyes on the screen or turn and give him my full face. Or the Saturday he asked if I'd come to a Cars and Coffee meet, and instead of brushing it off, I leaned in — and ended up fishtailing a Corolla wagon up the highway just to make him laugh.

It took me years to see the truth: values aren't what you say. They're what you choose, in action, repeatedly. [iv]

In business, I let millions slide because I wanted to be liked more than I wanted to be safe. Contracts came across my desk, and I softened every edge. I romanticized the handshake, the "we're mates" tone, the illusion that good faith was enough. My gut twisted when I skimmed clauses, but I told myself not to rock the boat. Don't ask for too much. Don't spook them. Keep the peace. The devil's-advocate training had inverted—instead of defending against every angle, I defended against no one, not even myself.

One partner talked big online but stayed small in person—quick with opinions, slow with decisions. Every choice was deferred to an accountant, a market, a phantom variable—anyone but himself. He spoke about his audience like a class below him, basked in their praise, and believed it proved intelligence. I mistook that for strength. When I wrote *Passion*

*Driven* and he told me he'd lost respect for me because I believed in God, it cut deeper than it should have. I'd made the classic mistake—confusing intellect with wisdom, dominance with depth. He let me in, and I'm still grateful. But it took years to see that what I'd admired wasn't strength at all. It was armor made of noise.

When I started, he was renting a semi-detached townhouse. By the time I exited, he'd leveled up to waterfront property—multiple holdings, complex structures, eight figures deep. None of it was secret—the frameworks began soon after a trip I made, when I'd spoken with him about setting up prudent protections for wealth.

Later, when the numbers didn't add up and the doors closed, the sick taste in my mouth wasn't just loss—it was self-violation. Not his. Mine. My own values unsigned. My own safety sold for the illusion of being easy to work with. The cost kept climbing. And the same blindness that cost me peace at home cost me millions in business. The pattern was identical pleasing first, boundaries last.

The worst part wasn't the money. It was the code I'd been running loyalty disguised as love. I carried a particular programmer for seven years. Paid him heavy to keep Google off his scent. Flew to his wedding in Eastern Europe—helped him buy beachfront property. Forgave him when he worked two jobs behind my back. When the buyer made the sale contingent on him, he tried to ransom me for a cut. My chest went ice-cold. For the first time in my life, I went clean, not cruel: "I'd rather kill this deal than let you hold me hostage." He soon signed. I'd already negotiated him a package fifty percent higher than the generous remuneration I'd been paying—before he showed his teeth.

Fourteen years I poured into that company. I covered wages for staff who weren't even mine. I turned down upgrade cycles that could've brought seven-figure paydays—just to keep the team aligned. I supported families when they were sick—some for months. I bought expensive laptops as gifts for good work. I flew across the world half a dozen times to see them. Ate with them. Drank with them. After the sale: not one call. Not one thank you.

That was the tell. My version of "fair" wasn't virtue—it was imbalance. I wasn't generous. I was tilted. A value system wired to over-give and call it character. And that same imbalance didn't stop at the office; it followed me home.

If people-pleasing ever worked, I'd be its poster elder. Fifty years of contortion—bending, softening, smoothing the edges. It doesn't make people happy; it just makes them hungry. It doesn't buy peace; it buys quiet resentment dressed as virtue.

That's the hidden tax of living by values you never chose. They run you. They bleed you. And they wear your kindness like camouflage.

The work begins when you stop performing goodness and start defining it. When generosity becomes boundary. When loyalty means truth, not tolerance. When you stop trying to be "the good man" and start becoming the real one.

At home, *"I'm fine"* was my shield. Back then, when I was asked what I needed, I'd shrug. I didn't want another late-night debate or a drawn-out dissection of feelings. It was easier to nod, easier to carry it, easier to smother what I wanted under a blanket of silence. But the silence wasn't soft—it grew teeth. It chewed through intimacy until our bed became a DMZ, two bodies in a ceasefire pretending peace were progress. I told myself it was noble to take the weight, to be the steady one. I'll say it straight—it was uglier: I was exhausted and scared of my own voice. By the time I found it, it was too late. The hardest blow didn't come from a man—it came from silence.

Months after the collapse, I realized how few people had checked in. Men I'd shared meals with, built companies besides, stayed up with on those late-night calls—all gone quiet.

At first, I told myself they were busy. Then I saw the pattern: when a man loses altitude, most of his circle waits to see if he pulls out of the dive before they wave the flare. No one wants to stand too close to wreckage.

That silence did what their words never could. It stripped the illusion that loyalty equals proximity. Some men aren't built for the burn; they're built for the after-party.

A few proved otherwise. Michael called just to say he understood, that when I was ready to reconnect, I could. Christian and Sepp gave me space even when they didn't agree with how I handled things. And there were others—Wayne, Aidan, Dalibor, John, and David. Seven out of about twenty-five mates I thought had my back. The rest were missing in action—or I felt had other motives for calling, so I ignored them.

I stopped counting who disappeared and started noticing who remained. The ones who called without agenda. The one mate who left a coffee on my doorstep and drove off. The one who texted, "Still here."

Trust rebuilt itself from that handful of gestures—not speeches, not promises. Just presence.

Sometimes the lesson doesn't come from betrayal at all. It comes from discovering who keeps showing up when there's nothing left to gain.

Values aren't slogans. They're not poster words you print and hang on an office wall. They're not lines in a mission statement. They're choices—sometimes quiet, sometimes costly, but always concrete.

One Tuesday afternoon, I decided to make the smallest, most ordinary test of this. I told myself: today, presence is the value. So, when my son walked into my home office, I put the phone down. Screen off. Eyes on him. Nothing dramatic, no lecture—just undivided attention.

"Dad, there's a Cars and Coffee meet Saturday morning. Want to come?"

I could've said I was busy. Could've kept typing. Instead, I leaned back. "Tell me about it."

He lit up, started talking about the cars that show up, how some idiot always ruins it with a burnout and the cops shut it down. Then we both started laughing about that night meet with the Japanese tuners. Me in my 2006 white Toyota Corolla wagon—automatic transmission, grocery-getter supreme. Rain slicking the roads. I'd dropped him off, then pulled into the Toyota dealership across the street.

When the light went green, I floored it.

The Corolla's wheels howled. Fishtailed for seventy yards up the highway, smoke pouring off the tires. I had my arm out the window, fist-pumping like I'd just won Le Mans. The entire car-meet erupted. Young guys doubled over, phones out, screaming with laughter at this middle-aged dad absolutely sending it in the world's most sensible wagon.

"How the hell did you get that thing sideways?" my son asked, still laughing.

"Bald tires and commitment," I said.

We sat there grinning at each other. No agenda. No lesson. Just a father and son, present in a Tuesday afternoon, connected by the absurd memory of a Corolla doing what Corollas should never do.

Values shine in those moments. Not in the big speeches. In the Tuesday choices. In putting the phone down. In saying yes to the car meet. In being the dad who'll smoke the tires on a station wagon just to make his kid laugh.

Living by the values you choose isn't about perfection. It's about alignment. Closing the gap between what you claim and what you do. When the gap shrinks, the static inside quiets. You feel coherence—the system finally running true. [v]

And here's why these matters.

Values bring clarity—decisions go from gray to black-and-white. Values bring protection—manipulators can't play you when you're anchored. Values bring simplicity—you save energy; no endless re-deciding. Values bring safety—those around you trust your steadiness. Values bring identity—they tell you who you are when everything else burns down.

That's why values aren't "nice to haves." They're the core software. When inherited scripts fail, values are the update. And when you choose them consciously, you stop running other people's programs.

## PRACTICES & DRILLS

### Reflection Prompt – The Audit

Complete the A3. Values Inventory first if you haven't identified your core values yet. Write down your top five claimed values. Then, for each, ask: Where does this show up in my actual week? Not in words—in time, money, energy. Circle one gap that stings. That's where to start.

### Drill – The Tuesday Test

Pick one value. For a single day, make it visible in every small choice. If it's honesty, tell the full truth once where you normally wouldn't. If it's presence, put the phone away during dinner. Notice how it feels when the code matches.

### Practice – Legacy vs. Chosen

List two values you inherited that no longer fit (e.g., "never ask for help"). Then rewrite them into chosen values that do (e.g., "strength is asking when I need support"). Put the new code where you'll see it daily.

### Gratitude Reframe – Proof of Alignment

At night, note one moment where you lived a chosen value. However small. Train your system to see the proof.

### Takeaway

Values aren't posters on the wall or lines in a mission statement. They're the operating system of your life. If you don't choose them, you'll run whatever scripts were handed down—and they'll crash under modern demands. Your calendar is your creed in motion. Coherence begins the moment you close the gap between what you say and what you do.

## Reflection Question

Which value do you claim to live by, but can't yet see in your calendar or in your actions?

# SEVEN
# WHEN YOUR WOUNDS REWRITE REALITY

"If you can't name it, it owns you." [i]

Most men navigate life through mental models they never chose. These models lie beneath awareness, tilting the frame: what you see, how you interpret it, and what you do next. When these models are outdated or distorted by wounds, they don't just color the past—they warp the present. A surprising number of men routinely misread motives and social cues, and those misreads cascade into unnecessary conflict, poor decisions, and chronic stress. [ii] [iii] [iv] This isn't a character flaw; it's a map problem. If your map is wrong, the road feels hostile even when it's not.

Jake knew how to find a single stray character in a million lines of code. He could spot the error buried in complexity. But when his wife said, "Can we talk about us?" his internal system lit up like a siren. His shoulders pulled up to his ears, hands balled, nails carving crescents into his palms. He didn't hear a request for closeness; he heard a tribunal. In his childhood home, "We need to talk" meant punishment. That old model still lived in his body. So, on a Tuesday night, when she asked about their finances—a simple ask for partnership—his system translated it as, you're failing as a provider. Within minutes, he was defensive, then sharp, then silent on the couch, stunned at how a neutral conversation had turned into a crisis. *The moment hadn't attacked him; his model had.*

Jake's turning point came months later. Same kitchen, same wife, same words: "Can we talk?"

But this time he caught it. He noticed the heat rising in his neck and the fists forming under the table. Instead of firing back or shutting down, he said the one thing he'd never said before:

"Give me a second. My body's reacting, but I know you're not attacking me."

The room shifted. She blinked, surprised. The air softened. They talked. Not perfectly, not smoothly, but without the explosion.

That single interruption — naming the model instead of obeying it — was the beginning of an entirely different marriage. He told me later, "I thought she wanted a stronger provider. Turns out she just wanted me present."

I knew exactly what he meant, because I'd run the same ghost code. My chest would clamp whenever someone said, "We need to talk." My throat tightened, as if words were jammed behind my sternum. It wasn't my wife in the room — it was my parents, my headmaster, my old prosecutors. Every conversation became a courtroom I had to survive. So, I minimized, disappeared, swallowed truth until my own body revolted.

The breakthrough came the first time I did what Jake did: named the ghost out loud. "I'm reacting like I'm being judged, but I know you're not my father." The other person in the room exhaled. And for the first time in years, I did too.

The pattern emerged: wounds rewrite reality until you interrupt them. The system fires old alarms at new faces, and you mistake the people in front of you for enemies long gone. The map lies. But if you pause, name it, and test it, the terrain comes back into view.

I ran my own version for years. My default setting was Perfectionist Provider. If someone I loved showed frustration, my brain snapped to: You should have prevented this—you're inadequate. I wasn't responding to the person in front of me; I was answering a ghost. That's what models do—they smuggle yesterday's fear into today's room, then call it truth. The cost is trust, energy, and connection. And because the processing is invisible, you don't notice you're doing it—you just feel exhausted and misunderstood.

I sneered at divorced men. Thought they were weak, thought they'd failed, thought they had no right to stand on a stage and teach others. Tony Robbins, whoever—if they had a marriage behind them, I dismissed them. That arrogance became a cage. Not me. I'll never be that guy. So, I stayed longer than I should have, told myself it was noble, told myself it was for the kids. It took me decades to admit I was hiding. I was terrified of being branded what I judged in others. My wound rewrote the room: divorce didn't mean freedom or truth; it meant shame. So, I stayed.

And yet, when the marriage finally ended, the world didn't spit me out. Some people stepped closer. Brothers trusted me more because I finally told the truth. My sons respected the fact that

I didn't hide. The wound had painted divorce as humiliation. Reality painted it as liberation. Staying to avoid shame is its own kind of failure.

I thought I'd lost a business. The reality was sharper: I lost myself every time I trusted handshakes instead of drawing a line in ink.

I kept misreading business as a place where warmth could replace clarity. I told myself contracts were cold, and honesty could live on handshakes. That wasn't honor; it was fear—an old model that said don't rock the boat or you'll be abandoned. The fallout you already know from Chapter 5. The important part here isn't the dollars; it's the distortion: I wasn't reading the room; I was reading my wound.

My sons needed university, needed private school, needed safety from the pain I knew too well. The truth? That was my wound talking. My school years in the UK were hell. Bullied, cornered, humiliated. At twelve, I was so desperate, I made up a story to the headmaster, convinced him to let me repeat a year just to escape. No one had ever done it before. The whole school laughed at me—the failure kid, sent back. But I didn't tell my parents. I swallowed the shame, carried it in silence, and bore the humiliation. Because to me, that was the lesser pain.

And here's the twist—the deal worked. I made the top streams. I got through school without the daily torment. I even ended up at Oxford.

But the win carried a hidden cost. The wound wrote a different code into my bones: *You're not smart. You didn't earn it. You cheated the system.*

That childhood story metastasized into a lifelong lie. For forty years it ran quietly in the background—corrupting work, love, body, confidence, everything.

I put other men and women on pedestals, handing them authority they'd never earned, doubting what I already knew.

It took me forty years to see it—the child's self-protection mechanism that once kept me safe had grown into the adult pattern that was hurting me and everyone around me.

That lie wasn't born from malice; it was born from fear. I couldn't stop the bullying or control how others saw me, but I could outthink the pain. Hiding the truth gave me back a sense of control—agency in a world that felt unpredictable and unsafe. It kept me from humiliation, from disappointing my parents, from showing weakness I believed would cost me belonging. It worked so well it went unnoticed for decades—an invisible code running in the background—until the same self-protection that saved a boy started suffocating the man he became.

The truth? That twelve-year-old didn't cheat anything. He pulled off one of the sharpest negotiations of his life—and then spent four decades forgetting what that proved: that he could think, adapt, and survive when the world turned on him.

Years later, that reframe changed everything. A client asked me to present a solution to their entire team—twenty people around a table, all looking at me. The old wound whispered: *You're the fraud who cheated to get here.* But I caught it. I remembered that twelve-year-old strategist. He wasn't lucky; he was resourceful. So, I stood there, pitched my solution with the same strategic mind that had saved me at twelve, and watched them lean in. They didn't see a fraud. They saw someone who could read the room and deliver. The wound had lied for thirty years.

These were the ghosts I fought for years. Rooms I once believed were loaded with judgment or danger turned out to be just rooms. Divorce didn't mean collapse—it meant truth. Contracts weren't daggers—they were paper. My sons didn't need the path I'd longed for—they needed me present. That twelve-year-old boy wasn't an impostor—he was a survivor with teeth. The wounds kept repeating one story. Reality whispered another. And the more I tested the wound's story against the facts in front of me, the truer the room became.

Here's the sober truth: emotions aren't the problem; unread emotions are. Threat systems that were once protective keep firing at neutral stimuli. Unresolved wounds bias perception so that ordinary moments feel loaded, and your nervous system treats yellow lights like red ones. [v] [vi] The work isn't to bulldoze feelings or run colder. The work is to bring the model into view—to notice the spike, name the story, and test it against what's here. That's how you start living in the world as it is.

*Your wounds tell stories; reality tells truth. Which one you live is the difference between ghosts and ground.*

## PRACTICES & DRILLS

### Reflection Prompt – Catch the Spike

Recall one recent overreaction. Write down the trigger and the instant story your brain assigned (e.g., She thinks I'm failing). Where have you felt that story before?

### Drill – Test the Story in the Present

Ask: Is that story true here and now? What evidence supports it? What contradicts it? If the fit is poor, write one truer sentence you can act from tonight.

### Exercise – Install the Update

Choose a recurring trigger (money talks, "we need to talk," teen eyeroll). Before the next instance, pre-write your new line of code (e.g., This is a bid for partnership, not an indictment). Read it, then practice it in the moment.

### Gratitude Reframe – Evidence of Safety

List two moments from the last month that contradict your wound's story (someone stayed, believed you, worked with you). Keep them visible. Train your system to register safety, not just threat.

### Takeaway

You don't have to be ruled by the story your wounds talk about reality. When you surface the model, test it, and update it, the room gets truer. You stop fighting ghosts and start responding to people.

### Reflection Question

What old story does your system keep auto-loading—and what one-sentence update would make today's room more accurate?

## INTERLUDE: WHEN THE PRESSURE LEAKS SIDEWAYS

### When the Pressure Leaks Sideways

He never raised a fist.

He raised his voice.

He slammed doors.

He went silent for days.

He called it space.

She called it fear.

Somewhere between those two definitions, a marriage dissolved. The wreckage didn't start with cruelty. It started with compression. Years of unspoken frustration, guilt, and exhaustion—bottled under the banner of composure—finally found a crack. And when pressure finds a crack, it doesn't vanish; it leaks. Sometimes through sarcasm, sometimes through control, sometimes through absence that cuts sharper than violence.

I know that leak. I've felt it in my lips—the pursing before the word, the heat behind the ribs. You tell yourself you're "just cooling off." But silence isn't cooling. It's weaponized distance. It's the body's way of saying *I can't hold this anymore.*

Unspoken pain doesn't die. It migrates—from self to spouse, from mind to body, from loneliness to control. You can bench-press it, breathe through it, pray over it; if you won't name it, it will find another mouth.

When that pressure goes unspoken long enough, it can do more than hollow a man — it can spill into harm.

The Australian Institute of Family Studies found what every honest man already knows: isolation and depression don't stay private forever. They leak sideways — as control, withdrawal, anger that lands where love should.

Brotherhood, truth, and emotional literacy aren't niceties. They're preventative medicine. Every time a man speaks instead of stews, he lowers the chance his silence becomes someone else's fear.

This isn't theory; its harm reduction disguised as healing. [vii] [viii] [ix] [x]

## BONUS PRACTICE & DRILLS

**Reflection Prompt — Map the Leak**

Think of the last time your reaction frightened someone you love. Not because of what you did, but because of the energy that came off you. What were you defending in that moment—your pride, your fear, your shame?

Write the first honest answer that surfaces.

**Drill — Pressure to Pattern**

Next time the surge rises, step outside—physically move. Breathe through the soles of your feet and ask, *What story am I protecting right now?*

Name it before you speak. Truth releases pressure faster than silence ever will.

**Exercise — Debrief, Don't Disappear**

When calm returns, go back.

Say: *I felt a spike and needed space. Here's what it was about.*

That sentence repairs more intimacy than any apology rehearsed in guilt.

**Reframe**

Conflict isn't proof you're broken; it's proof you care enough to risk truth. But honesty without regulation turns love into collateral damage. Mastery isn't never losing control—it's knowing where your control ends and your wound begins.

**Takeaway**

The man who names his wound stops making others bleed for it.

The work you just did in this chapter was getting the ghost code into daylight and stopping it from spilling onto people who didn't write it. Naming the story slows the leak, but the pressure you mapped still has to go somewhere. The next move is learning to read the signals in real time — chest, jaw, breath, gut — before they harden into another slammed door or a three-day shutdown. That's where we're going next. [xi] [xii]

# EIGHT
# DECODING THE DATA OF EMOTION

---

"If you can't name what you feel, you'll stay a stranger to yourself — and to anyone who tries to love you." [i]

---

Men are taught to treat emotions as glitches. Suppress the tears. Swallow the anger. Smile through the shame. But emotions aren't noise – they're signals. They're the operating data that tells you what's working and what's broken inside. When you cut yourself off from that data stream, you don't get stronger. You get blind.

The numbers tell the story. Almost four out of five men rarely or never talk about their struggles with friends – compared to less than a third of women.[ii] Men are three times more likely to suffer from alexithymia – the clinical inability to name and express emotions.[iii] Emotional withdrawal is the leading factor cited in two-thirds of divorces filed by women.[iv] And men still account for three out of every four suicides – with isolation and silence almost always present._v_

Jake's life made those statistics flesh.

He was forty-seven, a senior director at a Fortune 500 company. Cool under pressure, always composed. His team called him "ice water." To them, that was strength. To his wife, it was absence. On the day she delivered the ultimatum, they sat in the car outside the counselor's office. Eighteen years married. Kids in high school. She turned toward him and said the words that crashed his system: "You're emotionally unavailable, and I can't do this anymore."

Jake prided himself on never losing his temper. On staying level-headed while others cracked under quarterly targets. But his wife wasn't asking for composure. She was asking for him. She told him: "It feels like I'm married to a robot. You respond correctly to everything, but I never know what you're feeling." Her voice didn't rise, but the sentence cut like a scalpel. He had built a flawless interface with no internal signal. His emotional dashboard was frozen. The cost wasn't just his marriage. It was his own sense of aliveness.

Jake's composure was its own addiction. You know you're addicted to something if the absence of it robs you of hope, of happiness. Addiction is an emotional backed demand, not a preference. When motivated by preferences, we experience more balanced, lighter, more loving experience of life. But addiction is like holding a gun to your partner's head—force, pushes, frantic ego-based life, not just about drugs and alcohol but any pattern we can't release. Jake was addicted to control, to never losing face. The absence of that control didn't just disturb him—it destroyed him.

. . .

For years, I lived like a smartphone with notifications turned off. Outwardly functional – building businesses, raising kids – but missing every important alert inside. A sigh I never let out. I ignored them until they became static in the background of every day.

Sometimes the signals broke through in ways I couldn't disguise. A Ute cut across two lanes and nearly clipped my front bumper. My whole body lit up. Chest hot, jaw clamped, fists welded to the steering wheel, knuckles white as bone. My foot slammed the brake too hard, heart hammering in my throat, taste of copper flooding my mouth. The voice in my head fired before I could catch it: What the hell are you doing, you idiot? You nearly killed me. Who the hell do you think you are? The target was him, but the hit landed elsewhere. That rage had nothing to do with the Ute. It was about every time in my life someone cut me off, ignored me, dismissed me. My nervous system had tagged this as injustice. But when I pulled over and sat with it, my body wasn't glitching. It was sending data. The heat in my chest wasn't just fury. It was saying: you feel unseen. You feel disrespected. Once I decoded that, the anger lost its teeth. The horn wasn't for him – it was for every time I felt unseen.

My body wasn't breaking—it was broadcasting. Metallic taste in my mouth, buzzing in my ears, constriction in my throat, steering wheel slick in my palms—each sensation a readout on the dashboard. Rage wasn't random; it was data. My chest heat was a flare for injustice. My tighten throat was code for unspoken truth. My shallow breath my body warning that I was stuck in survival mode. None of it was weakness. It was information I'd never learned to read.

The body keeps the receipts while the mind keeps lying. Tight jaw, shallow breath, restless hands—these tell the truth before thoughts can dress it up. The nervous system doesn't negotiate or rationalize. It just reports threat here, safety there, truth needed now. Every sensation is intelligence if you learn the language.

Another time, it was shame, sharp as a blade. They asked me a simple question in the meeting: "Why did you choose that strategy?" My face flushed hot, ears buzzing, the fluorescent lights suddenly too bright. My throat dried out, palms slick with sweat. I could hear my own pulse in my ears, loud as a drum. I stumbled through an answer, but inside I was collapsing. The story in my head was loud and merciless: You're a fraud. They've finally worked you out. Later, when the heat drained, I replayed it. What it came down to was simple: my body was warning me — you're unprepared, afraid of being seen. That wasn't worthlessness. That was a system message. If I decoded shame as "I'm broken," I spiraled. If I decoded shame as "I need to prepare better, learn, and own my gaps," I grew. Shame isn't proof you're a fraud; it's proof you care what's at stake.

Then there were the freezes. One argument with a friend turned sharp, his voice rising. My chest locked. Shoulders curled in. Molars grinding. Words jammed in my throat, breath shallow as a puddle. I went silent. To him, it looked like stonewalling. Inside, it was panic. The story was, If I speak, I'll make it worse. If I go quiet, I'll stay safe. My body wasn't betraying me. It was broadcasting you feel unsafe. The way forward wasn't armor or withdrawal – it was honesty. I finally managed to say, "I need a minute, I feel overwhelmed." The air cleared. The freeze was a message. Once I read it, the system worked. Silence isn't emptiness – it's your body screaming: you don't feel safe.

The most painful signal came not from traffic or business, but from my own son. One night he asked, "Dad, are you okay?" I said, "Fine." He stared at me a second too long, then walked away. That moment still cuts. He didn't need me bulletproof. He needed me real. The sigh I wouldn't let out, the truth I swallowed, was the very thing that kept him at arm's length. The body keeps the receipts.

The work doesn't end with awareness. It evolves.

Months after I'd started decoding my dashboard, I thought I had it handled. Training done, legs humming, sun low. I'm coasting home on the old bush bike, protein shake in one hand, handlebars loose in the other. Body clean mind clear—the kind of afternoon where you feel like you've finally figured it out.

Then a gate bursts open.

Big woman, small dog, phone in hand. Not looking. I swerve early, half onto the grass—clean avoidance, no issue. But when she finally notices me, she jolts like I've leapt out of the trees.

"Fucking cunt!" she spits. "You're breaking the law, citizen!"

The words land like a slap. My body floods before my mind can intervene. Jaw tight, hands hot, pulse hammering up my neck, that copper taste rising. For a second, I'm twelve again in the schoolyard, being blamed for something that wasn't mine. The same heat, same injustice, same need to defend.

But here's the difference from the Ute incident: this time I catch it happening. I feel my chest tighten, notice my knuckles go white on the handlebars, hear my breath go shallow. The dashboard is screaming: *You feel attacked. Unfairly accused. Small.*

Except I don't use the tools. Not yet.

I circle back—ego steering now, old code running. "What did you call me?"

She doubles down. "A cunt."

The old me would have exploded. The new me knows better. But knowing and doing are different beasts. I throw back "stupid twat"—the kind of word that sounds justified in the mouth and rotten the second it leaves.

The silence after is pure adrenaline and shame mixing like acid in my gut.

I pedal off, cheeks burning, hands shaking slightly. The rest of the ride home I'm writing better comebacks in my head—clever, cruel, useless. My body is still flooded: tight shoulders, clenched teeth, that sick feeling when you know you've failed your own standards.

That night I decode it properly. Sat with the sensation instead of the story. The trigger wasn't her words—it was the accusation when I'd done nothing wrong. My nervous system had filed it under "injustice/blame" from decades of similar hits. The rage wasn't about her. It was about every time I'd been called wrong when I was just existing.

Next morning, I see her again at the same gate. She looks down; I look up. My chest tightens—the body remembering—but this time I breathe through it. Feel my feet on the pedals. Drop my shoulders.

"Morning," I say, adding a genuine smile. "Have a good day."

Her eyes flicker—recognition, discomfort, maybe her own shame—but I don't need the response. The repair isn't for her. It's for my nervous system, teaching it a new ending: *We can be attacked and not attack back. We can be triggered and still choose.*

The difference between the Ute rage and this? Not that I didn't get triggered—I did. Not that I handled it perfectly—I didn't. The difference was recovery time. What used to take weeks of shame and replay now took one night of honest decoding and a morning of repair.

That's the real progress: not never falling, but how fast you can read the dashboard, decode the signal, and steer back to center.

That was the shift: emotions weren't defects in the system. They were messages. (See A4. Emotional Maps for a complete guide to decoding what you feel through the body.) Fear meant something mattered. Anger meant a boundary was crossed. Grief meant I had loved enough to hurt. Joy meant, pay attention – this is what fills you. Rage, shame, silence – none of them glitches. They were system data. My body was the dashboard. Learn to read it, and the room becomes clearer. Your body isn't lying. Are you listening?

## PRACTICES & DRILLS

### Reflection Prompt – Name the Signal

Think of the last time someone asked how you were. What word did you give them? Was it true? Write the word you should have said.

### Drill – The Three-Word Check-In

Twice a day, pause for sixty seconds. Name three emotions you feel right now. No fixing, no judgment. Just recognition.

### Exercise – Drop the Mask

Next time your child or partner asks how you are, trade "fine" for one real word: tired, hopeful, anxious, grateful. Watch what happens when honesty opens the door.

### Gratitude Reframe – Decode the Data

At the end of the day, circle one signal you noticed – anger, shame, joy, grief – and thank your body for sending it. Gratitude turns raw emotion into useful data.

### Takeaway

Suppressing emotions isn't strength. It's blindness. Emotions aren't flaws in the code – they're the data that makes you human. Ignore them, and you lose connection to yourself and to everyone who loves you. Decode them, and you reclaim your capacity to lead, to love, and to live.

### Reflection Question

What emotion have you muted the longest – and what might change if you let it speak?

# NINE
# HOW TO ACTUALLY CONNECT

---

"A man who knows himself becomes unshakable. The man who doesn't becomes everyone else's project." [i]

"Authenticity is the alignment of head, mouth, heart, and feet — thinking, saying, feeling, and doing the same thing — consistently." [ii]

---

Men are failing in the one arena that matters most for sustained meaning and emotional stability: connection.

Only one in three men say they are "very satisfied" in their romantic relationships, compared to nearly half of women. [iii] Sixty-eight percent of men admit they suppress emotions in intimate relationships to "maintain strength." [iv] Women initiate sixty-nine percent of divorces, most often citing "emotional disconnection" as the reason. [v] Nearly half of men report having no close male friends at all—twice the rate of women. [vi]

These aren't small glitches. They're crashes in the relational operating system of modern men.

In my first marriage, silence became my mask. When conflict rose, I defaulted to the same shield: "it's fine. I'll handle it." On the surface, it sounded noble — the steady husband, the reliable man who carried the load.

But underneath, it wasn't quiet. It was loaded. Each "I'll handle it" came with clenched teeth, a tight jaw, a muttered "add it to the fucking list." Resentment hid inside the silence, turning it from peacekeeping into passive aggression. I thought I was being strong. I was bleeding venom into the foundation of the marriage.

My body kept the score before my mouth ever admitted it. The clenched jaw left my temples pounding by nightfall. My chest felt like concrete by dinner. That's what living behind a mask does—it exhausts you even when you're still. Silence doesn't empty you; it drains you.

Every unspoken truth was acid. It corroded intimacy one swallow at a time. The silence grew teeth. It chewed through our bed until it wasn't a place of connection anymore — just geography. Two continents drifting apart under the same roof.

I told myself it was strength — that staying silent made me noble. But underneath, it was uglier: I was drained, scared of my own voice, and terrified that honesty would spark another midnight war. So, I swallowed the words and let resentment speak for me.

Silence didn't keep peace. It kept distance. Every time I said, "I'm fine," the walls thickened. Every time I swallowed truth, the air between us thinned. Until one day the geography became permanent: two people still in a marriage but already living on different continents.

Months passed. The house went quiet in a way that wasn't just silence anymore—it was absence. I was separated, living alone, piecing together a new rhythm. By then I'd been in the work almost a year—therapy, journaling, training, rewiring the code. Slowly, something shifted. The shame didn't vanish, but the edges dulled. I started to notice small things I'd never seen before—strangers holding my gaze, an easier laugh, the first hints of lightness in the body.

I was in the chemist trying to look like a man who knew his way around toner. A small basket, a smaller box of blonde touch-up hiding under a packet of paracetamol. I wasn't ready to be a silver fox. I wasn't ready to be seen, either.

She passed me in the aisle, paused, turned back.

"Sorry—this is random—but you smell great."

I froze like a schoolboy caught nicking Mars bars. The basket flicked behind my thigh as if the box could learn shame. A deflection spilled out: "Ah—aftershave." I took a step back without meaning to, measuring the distance like a burglar to a window.

She smiled and kept walking. I kept retreating—slowly, diagonally—so she couldn't see the basket. Separated now, a year into doing the work, I'd started to notice these small oddities: strangers looking up, doors held a beat longer, a compliment in a pharmacy of all places. Maybe it was scent, or posture, or something subtler that leaked from the skin once a man stops lying to himself. [vii] [viii] Whatever it was, I wasn't ready to let it land. My body braced as if kindness were a punch.

At the till, I put the box on the counter and laughed at myself. The ridiculousness of hiding from a compliment while buying camouflage for my hair. The lesson was simple, and I hated how simple it was: receiving is part of strength. If you can't take a small gift—a word, an eye-crinkle in Aisle 6—you won't take help when it matters.

It took me years to see what was happening in that aisle: I could give endlessly, but I couldn't receive. A compliment felt dangerous. Help felt like debt. Even a kind glance bounced off armor I didn't know I was wearing. That was old code. Connection isn't just giving—it's letting the loop close by taking in what's offered. Until you can receive without flinching, you're only ever broadcasting, not belonging.

It wasn't modesty. It was old code. Somewhere along the line I'd learned that if I let something good in, it would be yanked away undercut by a joke, flipped into devil's advocacy, or turned into someone else's punchline so they could feel taller. Safer to shrug. Safer to deflect. My nervous system treated kindness like a setup and coded every compliment as a trap. That's not preference. That's a trauma response.

The same reflex played out everywhere else. At home, if my partner reached out with softness, I'd answer with logic. If a friend offered affirmation, I'd pivot to banter. Connection offered, connection dodged. What looked like composure was self-protection.

That's why the loop matters. Connection doesn't exist in a broadcast. It only lives when truth passes both ways—when someone offers and you don't swat it away, when you risk being known and they risk meeting you there.

By the time I found my voice, the bridge was gone. Scar tissue taught me this: silence isn't strength. Silence is surrender — and surrender soaked in resentment becomes poison.

I thought I was good at relationships too. I could talk about feelings. I could quote Jung and Buber. I could dive deep into philosophy and spirituality. On paper, I looked like the evolved man women say they want. But in practice, my connection protocol was faulty.

For three decades, I ran the same loop. I opened, explained, over-gave. What came back only sounded like understanding—it carried the language of depth without the presence behind it. I mistook fluency for feeling. I confused talk about growth for growth itself. The rhythm stayed the same; I gave until I broke. The return was a fraction. I pushed harder, trying to bridge the gap. Words flowed, but meaning never landed. The silence grew heavy until it broke under its own weight. What I lacked wasn't good intention or effort—it was reciprocity. Connection is a circuit. Without current on both sides, it's just one voice echoing until the line goes dead—or one body draining the other until the fuse burns out.

I've seen this same faulty script running in other men. A man comes home late, tension still in his shoulders. His wife asks, "How was your day?" The dam bursts. He unloads everything —stress at work, money fears, frustrations with his boss. Ten minutes straight. She sits quietly, nodding, her fork idle. When he finally looks up, the silence is suffocating. His chest burns: I've shared everything, and she's given me nothing. She doesn't care.

But that wasn't true. She was overwhelmed. He'd mistaken a monologue for intimacy. He'd broadcast, not looped. Connection requires exchange, not dumping. A monologue isn't intimacy—it's exposure without return.

These are the scripts men inherit. Open in a dump and feel unseen. Defend instead of disclosing and feel rejected. Broadcast without loop and feel dismissed. Each time, the pain grows, the resentment stacks, the numbness sets in. And beneath it all is the false signal: I tried, and it didn't work.

But that's not truth. That's faulty code.

Connection isn't built on effort alone. It lives in the feedback loop—truth offered, truth returned. Without that loop, relationships become scripts. With it, they become living systems. Connection is a loop—truth offered, truth returned.

And nowhere does this loop fail more painfully than in the bedroom—where performance replaces presence and scorekeeping kills connection.

A friend of mine, Adam, told me this story a few years ago.

(*Name changed to protect the guilty—and the married.*)

He said it quietly, like a man handing over a weapon he no longer trusted himself to hold. And as he told it, I recognized pieces of my own marriage in every word.

And it hit me harder than I expected.

The way he spoke—measured, ashamed, but honest—landed somewhere deep in my gut.

Because as he described it, I could feel the truth of it.

Not his exact story, but the pattern. The ache. The performance.

And I knew he was right.

He and his wife hadn't had sex in four months. No explosion. No betrayal. Just a slow fade.

The bed had turned into a border. Eight inches of cold sheet between them, an ocean of silence underneath.

He kept mental tallies—attempts, rejections, mechanical completions.

He called it *the spreadsheet*.

Last attempt: shut down.

Three weeks before: finished, but her eyes elsewhere.

Month before that: she cried afterward. Not from joy.

The truth finally surfaced over dishes.

She turned from the sink, hands still wet.

"You don't even see me anymore," she said. "You fuck like you're trying to hit KPIs."

Ice water on exposed nerve.

Adam told me he stood there frozen.

Because she was right.

He'd turned intimacy into performance review.

Duration: optimized. Technique: researched.

Her pleasure: proof he still had value.

He wasn't touching her to connect—he was touching her to confirm he wasn't broken.

Every time he reached for her, she could feel the agenda.

His hands didn't say *I want you.*

They said *please validate me.*

Later that night, he finally told her the truth.

"I don't know how to touch you without keeping score."

She looked at him, wary. "What do you mean?"

"Every time we're together, I'm measuring. How long I last. Whether you finish. If it's better than last time. You've become my report card. And when you don't respond how I need, I feel like I'm failing at the one thing men are supposed to master."

Her shoulders softened. First time in months.

Then she said, "I can feel you're counting. You're not with me—you're hovering above us both, judging your performance. It's like being fucked by someone who isn't there."

That night they didn't have sex. They did something harder—they named every way they'd turned intimacy into transaction.

- Him: using sex as validation that he still mattered
- Her: offering duty sex to avoid the silence that followed rejection
- Him: watching porn to "learn techniques" that had nothing to do with her
- Her: faking responses because real ones took too long
- Both: never speaking what they wanted

Three weeks later, something broke open.

He reached for her hip—no scoreboard, no outcome, just warmth.

She didn't tense. Didn't perform. Just breathed.

When they finally reconnected, it was slower. Messier. Real.

She looked at him—not through him.

They both cried. Not from sadness, but from the relief of being fully there.

Adam said the moment everything shifted wasn't when they had sex again—it was when he said out loud:

"I don't want to perform anymore. I just want to be here."


Presence isn't something you do.

It's what's left when the performance dies.

The bedroom taught Adam what every other arena confirms: connection dies when we perform instead of being present.

It lives when we risk being seen—truly seen—without the scorecard, without the mask, without the need to prove we're enough.

This is the code update most men need: stop broadcasting competence. Start looping truth.

What that night revealed—and what stayed with me long after—is that intimacy isn't just emotional or physical. It's biological.

We're wired for connection.

For hundreds of thousands of years, the chemistry that made us reach for one another—oxytocin, dopamine, serotonin, vasopressin—was the same chemistry that kept tribes alive.

It's what made trust possible, what made civilization hold.

When intimacy becomes transactional and attention becomes a commodity, we start dismantling that circuitry.

We rewire the reward systems of the brain away from presence and into performance.

And when that happens long enough, we don't just lose closeness—we lose orientation.

Connection isn't a luxury. It's the operating system of our species.

When we forget how to connect, we forget how to care.

And when we forget how to care, we stop protecting the one part of ourselves that machines can't replace.

## PRACTICES & DRILLS

### Reflection Prompt — Your Connection Loops

Think back to your last three important conversations with a partner, friend, or colleague. Did you share more than you received? Did you nod along without revealing anything? Write down which way the imbalance tilted.

### Exercise — Ask Before You Speak

Pick one important relationship. Before sharing something that matters, ask: "Are you available to talk about this now?" Notice how the tone shifts when the exchange begins with mutual permission.

### Drill — Say It Plain

In your next emotional conversation, state your truth in under twenty seconds. No philosophy, no abstractions—just the plain feeling. "I feel anxious about money." "I feel distance between us." Train clarity before complexity.

### Gratitude Reframe — Spot the Loop

At the end of the week, note one moment where the exchange truly looped—where you offered truth and received truth back. Write it down. Thank the other person for meeting you there.

### Takeaway

A monologue isn't intimacy. Defensiveness isn't disclosure. Vulnerability without reciprocity is just a broadcast. Presence beats performance. Connection is not a solo act. It's a loop. And the moment both people step into that loop, the system comes alive.

### Reflection Question

Where in your relationships are you broadcasting instead of looping—and what one step could close that circuit today?

Excellent. Below is the **fully formatted, Vellum-ready Markdown version** — styled in the *ManOS* voice and rhythm, complete with footnoted data sources and smooth transitions.

It's structured to drop directly after the *Connection Loops* section in **Chapter 8: "How to Connect."**

Everything — tone, spacing, punctuation, cadence — matches the rest of the manuscript.

## BONUS PRACTICE – FOR MEN READY TO REBUILD REAL INTIMACY

*Optional. But if you do this, you'll never relate to sex—or yourself—the same way again. It isn't about technique. It's about truth — the kind that can't coexist with performance.*

Men today are facing an intimacy crisis not because we're weak, but because we've been conditioned to perform instead of connecting. The data is confronting:

A 2021 international study of men aged 18–45 found that *over 21 percent* reported some degree of erectile dysfunction (ED), and higher scores on problematic pornography use strongly predicted ED. [ix]

Two decades ago, ED among men under 40 was 2–5 *percent*. Now estimates range from *14–30 percent*, despite no physiological causes in most cases. [x]

In one major study, *91.5 percent* of men had consumed pornography in the past month; adolescent lifetime use already exceeds *80 percent*. [xi]

Research now links heavy or early porn exposure with *desensitized arousal patterns, heightened performance anxiety, and preference for solo stimulation over relational sex.* [xii]

This isn't about shame or moral panic.

It's about awareness—about realizing that our attention and arousal have been quietly hijacked by a system that profits from our disconnection.

And while governments can regulate gambling ads, sugar, alcohol, and driving ages, we still leave eight-, nine-, and ten-year-olds one click away from unlimited, high-definition sex.

That's not just a policy failure. That's a collective one.

Parents, platforms, ISPs, app stores, advertisers, payment systems—every layer of society has a lever, yet by staying silent, we effectively sanction the exposure of our children to material their brains aren't equipped to process.

It isn't only boys. Girls are also being shaped by the same machine—through comparison, pressure, and premature sexualization.

We criminalize adults who exploit minors—and rightly so—yet we permit a quieter exploitation: the constant voyeurism of underage eyes. It's a perversion of our own making.

By saying nothing, we become complicit. By doing nothing, we pass that complicity down as legacy.

A simple, lawful, privacy-respecting fix already exists:

- Default adult-content filters switched **on** at the network level, with an opt-out requiring verified adulthood. Verification doesn't log viewing habits; it confirms age once, then forgets
- App stores enforcing the same.
- Ad and payment networks cutting ties with any site that refuses compliance.

It wouldn't end everything—but it would raise the friction and buy our children time to become human before they become voyeurs.

Governments have the power; the technology is trivial. The only thing missing is will.

If this matters to you, there's an appendix at the end of this book outlining how such a plan could work, step by step.

It isn't a crusade. It's a blueprint.

Take it, adapt it, and help it take shape where you are.

We don't need outrage. We need grown men standing up for the innocence of the next generation. That's what legacy looks like.

## 1. The 7-Day Presence Reset

For seven days, stop chasing performance—sexually or mentally.

You may still have sex or masturbate, but only with full awareness.

Rules:

- No porn, erotic scrolling, or highlight-reel fantasy.
- When arousal comes, breathe. Feel the tension instead of escaping it.
- If you release, do it without fantasy—eyes open, breathing steady, grounded.

Purpose: retrain the dopamine system from *novelty and performance* back to *embodiment and connection*.

## 2. The Mirror Confession

Stand naked before a mirror.

Ask yourself out loud:

"What am I trying to prove when I touch myself?"

Stay there until the shame dissolves into curiosity.

If you want to go deeper, ask:

- When did I start performing instead of feeling?
- Whose approval am I chasing when I call myself a good lover?
- What would it look like to touch myself as an act of *presence* instead of *proof*?
- What emotion hides behind my desire for control?

Most men can't hold their own gaze for more than five seconds.

Stay until you can.

### 3. Partner Practice — The Slow Touch Loop

If you have a partner, tell her: *"I'm practicing presence, not performance."*

Set a 20-minute timer.

- First 10 minutes: you touch her—slow, curious, without outcome.
- Next 10 minutes: she touches you—the same.
- No talking. No escalation. Afterward, share what you *felt*.

Purpose: teach both bodies to associate safety and connection—not evaluation—with touch.

### 4. The Porn Truth Drill

If you feel the urge or open a porn tab, stop before pressing play. Ask:

1. What am I looking for—release, control, or escape?
2. What emotion am I avoiding right now?
3. What would happen if I sat with that emotion for five minutes instead?

Write down three sentences in answer.

Then, if you still want to watch, go ahead.

No judgment. Just awareness.

Do this every time for one week.

You'll start to see patterns. Patterns reveal truth. Truth changes behavior.

### 5. The 30-Day Challenge

For thirty days, eliminate all artificial arousal triggers—porn, erotic media, or "maintenance" masturbation.

Instead, channel that energy into creation: train, paint, build, write, move.

When sexual energy rises, breathe it through the spine—inhale from base to crown, exhale down through the feet.

You'll feel raw and restless. Good. That's power returning to the system.

### Reflection Questions

1. Where in my life do, I still perform instead of feel?
2. What would sex look like if it was about connection, not validation?

3. When do I use fantasy to replace honesty?
4. How does my body respond when I slow down instead of chase release?
5. What one action today moves me closer to presence?

## Closing Note

Most men think freedom means access—more porn, more partners, more performance.

That's not freedom. That's dependency.

Real freedom is the ability to *choose presence* when performance would be easier.

When you can do that—in sex, work, or love—you stop needing to prove you're enough.

You finally are.

# TEN
# BROTHERHOOD OR BUST

---

"Alone, a man's fears hunt him. With brothers, he becomes the storm they can't touch." [i]

---

Men are dying in silence. They take their own lives at nearly four times the rate of women, with middle-aged men at highest risk. [ii] Fewer than one in eight men under forty-five receive any form of mental health treatment each year, compared to more than one in five women. [iii] And fifteen percent of men now admit they have no close friends at all. [iv]

On paper, men look connected thousands of followers, full calendars, endless notifications. Many of us have no one to call when the dark hours come. Networking gives reach. It doesn't give roots.

Jason knew it too. He stared at his phone's screen-time report: seven hours yesterday, eight the day before. Instagram. Twitter. YouTube. LinkedIn. News sites filling the gaps. In those same two weeks, not one meaningful conversation with a friend. His feeds were packed with "connections," but when he asked himself who would answer at two a.m. if everything collapsed, the answer was no one.

Jason wasn't broken. He was starved—drowning in the illusion of connection, cut off from the substance of it.

The starvation wasn't just social—it was spiritual. Every man who's spent too long online knows it. The feeds give stimulation, not substance; they reward noise, not presence. And underneath it all sits something deeper than loneliness — a fracture in how we relate to power itself.

Because before a man loses connection with others, he usually loses connection with himself. That's what happened to Jason—and millions like him. That's where the distortion begins — where masculinity turns defensive, hardens, and starts mistaking control for safety."

We talk about "toxic masculinity" as if it's a movement or a meme, but it's older than language. It isn't masculinity at all. Its masculine energy cut off from consciousness—strength without self-awareness, will without direction, power without love.

It isn't men being strong, decisive, or ambitious. It's when those same traits lose their anchor. It's when confidence becomes performance, discipline becomes domination, leadership becomes control. *He can win the fight but can't name what he's fighting.* It's the voice that says, *don't feel, don't need, don't trust.*

At its core, toxic masculinity is a defense strategy that's gone septic born in a boy who learned that tenderness was dangerous, then carried that armor into adulthood. It once kept him safe; now it keeps him separate. It shows up everywhere: In the gym rep that's punishment, not purpose. In the business built to prove worth instead of create value. In the silence between father and son when love is there but language is gone.

It is not strength. It is fear wearing strength's skin. Masculinity itself is sacred—the force that builds, protects, penetrates, and provides. It becomes toxic only when it forgets what it's for.

When masculine energy severs from love and truth, it becomes voltage with no ground—a live wire sparking in the dark. The work isn't to kill that energy. It's to reconnect it—to bring will back under the guidance of awareness, to let power serve rather than prove.

Toxic masculinity isn't strength—it's strength without direction. It's what happens when discipline becomes domination, and confidence forgets humility. Power, left unanchored, turns inward and builds a cage around the man who forged it.

Toxic masculinity isn't men being strong. Its men being *trapped* —inside a performance they never consented to. It's the prison built from every lesson that said, *don't feel, don't need, don't ask for help.* It's a life powered by control instead of connection. It's what happens when strength forgets what it's for.

Every man inside it feels the same ache: the body is tight, the jaw clenched, the heart locked behind logic. He isn't a monster. He's a man still living by the code that once kept him safe. It taught him to conquer, not to connect. To achieve, not to feel. To win, even when there's nothing worth winning.

. . .

That's the cage. And to break it, he must walk back through every gate he built to survive.

He starts with the one called winning. For years, he thought victory would quiet the noise. If he just achieved enough, proved enough, pushed enough — the shame would shut up. But it never does. The applause fades and he's still alone with the same ache. That's when he realizes: creation heals what conquest can't.

Then comes the mask. The version of himself he shows the world. The calm, capable, unbothered man. It's armor — and it works, until it doesn't. It keeps out judgment but also love. He wears it so long he forgets there's a face underneath. When it finally cracks, what spills out isn't weakness; it's the truth he's been choking down for decades.

Next is ego. He sees how much of his drive was just fear in a better suit. The hunger to be seen, to be admired, to be untouchable — all of it was just a boy still trying to prove he mattered. The man he's becoming doesn't need that anymore. Purpose has replaced performance.

Then he faces the fortress. That private kingdom he built to stay safe. Four walls of independence and control. No one gets in, no one gets close. But safety isn't the same as peace. He realizes brotherhood isn't weakness — it's medicine. Letting another man stand beside him doesn't take his power. It gives it direction.

Then the lesson of sovereignty. He once thought power meant dominance. Now he sees it for what it is: responsibility. Real power protects. It builds. It makes others safer in its presence. The strongest man in the room is the one who doesn't need to prove it. The real proof of sovereignty is coherence — not what he says, but the fact that every layer of him agrees.

And finally, silence. No crowd. No validation. No noise. Just breath. The hum of his own pulse. For the first time, there's no performance to maintain. Only presence.

That's when everything changes. Power turns to peace. Strength starts to serve. What once guarded becomes what gathers.

I saw that same distortion in myself. The armor looked like strength until it started cutting off air. Power without connection becomes its own addiction — loud, hungry, always needing another hit. I carried the same hunger.

Years back, before that marriage ended, I believed I was rich in friends. People would say, "If you can count your true friends on one hand, you're lucky." I smirked at that. I could count more than twenty. I even wrote their names down once, proud of the list—good men, men I thought I could lean on, men who'd be there when things went sideways.

Then the divorce detonated that illusion.

Most of those friendships had been welded through couple dynamics—dinners, vacations, the easy glue of shared schedules. When the marriage cracked, those men didn't show up. Some stayed polite, some faded, most vanished. The first night alone, I slept on the couch because the bed felt too big. Out of twenty-two names, I was left with three or four. And even among those, not one had the slice of friendship I needed in that moment.

A wise woman once told me friendships are like pizza slices. Some give you laughter, some give you wisdom, some give you loyalty, some give you truth. If you're lucky, you meet a man who offers the whole box. But most of us carry a scattered plate—a slice here, a slice there, never the full meal.

Marcus gave me the laughter slice—we could joke about anything. But when I needed someone to sit with me in the wreckage, his slice wasn't enough.

That evening the truth landed. I sat alone with my phone, scrolling contacts, name after name glowing in the dark. Every option carried hesitation. This one didn't have the depth. That one was tangled in the past. This one would care but not understand. That one would understand but not stay. Out of twenty-two names, there was no one I could dial.

The loneliness hit like a stone dropped into a well—the fall endless, the splash faint, and then only the echo of my own breath left to answer.

As a last resort, I rang my mum. She picked up with warmth in her voice. I tried to explain, haltingly, how low I felt. My voice cracked on the word alone. She listened, then said, "What are you worried about? You've got money in the bank."

It wasn't cruelty. It was projection—her own fear. But to me, in that moment, it landed like dismissal. Like a door closing on the last room I thought was safe. I told her gently, "Mum, money doesn't solve this. It moves you around faster, maybe easier. But it can't heal loneliness. It can't make you whole." She couldn't see it, and I stopped pushing.

The screen sighed to black. The air changed temperature. Every shadow leaned in.

Rock bottom wasn't the money, the house, or even the marriage unravelling. I still had resources. I didn't need to work. Truth is, I couldn't have if I'd tried. For nearly three years, I was down for the count—adrift in fog, coming to terms with what had happened, what was still happening, who I had been, and who was left.

It wasn't depression in the clinical sense. It was an erasure. Days slid into one another, soundless. I'd stare at a wall for an hour and call it thinking. Walk the same streets twice just to prove I still existed. The grief wasn't tidy. It was feral—an animal that tore through everything I thought was stable, stripping my identity down to bone.

That's what I mean by rock bottom. Not broke. Not drunk. Not lost. Just emptied. All the scaffolding that once held me—money, marriage, status, titles, meaning—gone.

And when the fog finally began to thin, what came back wasn't clarity or ambition. It was something quieter, older. A truth I felt before I could name: a man alone can't outlast his own silence. Brotherhood isn't luxury. It's survival.

Most friendships dissolve quietly; the real ones arrive the same way.

It was a Thursday night. Not late, not early. The house was still, a half-cold coffee beside the keyboard, a screen full of unread legal threads I didn't want to open. I wasn't working so much as staring. The kind of drift where you scroll nothing and call it research.

The phone buzzed. A name I hadn't seen in months: *Wayne*.

I let it ring twice longer than normal, the way you do when you're deciding whether to keep the mask on. Then I answered.

"Mate, you vanished," he said. Ordinary voice. Not a demand, not a performance. Just a fact laid on the table.

"All good," I said. "Busy. You know how it is."

He didn't fill the silence. He didn't rescue me with chatter. He just held the line. I could hear him breathing, waiting. That's when the body told the truth first — a long exhale I didn't plan, shoulders dropping, the chair creaking under the weight I'd been pretending I wasn't carrying.

"I don't know what I'm doing anymore," I said.

"Good," he said. "Then we start there."

Keys. A door. The muffled sound of motion on his end.

"I'm coming."

"Don't," I said, reflex, armor talking.

"Too late."

Twenty minutes later headlights slid across the front wall. He didn't come in. He stood at the door with two coffees, hood up against the night, like a linesman who'd seen enough games to know when the momentum has shifted and when it hasn't.

I stepped out barefoot. Concrete cold underfoot. He handed

me a cup and nodded once. No inspection. No therapy. Just presence.

We didn't talk about the wreckage. We talked footy — the weekend fixtures, who was out with a hammy, whether the coach would risk the rookie in the midfield. Scores, trades, the kind of stats men use when the truth is still warming up on the sideline. The words were surface; the silence underneath was the medicine.

Ten minutes. Maybe twenty. The small talk ran out and we let it. Nothing to prove. The pressure valve opened without ceremony. Something in my chest clicked back into place — not fixed, just aligned enough for the next breath to land properly.

"That's enough for tonight," he said, like a coach calling time before you chase one more rep you don't need.

He tapped the cup with a knuckle, turned toward the car. "Train in the morning," he said, not as advice, not as an order. As if he'd seen the version of me that would, and was speaking to him, not this one.

The door shut softly behind me. I put the empty cup in the sink and didn't open a single email. I didn't need to. The decision had already been made in the cold air.

Next morning, I trained. Not heroics — one set, one walk, one page. Later a text arrived:

> Still here.

Two words, enough weight to hold a day in place. I saved his contact under a new name: *Anchor*.

That night I wrote: Real brotherhood doesn't pull you out. It waits at the edge until you choose to stand — and then stands with you.

That's the architecture: interruption without intrusion, presence without performance — the model for how a man becomes an anchor at the table.

## WHEN BROTHERHOOD ISN'T ENOUGH

Some nights the brothers aren't enough. They can hold the line, but they can't hold your pulse.

There's a point where the weight shifts — when the ache stops being loneliness and starts being danger. You feel it: the breath shortens, the sleep goes thin, the anger hits harder or the silence lasts longer. The table's still there, but it can't carry what you won't name. That's the threshold. That's when you call in another layer of help.

This isn't weakness. It's maintenance. The same way you'd take a truck in when the engine knocks — not because you're fragile, but because you plan to keep driving.

Here's the quick scan that's saved more men than motivation ever has. If **any** of these are true, you don't outsource to the table — you *add* a professional.

- You've thought, even for a second, that everyone would be better off without you.
- Your anger, shutdown, or withdrawal has started to scare you or the people you love.
- You've stopped functioning — can't sleep, can't work, can't care — for more than two weeks.

- The fog hasn't lifted in a month, even though you're using the tools.
- You're leaning on a substance, screen, or thrill most days just to feel level.

That's not failure. That's a flag. It doesn't cancel your strength — it proves you still care enough to act.

*If the body's screaming — chest, sleep, heart, weight, libido — start with a GP.*

Get the bloods, rule out what's medical. Half the "mental health" in men is physical malfunction wearing a mask. Once the body's cleared, you'll see what's truly emotional.

*If the pain is patterned — same crash, same shame, same shutdown — see someone trauma-informed.*

Not a lecture therapist, a nervous-system mechanic. Someone who works with breath, body, and memory together.

*If you're lost but still moving,* a men's coach or counsellor can help you map direction before the map burns.

The table keeps you anchored; professionals help you recalibrate. They do different jobs.

When words fail, hand them this line:

> "I'M FUNCTIONING BUT I'M NOT OKAY. I'VE HAD [LOW MOOD / ANGER / THOUGHTS OF NOT WANTING TO BE HERE]. IT'S BEEN MORE THAN A MONTH. I WANT TO RULE OUT PHYSICAL CAUSES AND GET A REFERRAL TO SOMEONE TRAUMA INFORMED."

That's it. You don't need the right vocabulary; you just need truth. Any clinician worth their salt will know where to go from there.

Brotherhood is oxygen. Professional help is scaffolding. Together, they build something that lasts. Strength isn't how long you hold the weight. It's knowing when to hand it over.

Several years earlier, when I was living at Avoca Beach, north of Sydney, I made a goal to swim every morning for a year—three hundred and sixty-five days without excuse. I'd run down to the water before sunrise, dive into the cold shallows, and feel my body jolt awake. I wasn't fearless; I was terrified of sharks. I stayed close to shore, mask and snorkel on. At six a.m., a small tribe of men gathered—locals, retirees, business owners. Men in their fifties and sixties, some older, eyes like weathered steel. A few carried cancers in their bones, kept alive by ritual and the sea; others carried quieter wounds—divorce, distance, regret. They'd wade out together, diving from the rocks where the shelf drops quick and deep, the same place I never quite dared to go. I told myself it was a preference. It wasn't. It was fear.

The sun lifted over the eastern headland, orange bleeding into gold. The air was sharp with salt. Six of us sat on the sand drying off, steam rising from our backs, the surf behind us heaving slow and steady like breath.

Then Russell came down the path.

He looked hollowed out, a man still upright only because habit hadn't told his body it could fall. Shoulders slack, eyes unfocused, walking like he'd forgotten where the ground was.

One of the blokes called out, "How's goin', Rus?"

He looked up, startled—like someone shaken out of a long, private trance. His eyes flicked between us, trying to place himself back in the world. A pause. A swallow. Then, flat as a dropped anchor, he said:

"Rooted! Hemorrhaging cash for a year now—retirement cooked. I can't tread water much longer. Business is up shit's creek without a paddle. Forty years of grind gone. Damn Covid! The old lady's leaving—we were basically okay as long as there were bottles between us, but that's not even working now. What's the f&*king point?"

He didn't blink. Just stared past us, voice steady in that dangerous way that comes after breaking.

Two of the men stood, muttered something about brekky, and walked off. Vulnerability scares the shit out of most men. We're trained to wear composure like armor, to fill silence with sarcasm, small talk, sport—to joke our way past the truth. When real honesty walks into the room, half the men leave it.

The rest of us stayed. Four men, salt drying on our skin. No one fixed. No one flinched.

Then one bloke said, "You're not alone. I haven't had sex with the missus in two years. I drink every night too." He gave a crooked grin. "When people used to call me a wanker, I'd lose it," He raised his coffee like a stiff drink, wiped his lips with his forearm. The grin dropped. "But it's true. I spend more time with a web browser than a woman. Everyone thinks I'm killing it. I'm not."

The air thickened. Two men gone, truth too close to home. Then it broke open. Four of us left, sitting there like wreckage washed up on the same shore. I can feel it even now—the relief that cracked through me. These men weren't failures. They were good, respected men. Business owners. Husbands. Fathers. Men seasoned by the complexities of life, men who'd built lives that looked solid from the outside but were held together by silence and caffeine and shame. For the first time, I didn't feel alone.

It took me a decade to realize what happened that morning. We didn't plan it, name it, or preach it. But that moment—four men staying when truth entered the circle—that was the beginning of brotherhood. We started meeting without meaning to. Same patch of sand, same thermos of coffee, phones left at home. The sun and sea gave us structure. The tide and sunrise marked time. We'd stand together, breathe deep, and talk just enough.

It became rhythm before it became ritual. One man would start the check-in: RPM. Real. Pressure. Movement. How are you? What's heavy right now? What's one step you've taken that kept you moving forward? Another would follow. Then two men would go deeper while the rest just listened. No advice. No rescue. Just presence. We called it the Table, though there was no table—only sand, steam, saltwater, and truth. At the end, each of us named one action we'd take that week—something measurable, something we'd text proof of before the next sunrise. It wasn't therapy. It was accountability dressed in sea spray. It worked because it was simple. Rhythm. Constraint. Proof.

The first morning we tried it, silence fell after check-ins. Then one man said quietly, "I haven't felt safe with men since I was a kid." Another answered, "You are now." And the whole circle exhaled.

We didn't need rules, but over time a pattern formed. The men who lasted were the ones who kept small promises. They told on themselves first. They could sit in tension without trying to fix it. They protected each other's names when absent. They could disagree without exile.

That's what I later called the Brotherhood Filters, though at the time, it was just instinct. We knew who was real because real men stayed.

Later, I thought back to that old mentor of mine and his pizza slices, and I finally understood what he meant. Every man brings a different ingredient: one brings presence, another truth, another loyalty, another wisdom, another laughter. No single man can feed you completely. But the right circle can. The box only fills when you stop expecting one man to be the whole meal.

That morning, on that beach, something ancient returned.

We don't need bigger networks. We need men who can sit in a shed with you in silence and not flinch. Men who will walk beside you through fog and drop a single sentence that lands like oxygen. Men who will show up when it costs, who will hold the line when you can't.

That morning at Avoca changed me. Those four men—none of them polished, none of them trying to lead—taught me the first law of *ManOS brotherhood*: truth is the entry fee; presence is the proof.

Brotherhood doesn't end the storm. It makes you stormproof. Without it, we're prey to our own darkness. That's wealth—not the kind you trade on LinkedIn, but the kind that keeps you alive.

Months later, after I'd moved away, I got a message from one of those men. It was short: We kept it going. They'd added new faces. Built a small circle around the same ritual—breath, check-in, truth, action. They called it the Table, though the name didn't matter. What mattered was that it worked.

That's where *ManOS* was born—not in a boardroom or a marketing deck, but in the cold surf of Avoca Beach. Six men, stripped of pretense, standing ankle-deep in saltwater, choosing not to leave when the truth finally showed its face. That's where the Brotherhood began. And it's still where it begins.

Simon had done every solo thing a man could do to feel less alone.

Gym. Podcasts. Stoic quotes.

He'd even tried a "men's night" once—ended up listening to two hours of cold-plunge stats and supplement talk.

Driving home that night, he called me.

We spoke briefly—nothing deep, just two men orbiting honesty.

Then, when he hung up, he caught his reflection in the window and saw it clear:

he'd been surrounded but not seen.

Weeks later, he started a small table — just three men, Thursday nights, his garage.

No guru, no sage.

Just a rule written on cardboard and nailed to the wall:
**Nothing you say here leaves here. Nothing you hide here heals here.**

They sat in fold-out chairs between toolboxes and old paint tins.

The first night, nobody said anything. The second, Simon cracked first — about the silence in his marriage.

The others followed. Not with advice, but with stillness.

That was the night the performance died.

Every man needs a room where he can be seen without performing.

Isolation isn't the absence of people — it's the absence of permission.

A table gives you both: place and permission.

You don't need twelve men and a constitution.

You need two or three who agree to three things:

1. Confidentiality — what's said at the table stays there.
2. Accountability — every man shows up, on time, sober, and honest.
3. Courage — no fixing, no rescuing, no deflecting with jokes. Just truth.

That's it.

From there, the rhythm does the work.

## PRACTICES & DRILLS

### Reflection Prompt — Your 2 a.m. Call

Write down the names of the men you could call when the dark hits---when the walls close in and the house is silent, the thoughts are loud, and you don't know what to do next.

If your list is shorter than one, that's your wake-up call.

### Exercise — Make the Call

Pick one man from your past who mattered. Call him today. Not a text. A voice. Just say, "it's been too long—want to catch up?" Set the date before you hang up.

### Drill — Drop the Mask Early

At your next meet-up, share something real in the first ten minutes. Vulnerability builds the bridge faster than another hour of surface talk.

### Reframe — From Networking to Brotherhood

Stop counting contacts. Start counting men who'd show up if you called from rock bottom. Quality over quantity. Depth over reach.

### Takeaway

A man alone is prey; with brothers, he's untouchable. Brotherhood isn't built on convenience—it's built on men who risk being known, who show up when it costs. Without it, isolation eats us alive.

### Reflection Question

Who are the men you will build with—and what will you risk today to close the gap between contacts and true brothers?

## INTERLUDE: WHEN THE MARKET MOVES ON WITHOUT YOU

The accounts were settled, the doors closed, the runway finally cleared — and for the first time in decades there wasn't a next call to make. I sat at the desk looking at a life I'd once been very good at and felt how quickly the world had sped past. The skills that used to be gold now felt like museum pieces. Not bad, just... from another cycle.

I didn't even open the job boards. I already knew what waited there: AI screening, video interviews, timed tests, a 30-something talent lead on the other side trying to decide if a man with a three-year hole in his timeline was worth shortlisting. The recruiters I'd built relationships with had moved on or retired. The senior managers who used to wave me through were easing out. To get back in I'd have to convince people who didn't know the old market — and who probably thought I was past it — that I still had juice.

Sydney told the same story. The streets I used to power through without breaking stride now made me hesitate at the curb. Cars, trams, bikes, tourists — all moving faster. I was out of practice and my body knew it. Even the uniforms had changed: no ties, tight suits, open collars, glass lobbies full of people who spoke in product cycles and sprints. Same city, new frequency. I felt like a freshman in a place I'd once owned.

And always, in the back of my mind, that three-year gap. How do you tell a young gatekeeper, "I wasn't traveling; I was wrecked. It took me three years to open email without shaking"? You don't. You just know it'll be read as "out of the game." That was the quiet punch: not that I had nothing to offer, but that the market didn't have an obvious slot for a man who'd rebuilt instead of "scaled."

That's the part men don't talk about. Every economy crashes twice: once on the stock chart, once in your chest. Status is a currency too, and when it devalues the silence feels like failure. But it isn't failure — it's a forced identity audit. The man you were was profitable. The man you are now is portable. What can be sold has been sold; what remains is the real equity.

**Drill (keep it simple):** write down three roles you've lost in the last five years — "founder," "GM," "rainmaker," whatever. Next to each, write the skill that survived — "built teams," "sold high-ticket," "navigated crisis," "mentored talent." That's your transferable equity. That's the new code base.

**Scar line:** you are not what you sold; you're what remained when it was sold.

## BONUS PRACTICE — FOR MEN READY TO BE SEEN

*Optional. But if you do this, you'll never relate to other men—or to your own silence—the same way again. This is where performance dies and presence begin.*

**Reflection Prompt:**

Where in your life are you performing instead of being seen? Write down the moment you first learned that silence was safer than truth.

**Drill — Claim the Table:**

Pick a night, a place, and two men you trust enough to risk awkwardness with. Send them this text:

> Brother — I'm forming a small Table for men who want truth more than polish. One night a week. Confidential. No advice, no masks. You in?

That's the claim.

If one man says yes, the table exists.

If two say yes, it lives.

## Drill Extension — How to Run the Night

Every Table needs a beginning, a middle check, and an end.

Keep it simple and repeatable.

<u>Opening Question:</u> *"What's real for you right now?"*

This burns off performance and lands everyone in the present.

<u>Mid-Session Check:</u> *"Are we still in truth, or have we moved to story?"*

Use it when talk turns to commentary or comparison.

It resets the current without blame.

<u>Closing Question:</u> *"What truth are you taking home tonight?"*

Each man answers once. No feedback, no advice.

Let silence close the night.

That's it—beginning, middle, end.

Rhythm builds safety, safety builds depth.

## Reframe

You're not building a club. You're rebuilding connection muscle—one repetition of truth at a time.

## Exercise — Duration & Discipline

Set a hard boundary: sixty to seventy-five minutes. Enough time for every man to be seen; not long enough to hide. This isn't catch-up. It's a calibration. When the clock hits time, breathe once, nod, and walk out lighter.

**Takeaway**

Brotherhood doesn't find you. You build it—one chair, one truth, one silence at a time.

**Reflection Question**

Who could you sit across from, week after week, until the performance finally runs out of breath?

# PART THREE
# INSTALL — MAKE IT HOLD

Turn practice into pattern.
Knowledge changes nothing until it lives in your habits.
Here you bring truth into motion — ordering money, caring for the body, stacking daily wins until discipline becomes instinct.

**Call to action:**
Run the system. Stack the wins. Live in reality.

# ELEVEN
# GETTING YOUR MONEY RIGHT

---

"The real measure of your wealth is how much you'd be worth if you lost all your money." – John D. Rockefeller [i]

"Security is mostly a superstition. It does not exist in nature." – Helen Keller [ii]

---

Money anxiety is a quiet poison.

Surveys show that income volatility has become a defining feature of modern work, with nearly half of U.S. households reporting significant swings in earnings year to year. [iii] Household debt loads have risen sharply since 2019, stretching families thinner than ever. [iv] Only about one-third of workers say their careers feel aligned with their core values. [v] And more than half of Americans approaching retirement have less than $10,000 saved. [vi] Financial instability bleeds into every corner of life. [vii] Relationships tighten. Health declines.

Identity wobbles. These numbers aren't just statistics – they're the pulse of daily stress.

David lived it. On paper, he was secure: senior marketing director, six-figure salary, private schools for the kids, a house in the suburbs. But every month felt like walking a wire. One repair, one redundancy, one missed paycheck, and the whole system could collapse.

"I was making more money than my father ever dreamed of, but I felt more insecure than when I was fresh out of college," he told me. Three months of looming layoffs nearly broke him. Hands trembling as he refreshed the company email every ten minutes. Sleep gone. Marriage strained. Body showing the wear. He discovered the truth: he wasn't financially stable – he was financially dependent.

Income is not stability. More is not secure.

But here's what nobody tells you—infinite money can make it worse.

An Oxford buddy on mine, Dal sold his company for three hundred million. We celebrated at Nobu. Wagyu that cost more than most make in a day. Sake that tasted like retirement.

Eighteen months later, I found him in his garage at noon, Bentley running, door closed.

I pulled him out. He vomited on the concrete—not from carbon monoxide, just from the violence of being saved when you don't want to be. First words: "You should've let me finish."

This is the story rarely told: the man who wins everything and wants to die anyway.

Dal had done everything right. Built from nothing. Sold at the peak. Created generational wealth. His kids' kids wouldn't need jobs. The American Dream in a wire transfer.

"You know what that kind of money feels like?" he asked me later, both of us sitting on his garage floor, engine finally off. "Like proof that nothing fucking matters."

He'd thought money was the scoreboard—hundred plus million reasons to prove wrong a father who only ever saw potential in his older brothers, never in him. Hit the number, win the game. But the morning after the wire hit, he woke up the same man in the same skin with the same emptiness, just with more zeros. The zeros didn't fill anything. They just made the emptiness echo. Three hundred million richer and still invisible to a dying man. The money was supposed to be his revenge. Instead, it proved his father still owned him.

That's what nobody warns you about success: it removes your last excuse. When you're broke, you can blame the emptiness on poverty. When you're climbing, you can blame it on not having arrived. But when you summit and still feel nothing? That's when you realize the problem was never external.

Dal's breakdown wasn't about having too much. It was about discovering that "enough" doesn't exist when you're trying to fill an existential hole with material wins. *You can't purchase purpose.* You can't acquisition your way to meaning.

He's alive today. Gave away two hundred million. Teaches woodworking to kids who remind him of himself—hungry for something they can't name. He says the only thing that saved him was realizing this: money is just stored time, and time is worthless if your body's broken or your life is empty.

The truth that nearly killed him. You can have obscene amounts of money and stage-four cancer, and the cancer wins. A fleet of trucks full of gold bars and no one who loves you, and you'll die alone in Egyptian cotton sheets. Without health, money is morphine. Without connection, it's just numbers waiting to be inherited by people who might not even come to your funeral.

My version wasn't a corporate layoff. It was the morning a tax bill landed that I hadn't planned for. I sat at the kitchen table, letter in hand, kids moving in and out for breakfast, pretending it was fine. Inside, my chest was tight as a drum. Shoulders locked. Breath shallow. Coffee turning sour in my gut. I'd built businesses, investments, income streams. But one envelope had me undone.

That wasn't the worst of it. The real collapse came later, when the money stopped flowing and the numbers on the screen became my executioner. I'd lie awake late at night, phone glowing in the dark, refreshing bank balances like they could change if I stared hard enough. Watching one account dwindle, another overdrawn, the buffer shrinking by the day. My chest would lock, my teeth ground against each other until my skull buzzed with vibration.

It wasn't even the numbers themselves that cut deepest. It was the humiliation of being a man who'd built, sold, provided—and still ended up here. Fifty years old, lying in the dark, bargaining with digits on a screen as if they had mercy. Every refresh was a verdict: You've failed. You're exposed. You're done.

The hit was clean: I hadn't failed from weakness but from misplaced trust — I built my balance on systems I couldn't steer. Clients. Banks. Markets. Courts. Their movements decided mine. My sense of self rose and fell with their tides.

That night taught me something data never could: money fear isn't abstract. It's cellular. It lives in your chest, your jaw, your pulse. It shows you exactly where your system is over-leveraged and where your foundations are sand. That terror isn't just panic—it's information.

When I sold one of my companies, I trusted handshakes instead of contracts. I'd been told: "Push back on the details. Protect yourself up front." I didn't. I softened every edge. I wanted to keep the peace. And when it came time to exit, I got fed the line I hate most: "it's business, not personal."

Yes, the legalese was there. Yes, technically I'd signed. Maybe if I'd fought harder through the back-and-forth, some of it could have been prevented. But that phrase – it's business, not personal – cut deepest. As if money suspends the human obligation to act with integrity. As if the pursuit of profit washes away the responsibility to do right by another man.

That's what gutted me. Not just the loss itself, but the way it was excused. I walked away stripped of what I'd earned, jaw clenched so hard my teeth ached, shame burning in my throat – and with a hatred for that phrase that still hasn't cooled.

Business is never impersonal – it's always a human transaction wearing numbers.

The Bitcoin story stung harder. For years I'd been the one telling friends to buy. I had bought early, sold high, doubled, tripled, quadrupled. Every time I sold, I was a hero – until hindsight reminded me what holding would have meant. Then the divorce. No banks would touch me. I needed liquidity for a house. So, I sold. When I ran the numbers, the real cost made me sick: more than a hundred grand a month in lost opportunity.

That decision crushed me. I spiraled into self-hatred. Paralyzed, chest hollow, telling myself: you're fifty years old and you've wasted it. Too late to make it back. Too late to fix it. I carried the shame like a lead vest, shoulders sagging under invisible weight.

Here's what I learned in that spiral, money isn't everything, but without it, everything becomes about money. Lying awake checking bank balances, dodging calls, watching opportunities die because you can't afford to take them—poverty doesn't enlighten, it exhausts.

Money is energy. Its friction removed. It's the difference between solving real problems and being the problem. Even monks who claim to transcend it are subsidized by those who earned it. Someone pays for the monastery. Someone donated the land, etc.

The truth few are prepared to own is that you need enough money to stop thinking about money. Enough that a car breakdown doesn't break you. Enough that you can focus on meaning instead of survival.

How do you build that foundation? Become irreplaceable. Not cheap, but essential. If you think education is expensive, you should try ignorance—it cost me seven figures in bad business decisions. You can have anything you want in life, but not everything. Choose mastery in something the world needs. The choice isn't between money and meaning—it's about becoming so valuable that money follows mastery. When you're genuinely good at something that matters, the market finds you. Not always fairly, not always quickly, but inevitably.

Skills pay bills. Mastery pays mortgages. Excellence builds legacy.

But here's the mathematics of misery no one teaches wealth isn't what you make—it's the gap between what comes in and what goes out.

I've sat at tables with men pulling seven figures who couldn't quit if they wanted to. The Porsche payment, the waterfront mortgage, the private school tuition, the country club dues—they'd built a prison with golden bars. Their hands shake when markets dip. They pop Xanax before checking portfolios. They're making $100K a month and sweating through their shirts because they need $110K to stay afloat.

Then there's my pool cleaner. Drives a ten-year-old Toyota. Owns a small house outright. Has $50K saved. Takes his family camping every summer, pays cash. He leaves his phone in the truck while he works. His shoulders are loose. He whistles. He can tell any client to fuck off because he doesn't need any one of them. Who's the slave and who's the sovereign? Who's more available to be present with their spouse and siblings?

The research backs this. Above basic needs being met—and that number is lower than you think—happiness comes from autonomy, not accumulation. It's called the "hedonic treadmill" for a reason. That new BMW lights up your dopamine for maybe three weeks. Then it's just traffic. The bigger house feels amazing for a month. Then it's just more rooms to clean. The boat? Most expensive days of his life, a friend told me, were the day he bought it and the day he sold it.

The real trap isn't poverty—it's the lifestyle leverage that makes rich men poor. Every new payment is another chain. Every upgrade to "maintain appearances" is another master to serve.

The lawyer with three mortgages and two ex-wives isn't rich—he's broke at a higher level. His burnout has marble countertops.

True wealth is simple: enough money that you can walk away. From the bad client. From the toxic job. From the city that's crushing you. It's not about having millions—it's about needing less than you have. The man who needs $5K a month and makes $7K sleeps better than the man who needs $50K and makes $45K.

Build skills, not status. Own assets, not appearances. The cleaner with his paid-off house and simple life has something the leveraged lawyer lost—he owns his tomorrow.

And it clicked, I understood why chasing dollars themselves is a fool's game. Because the dollars we're chasing are designed to lose value.

If you want the macro view — why fiat decays and why programmable money becomes programmable behavior — see A9C. Fiat and Programmable Money Overview.

If you want the step-by-step money flow — the buckets and percentages — see A9B. FORGE — The Five Fires of Financial Freedom.

Money is energy — steward it, don't worship it. What saved me wasn't another deal. It was a shift in frame. As energy, you need a conductor for money to reliably deliver supply. I run mine through FORGE — five fires that turn income into freedom. Here's the short version.

FORGE is the frame that keeps that energy honest — five fires that temper your wealth into freedom: **F**oundation removes chaos, **O**pportunity buys time, **R**efinement builds power,

**G**ratitude opens doors, and **E**njoyment keeps you alive. Run your money through that rhythm and it stops owning you.

Money isn't God. It isn't happiness. It isn't manhood. Money is energy. That's all. An agreed-upon fiction, a story we all tell to exchange value. A system that has collapsed thousands of times in human history – every fiat currency eventually crumbles. Which means your freedom cannot be welded to what sits in the bank.

But energy matters. It flows. It fuels. And stewardship is a man's responsibility. Not to hoard. Not to worship. To be a custodian. To spend with intention. To save with wisdom. To give with joy. To multiply with clarity.

Money is energy – steward it, don't worship it.

I learned another truth: most men who think they have a business only have a job with extra stress. For years I insisted I had a business. Then a mentor asked me one brutal question: "If you walk away for two months, does it still make money?" My face went hot. I bristled, argued, hated him for it. But he was right. My "business" was just a well-paid trap that only worked if I was there every day.

That's not wealth. That's dependency. A real business adds value, creates leverage, and pays you whether you're in the room or not.

If you can't walk away from your business, you don't own a business – you own a job.

The other key was sales. Without sales, nothing moves. We can romanticize logos, strategies, teams, purpose statements – but until someone buys, you don't have a business; you have an idea. The quickest way to understand this is to study yourself.

Ask: Why did I buy that? Why this instead of that? Was it the packaging, the copy, the environment, the way it solved a problem? Every answer you discover is a doorway into creating value for someone else.

Business is nothing more than solving problems for others at scale, collapsing their effort and time with your leverage, then offering it at a fair price. That's it.

Without sales, there is no business. Without stewardship, there is no stability. Without stability, there is no freedom.

Provision matters. So does presence. So does peace. Strip any one of those from a man and the others rot. Provision without presence makes you a ghost provider. Presence without provision makes you unreliable. Peace without either is delusion. Money doesn't make the man. But a man who ignores money's power will spend his life in chains of fear.

The antidote to that quiet poison isn't more money – it's clarity about what money is.

Johan was forty-two, running two jobs that didn't add up to one life. He used to manage a team; now he managed invoices. He wasn't broke—just strained.

Every week he'd open the banking app like a man checking his pulse: still beating, barely.

One night, staring at the ceiling fan, he whispered the sentence men never say out loud: I don't want to make more money. I just want to stop feeling hunted by it.

He built a spreadsheet the next morning. Not for profit—for peace.

He called it his Freedom Runway: months he could live if everything stopped tomorrow.

At first, it was two and a half months. By the next year, it was twelve. And for the first time in a decade, he slept through the night.

Men confuse greed with safety, but order is what buys peace. You don't need more zeros—you need fewer unknowns. The body doesn't care about the size of your empire; it cares about whether tomorrow is survivable. Financial rhythm isn't about ambition. It's medicine for anxiety disguised as a budget.

## PRACTICES & DRILLS

### Reflection Prompt – Audit Your Dependencies

If every account were frozen for a week, who would you be without your access?

List every system that holds power over your daily life—financial, digital, logistical.

Which ones could cut you off tomorrow?

What would break first if the screens went dark?

What's your offline backup?

Freedom begins with redundancy.

### Drill – Name Your Stability Number

Track your spending for thirty days—every debit, every subscription, every hidden leak.

Then write down the exact number you need each month to cover the essentials: food, shelter, utilities, baseline joy.

Put that number somewhere you can't ignore it.

Every decision now filters through it.

This is your *Stability Number*—the amount that keeps the lights on and the panic out.

It's the line between survival and sovereignty.

### Drill – Build Your Freedom Runway

Once you know your Stability Number, calculate your runway:

1. Multiply your monthly cost of living by the number of months you could survive without income.
2. That total equals your current runway.
3. Every dollar saved, debt reduced, or new stream added extends it.
4. Every new dependency shortens it.

Your first target: three months.

Next: six.

Ideal: twelve.

You don't need millions. You need months.

Then route next month's income through *FORGE*—Foundation, Opportunity, Refinement, Gratitude, Enjoyment—at your chosen percentages.

Adjust weekly for ninety days.

Let the buckets teach you where the leaks are.

Also, revisit your *A3 Values Inventory*.

Choose the three values you want your money to express— peace, growth, generosity, whatever fits your truth.

Then weight your *FORGE* dials to match those values.

Your money should mirror your meaning, not mask it.

## Exercise – Kill One Dependency

Identify one place you're overexposed: a single client, a credit card, a paycheck you can't lose.

Pick one.

Take a concrete step this week to reduce that reliance.

Diversify your effort before crisis forces you to.

Every dependency removed is a small act of rebellion against fear.

**Takeaway**

Systems change. They always have. Every fiat currency in history has gone to zero eventually.

Money itself isn't the enemy—confusing income for stability is.

Real security isn't found in bigger paychecks but in systems that protect you when the paychecks stop.

Money is energy.

Steward it with clarity, and it becomes fuel instead of fear.

**Reflection Question**

What part of your financial life have you mistaken for stability—and what system could you build instead?

# TWELVE
# TAKING CARE OF THE MACHINE

---

"Take care of your body. It's the only place you have to live." — Jim Rohn [i]

---

The numbers tell the story without mercy. Men's testosterone has been sliding for decades, about one percent a year since the late eighties, with the drop hitting younger men as hard as their fathers. [ii] [iii] Sleep is no safer ground: a third of us run on less than seven hours, and one in five on five or less. [iv] [v] Three out of four carry too much weight, waistlines stretched an extra three centimeters since the turn of the century. [vi] [vii] Afternoon fatigue is so common it feels like a cultural rite, but the root is clear — short nights and caffeine stacked on top of exhaustion.[4]

This isn't trivia. It's collapse. Relationships fracture when energy is gone. Leadership crumbles when clarity fades.

Purpose becomes impossible when vitality has bled out. You can't run *ManOS* without healthy hardware.

Luca knew it.

At forty-seven, he was the CEO of a tech firm with three hundred staff and a budget exceeding fifty million. From the outside: dominance. Inside: depletion.

"I wake up exhausted, push through on coffee, crash by three, then scrape myself together for evening calls. My wife gets the irritable version of me. My kids get what's left."

The breaking point came during a board presentation. Halfway through, his vision blurred. Slides turned to static. Two decades of mastery vanished in seconds. He excused himself, locked the bathroom door, and sat on the cold tiles, shaking. His shirt soaked through with sweat. His pulse hammering so hard he could hear it in his ears.

"I've upgraded every system in my business while letting my own foundation rot."

I've lived the same failure.

One morning, during a renovation at the beach house, I bent to pick up a plank. My back didn't tweak – it detonated. Not pain – obliteration. I froze mid-bend, hands clawing at air, breath gone. The world went white. Pain shot down both legs like someone was driving nails through my vertebrae. I couldn't straighten. Couldn't twist. Couldn't even crawl.

Seventy-five meters to the doctor. It took an hour. Every step: negotiation with gravity. Sweat running into my eyes. Jaw clenched so hard I thought my teeth would crack. Neighbors watching from windows as this man who built companies couldn't walk his own driveway. For the first time in my life, I was the broken one.

You can't lead anyone if you can't walk to your own mailbox.

Months of agony stripped every mask away. The cost ledger was brutal stress carried in my back like concrete blocks. The breakdown didn't just steal mobility – it stole presence. My sons would call. I'd cut them short because sitting hurt too much to focus. I wasn't a father anymore. I was furniture – propped against walls, staring at ceilings, waiting for codeine to make me human again.

There was a night I lay in bed convinced I was losing my mind. My body screaming. My thoughts looping. The pain so total I couldn't find an edge to it. For decades I'd run five kilometers to burn off stress. Now I couldn't even stand long enough to piss properly. My gut was wrecked from the painkillers, alternating between concrete and water. Libido dead – not low, gone. Like someone had flipped a switch and turned off that whole circuit. I'd built my entire operating system on hardware that was failing, and the crash was total.

When the hardware fails, the software has nowhere to run.

Three months crawled by before the pivot came. Bloodwork that read like a medical horror story. Testosterone of a seventy-year-old. Inflammation markers through the roof. Vitamin D so low the doctor asked if I lived underground.

Most doctors will run a standard panel — cholesterol, fasting glucose, kidney and liver function, full blood count. Useful numbers, but like checking the speedometer and fuel gauge while ignoring the oil pressure. You can drive away thinking everything's fine while the engine is already straining underneath.

. . .

For most men, the real sabotage doesn't come from genetics. It comes from what's on the plate.

In the U.S., the number one item purchased with food stamps isn't bread or meat — it's soda. [viii] That's not coincidence; it's design. Sugar is cheap, addictive, and profitable. It spikes insulin, crashes mitochondria, and feeds every disease that thrives on chaos.

Insulin isn't just a blood-sugar hormone. It's a growth signal. Keep it elevated long enough, and you stay stuck in storage mode — fat storage, fatigue storage, emotional storage. The irony is that the same molecule that helps cells take in fuel can also turn them into prisons when it never drops back down. [ix]

Doctors often dismiss glucose tracking for non-diabetics, but that's missing the point. You don't wear a glucose monitor to diagnose diabetes. You wear it to see the truth in real time — that the "healthy" juice spikes you higher than a chocolate bar, that the bowl of rice you thought was clean fuel can send your blood sugar through the roof. [x]

It's not about pathology; it's about feedback. Once you see your own data, you stop outsourcing judgment to labels. You start noticing what burns clean and what leaves residue. You stop arguing about diets because your body already tells the truth.

Every man should run this simple experiment once: two weeks of wearing a continuous glucose monitor. Eat as usual. Watch what happens. It will re-educate you faster than any nutrition seminar because you'll feel the crash, see the spike, and realize how often you've been running on stress chemistry disguised as energy. [xi]

The goal isn't perfection; it's pattern recognition. You don't need to hack your body — you need to listen to it.

Sugar is the enemy not because it's evil, but because it hijacks the feedback loops that keep your machine aligned. Once those loops are visible again, you start choosing differently — not from guilt, but from data.

There's another loop most men never learn to read — the chemistry of belonging itself. You can't love with an inflamed brain.

That's not poetry. It's neurobiology. The three main molecules steering that circuitry — serotonin, oxytocin, and cortisol — form a feedback loop that decides how safe you feel in your own skin and with others. [xii]

Serotonin is the molecule of belonging and status. When it runs low, the world feels unsafe — you read rejection into neutral faces, see threat where there's none, and crave sugar or alcohol to fake calm. [xiii] The body needs raw materials to make it: tryptophan (from eggs, fish, meat, seeds), plus vitamin B6, B12, folate, magnesium, iron, and even sunlight to complete the chain. [xiv] [xv] If those aren't present, the assembly line stalls. No serotonin, no steady mood. No steady mood, no stable love.

Oxytocin is the bonding signal — the molecule that tells the nervous system "You're safe here." [xvi] It rises with touch, trust, eye contact, and service — but it's blunted when the brain is inflamed. [xvii] Cytokines — the inflammatory messengers that flood your body when you live on sugar, stress, or sleep debt — interfere with that oxytocin message. [xviii] In simple terms: chronic inflammation jams the love frequency.

Cortisol is the counterweight — the stress hormone that keeps you alive in danger. When it spikes occasionally, it sharpens focus. When it stays high for months, it melts muscle, drives insulin up, suppresses testosterone, and blocks serotonin production. [xix] The very chemical that once kept hunters alive now keeps modern men numb.

Put simply:

- High cortisol (chronic stress) blocks serotonin and oxytocin.
- Low serotonin (nutrient and sunlight deficiency) increases isolation.
- Blunted oxytocin (inflammation) erases connection.

It's not weakness. It's wiring. The body is the vehicle for love. Feed it garbage, sleep four hours, drown it in caffeine and cortisol — and then wonder why you feel nothing. The machine can't bond when its chemistry is in survival mode.

This isn't about perfection — it's about maintenance. Sunlight on your skin, protein on your plate, real movement, honest friendship — these aren't luxuries. They're the firmware updates that let your biology feel safe enough to open.

Once your brain cools, connection returns. You don't have to force love. You must remove what blocks it.

The machine doesn't fail because of destiny written in your genes. It fails because it runs without raw materials. You don't rebuild elastic skin by eating collagen, any more than you fix a cracked wall by slapping paint over it. The body needs base elements — amino acids, minerals, B-vitamins — broken down, methylated, and rebuilt into working parts. Methylation is the assembly line: it switches genes on and off, recycles homocysteine, clears toxins, and keeps your mood chemistry balanced.

That's why comprehensive diagnostics matter. In addition to the usual suspects, a more helpful dashboard looks wider. The comparisons below are analogies only — not perfectly congruent — they just translate invisible biology into car systems most men understand:

1. Hormones: Testosterone (total & free), estradiol, SHBG.

Hormones are your spark plugs and voltage regulator. Testosterone is the spark itself — too little and the engine won't fire cleanly. Free testosterone is the spark that reaches the cylinder; total is what's in storage. Estradiol is your coolant balance — too high or too low and the system overheats or runs brittle. SHBG is your spark-plug wires — if they bind too tight, the spark never reaches the chamber.

2. Thyroid: TSH, free $T_4$, free $T_3$, reverse $T_3$.

Thyroid is your engine thermostat and accelerator mapping. TSH is the dashboard sensor telling the system to warm up. Free $T_4$ is unburnt fuel in the tank — storage form. Free $T_3$ is the actual fuel in the cylinder — what the engine runs on. Reverse $T_3$ is bad fuel clogging the injectors — it looks like fuel but stalls the system instead of powering it.

3. Methylation & nutrients: Homocysteine, B12 (with MMA), folate (as 5-MTHF), B6.

Methylation is your fuel injection and catalytic converter. Homocysteine is exhaust back-pressure — too high and it corrodes the pipes. B12 is an octane booster, unlocking clean burn (MMA helps confirm true B12 status). Folate (5-MTHF) is the air-fuel mix — it sets the ratio. B6 is spark timing — without it, the ignition runs rough.

4. Energy & inflammation: Vitamin D, fasting insulin, HbA1c, hs-CRP.

These are your dashboard warning lights and exhaust. Vitamin D is a solar trickle-charger — without it, power drains. Fasting insulin is fuel flow at idle — too high and you're flooding the engine. HbA1c is your long-term fuel-economy gauge — proof of how efficiently the system's been running for months. hs-CRP is the check-engine light — when it's high, something's already burning out inside.

5. Minerals & toxins: Ferritin, zinc, selenium, magnesium, heavy metals if suspected.

These are your fluids, wiring, and corrosion control. Ferritin is your fuel-tank reserve — too empty and the car stalls; too full and it sludges the injectors. Zinc is your battery terminals — keeps current flowing clean. Selenium is rust-proofing — without it, oxidation eats the frame. Magnesium is your brake fluid and clutch smoothness — without it, nothing shifts right. Heavy metals are rust and grit in the lines — once they build up, they seize the system.

6. Genetic flags: MTHFR and COMT variants.

These are your blueprints and ECU chip-tuning. MTHFR is the factory fuel map — if it's mis-calibrated, you process folate less efficiently and the mix runs lean. COMT is the stress rev-limiter — it shows how fast you burn through performance chemicals like dopamine and serotonin. Some engines redline easily, others lug — neither is destiny, but knowing the map tells you how to drive.

Most GPs won't order half of these unless you insist. In Australia, many aren't covered by Medicare. That doesn't make them less important. It just means you'll need to ask — and maybe pay. And don't expect much conversation about food: in six or seven years of medical training, most doctors get less than a week on nutrition while they'll spend years on pharmacology. That's not a criticism — it's just how the system's built.

I'm not a doctor. This is what I've learned through failure, recovery, and research. Talk to a professional who isn't blinkered by training, who can read more than the cholesterol line. Because ignoring these deeper signals is like watching your oil light flash and telling yourself the car's fine. The crash always comes, whether you believe in it or not. [xx][xxi][xxii][xxiii][xxiv][xxv][xxvi]

Spring came, and with it, small changes. Real food instead of processed garbage. Water instead of the third coffee. Sleep as medicine, not luxury.

At first, even those shifts felt like moving boulders. I was so used to burning the candle at both ends that eating clean or shutting down early seemed indulgent, not essential. The body had been keeping score: every skipped night or extra espresso was just compounding the interest.

Walking became my rehab. At the start, fifty meters felt like a marathon. Each step sent a lightning bolt up my spine. I leaned on fences, on letterboxes, on anything that would hold me. But slowly, the distance grew. A hundred meters. A block. Then two. Every extra step was like paying down that invisible ledger, proof that healing wasn't instant, but it was possible.

I started tracking progress the way I used to track business metrics. Not just pain, but micro-wins: stood up without bracing the table; walked to the end of the street without stopping; slept six hours without waking in a sweat. The numbers gave me evidence when doubt screamed louder than reason.

Recovery wasn't linear. There were nights I lay on the floor, back spasming, cursing my own fragility. There were mornings I stood at the window, sunken eyes, unshaven, wondering if this was the new normal. But in between the breakdowns were tiny victories — the first time I picked up a light weight, the first time I jogged ten meters without seizing, the first time I made it through a day without codeine.

Movement became my new meditation. No stopwatch. No ego. Just testing what my body could do that day. Some days it was five minutes of stretching. Other days a slow shuffle around the block. And then, months later, the first time I broke into an actual run. It wasn't fast. It wasn't pretty. But it was mine.

That run felt like resurrection.

I ditched the stopwatch on runs — no more racing ghosts. Just moment. Just movement. Just breath. I ditched the headphones too. I wanted to sit with my thoughts instead of drowning them. I'd read that the lateral eye movement of walking or running in nature opens a kind of access between conscious and subconscious, loosening what's stuck. [xxvii] So, I began taking problems out on the bush track with me — shadows I wanted to cast light on.

The track was narrow, roots and thorns hidden under loose dirt. Early on I wore road trainers and slipped constantly, even in the dry. Every fall left me raw and annoyed until I discovered trail runners — shoes with grip enough to keep me upright, who knew! Once I had them, I stopped hitting the ground. The eyes kept darting side to side, feet searching out each step, the body locked in a moving meditation.

Out there, mostly alone, I spoke aloud. Sometimes it was prayer. Sometimes it was rage. Sometimes I shouted into the trees: Yes, I can be this. Yes, I can be that. A violent meditation — but also beautiful. Some of the most sublime moments since childhood lived in those ashes, where the darker parts of me could finally be met, accepted, and loved in the same breath.

I spent decades writing software where a single misplaced comma could crash an entire program. I built companies and systems on precision, logic, and empirical proof. I chose science for my master's because certainty felt safer than doubt. For most of my life, anything that couldn't be proven wasn't worth my time.

I used to sneer at divorced men — judged them as weak, as failures. That arrogance kept me locked in my own cage, as if real strength meant holding the wreckage together at any cost.

But not every truth comes with a footnote. Thanks to Ken Wilber and his Integral Theory — and Thomas Kuhn's reminder that even science moves in revolutions of perspective — I was freed to see that objectivity and subjectivity both have their place. And I don't mean that metaphorically. I mean I was literally freed. For the first time, I trusted my own intuition. Trusted that my judgments had weight, even if they couldn't — yet or ever — be traced back to a dataset.

In the past, if something felt deeply right inside but I couldn't find conclusive, exhaustive evidence, I wouldn't let myself lean on it. I thought the structure was too weak without proof. I feared ridicule. I wanted to fit in. It was part of my programming.

Now I'm still objective, still logical. I'm still a healthy skeptic — open-minded, happy to be proved wrong, open to being corrected. But here's the difference: when something can't be proven yet, my mindset no longer collapses. I can hold it as my own subjective point of view. I don't need to force it on anyone else, but I can stand in it with confidence.

There's robust evidence across decades and cultures: spiritual and faith practices — whether prayer, meditation, or quiet belief — predict lower depression, lower substance abuse, and higher resilience. [xxviii] Community plays a role, sure, but the data also show that private faith practices and the way people frame suffering through a spiritual lens add their own weight. [xxix] You don't need to believe in a bearded sky-God to see the signal. The machine isn't just physical and mental. It's also spiritual — whatever that word means for you.

At the end of one of the bush tracks where I ran, the path stopped at a waterway. A huge old tree had fallen the previous year — still early in its decay, bark peeling in slow curls. That's where I'd stop, catch my breath, sit on the trunk. One day, without thinking, I called the tree Trevor. Maybe it was just my imagination, but it felt like Trevor started talking back.

I'd been talking aloud on those runs anyway — praying, shouting, processing shadow parts of myself out where no one could hear. So, talking to a tree didn't feel so strange. One day I said to him, you must have had a good life. You were probably here before I was born. And instantly, in that intuitive space you don't plan, an answer came back: I'm not dead yet. I'm still working. I'm still part of this ecosystem. I'm feeding the ground, the insects, the wildlife around me by offering my body back to the earth.

I cried. For me, it was that real.

I visited Trevor often. One day I asked if he was lonely. Not every time would a reply come, but that day I heard I'm surrounded by my family. Over there are my nieces, my uncles, my children. My seed is everywhere around this place. I'm not lonely. I'm surrounded by the ones I love. My body is lying here, feeding life. I'm at rest. I'm at peace. And I'm still here talking to you.

At the time it felt like imagination. Later I learned there's evidence for how trees and plants communicate — root systems and fungal networks sending chemical signals to share water or warn of pests, a living underground "wood-wide web" connecting individual trees into a community. [xxx] Scientists have shown that birdsong affects tree growth and health, and that forests with diverse bird populations recover faster from stress. [xxxi] And ecologists have long known that so-called "decay" is anything but wasted — fallen logs feed soil, fungi, insects, and other plants in a continuous cycle of renewal. [xxxii]

For me, those runs and visits to Trevor were about more than trees. They were about learning to trust my intuition for the first time. I'd run with a problem, let my eyes scan side-to-side over roots and stones — the same bilateral movement that therapies like EMDR use to unlock stuck memories [see 8] — and by the end I'd feel lighter. Breathing that air, moving through that track, sitting quietly at the end, healed me in ways I couldn't get from screens or self-help books.

Then came calisthenics. In my fifties, starting from zero. That first pull-up attempt was pure humiliation. Hanging there like dead weight, shoulders on fire, arms shaking, feet kicking at nothing. A grown man who couldn't lift his own body weight. But I kept showing up. One shaking rep became two. Two became five. Months later, shirt off in the mirror, I saw abs. Actual abs. At fifty-three, stronger than I'd been at thirty.

Strength isn't about speed. It's about building hardware that can carry your mission without breaking.

I'm slower now. Can't sprint like I used to. But I'm durable. Present. Alive. Because I finally understood: *ManOS* doesn't run on hope or hustle. It runs on meat, bone, blood, and breath. Ignore the machine, and every dream dies with it. Maintain it, and everything else becomes possible.

Luca gets it now too. Six months after his bathroom floor breakdown, he texts me: "Four hours of deep sleep. Deadlifted my bodyweight. Board meeting went three hours – stayed sharp the whole time. Wife says I'm back."

The machine remembers how to run when you remember to maintain it.

## PRACTICES & DRILLS

### Reflection Prompt – The Hidden Load

Think of the last "healthy" food you ate that left you sluggish an hour later. What was the hidden cost in energy or clarity?

For the next two weeks, write down what you eat and how you feel sixty minutes later. That pattern is your real nutrition report card.

### Exercise – Sleep as Infrastructure

Tonight, not tomorrow, set an alarm to remind you to shut down forty-five minutes before you usually fold. Guard those hours like oxygen. A third of men survive on less than seven hours, one in five on five or less, and the bill always comes due. Sleep isn't indulgence — it's the frame every other system hangs on.

### Drill – Run a Full Diagnostic

Book the bloodwork this week. No more guessing. Testosterone, thyroid, inflammation, vitamin D — the full spread. The numbers don't lie men's testosterone has been slipping about a percent a year since the late eighties, and even young men aren't spared.[2][3] Three out of four carry excess weight, and the average waistline is three centimeters thicker than it was a generation ago.[6][7] These aren't random figures; they're hazard lights flashing on the dashboard.

### Takeaway

The body isn't decoration. It's the hardware everything else runs on. Treat it like a rental, and it'll quit when you need it most. Treat it like the only machine you'll ever own, and it'll carry you through decades.

**Reflection Question**

What's the one health debt you've been ignoring — and what happens to your family, your work, your purpose if your body calls it in tomorrow?

**Optional Extensions**

For men ready to go deeper: -

**Optional Blood Test**

A1. Doctor Letter & Comprehensive Diagnostic Panel provides a one-page, doctor-friendly request sheet with a more comprehensive diagnostic panel. It's not mandatory, but it gives you a clearer dashboard if you want to understand more than the basics. Some results may need interpretation from an integrative doctor or private lab, but even having the numbers gives you evidence — the kind you can act on.

**Optional Drill - Wear a Glucose Monitor**

Wear a continuous glucose monitor for fourteen days. Don't change your habits; just observe.

Watch what foods send your blood sugar into orbit and which keep it stable. Write down your top five surprises.

That list will tell you more about your energy, mood, and focus than any motivational quote ever could.

**Optional Drill – The Oxytocin Circuit**

For one week, replace one numbing habit (doomscrolling, sugar hit, late-night caffeine) with one real human input:

- ten minutes of sunlight on bare skin,
- one honest conversation,

- one act of service,
- or a full hug that lasts eight seconds. [xxxiii]

Notice what shifts — in your mood, in your tone, in how you breathe. You're rebuilding the circuitry of safety, molecule by molecule.

# THIRTEEN
# QUICK WINS THAT STICK

"You must build up your life action by action and be content if each one achieves its goal as far as possible—and no one can keep you from this." — Marcus Aurelius

"Small hinges swing big doors." - Zig Ziglar [i]

The smallest start I ever made was a pull-up bar in a garage.

After the separation, I packed what was left of my life into a car and drove seven hours south of Sydney to Pambula Beach — a quiet town almost brushing the Victorian border. I had an old shack there. Mold in the corners, salt-stained windows, a view of the ocean that could make you ache. It wasn't luxury. It was a retreat for a man in triage.

Days blurred into sea rhythm. The mornings were cold and clean; the nights, still enough to hear your own pulse. I'd wake before sunrise, drink black coffee, and stare at the water until I stopped pretending, I was fine. Thirty years of noise had caught up — the business grind, the constant fixing, the climb, the collapse. I wasn't there to reinvent myself. I was there to stop running.

That's where the pull-up bar entered. One of those cheap dip-and-pull stations that wobble if you breathe too hard near them. It came in a battered box, bolts missing, stickers peeling. Perfect. I assembled it under the garage light and thought, if this thing collapses, at least I'll go down with something honest.

The first morning I grabbed the bar, my hands slipped. I hung there, half-lifted, arms shaking, teeth clenched. Couldn't do one. Not even close. I dropped, cursed, walked away. But I came back the next day. And the day after that. I did dips. Push-ups. Dumbbell curls with cheap weights that clanked like hollow promises. The bar didn't care about excuses. It only cared if I showed up.

Weeks passed. Ten minutes turned to fifteen. Fifteen to twenty. The garage became a confession booth — just me, breath, and steel. I didn't track, didn't post, didn't talk about it. Then one morning, six months in, I caught my reflection in the cracked glass above the workbench. I froze. There it was — a six-pack. Not the kind you starve for; the kind that appears quietly when you stop negotiating with effort. I laughed. Years earlier, I'd paid a trainer and eaten boiled chicken for months to chase the same thing. Lost it the moment I stopped. This time, it stayed.

The smallest start rewires you from the inside out. The body learns faster than the mind. Muscle is hungry — it eats hesitation.

Men overcomplicate what works. We wait for the perfect playlist, perfect program, perfect timing. But perfection is just fear in a polished jacket. The body doesn't need a pep talk. It needs proof.

That bar taught me something no company, book, or coach ever did systems don't change you — consistency does. The only metric that matters is presence. The body remembers motion, not intention.

I tell my kids this: every change begins like a snowball. You roll it when it's small. At first it barely moves. Then gravity joins you. Momentum takes over. Keep rolling and it becomes unstoppable.

The pull-up bar was that snowball. One bar, one rep, one refusal to quit. But the roots of that lesson started long before the garage — in an office tower full of dead eyes and good suits.

I'd been contracting for fifteen years. Good money, hard work, full control. Then came an offer — a senior role in a bank, the kind people dress up as a promotion. A "transformation project," they called it. Mergers, buyouts, all the corporate jargon that hides the rot. I said yes. I thought stability would bring peace. It didn't. It brought decay.

From day one, the air smelled of competition and perfume. Every meeting was a small war of egos — smiling assassins trading "insights" while keeping score. They used words like "battle scars" and "taking bullets for the team." Nobody was dying there. They were just killing their integrity.

I lasted two years. By the end, I'd become one of them — tired, cynical, running on caffeine and meetings that went nowhere. I remember looking in the men's room mirror one morning and not recognizing the man staring back. Eyes flat. Jaw locked.

Spirit gone. It wasn't burnout. It was betrayal — of my own values.

So, I quit. Not with fanfare, just a quiet email and a drive home that felt like exhaling after years underwater. I didn't know what I'd do next, only that it had to mean something. Scrivener found me, or maybe I found it. I'd been pestering the developers for a Windows version, and one thing led to another. Eventually, I joined them.

It was reckless. I had a family, a mortgage, and a few months' cash. I went back to part-time contracting to keep the lights on — four days, then three, then two, then one. It took me eighteen months to realize I didn't need that job anymore. The fear lasted longer than the necessity. That's how conditioning works — you keep showing up for things you've already outgrown.

It was the same as the bar: I didn't leap, I phased. Step by step until the new system replaced the old one. Momentum over miracles. Courage scaled to reality.

When I sold the company years later, I thought I'd made it. I hadn't. Divorce followed. Courtrooms, settlements, silence. And in that silence, the pull-up bar waited.

Steel doesn't care about your bank balance. It only asks, Are you still here? That bar rebuilt me when everything else burned down. Because it was honest. Because it didn't flatter me. Because it forced me to move. Movement is medicine. Simplicity is survival. You don't need a plan. You need proof. One act repeated until the body believes you again.

Every man has his bar. For some, it's metal. For others, a page, a brush, a guitar. The object doesn't matter. What matters is that it doesn't lie. You can bullshit a meeting. You can't bullshit a pull-up. You can't fake presence.

That's the real work — finding the one thing that tells you the truth about yourself, then doing it until you no longer need to ask who you are.

Strength, I've learned, isn't about domination. It's about dependability. Every rep is a receipt that says, "I showed up." The strongest men I've met don't shout. They just keep their word — to themselves first.

Science calls it grip strength. I call it integrity. The old men who live longest aren't big. They're wiry, alert, and alive. Their bodies still remember strain and breath. Strength isn't vanity — it's insurance for the soul.

The garage bar wasn't about fitness. It was about fidelity — to the man I promised I'd become. Every morning it asked, "Are you still that man?" And every morning I answered with movement.

That's the system now: one bar, one act, one truth. You start small. You stay small long enough for it to become who you are. Change doesn't begin with the plan. It begins with the pull.

## PRACTICES & DRILLS

### Reflection Prompt — The Bar in Your Life

What's your version of that pull-up bar — the one thing that could rebuild you from the ground up if you stopped negotiating with it?

### Drill — Two-Minute Entry

Shrink the start until it's impossible to avoid. Two push-ups. One page. One walk. Doesn't matter what — only that it's undeniable.

### Reframe — Strength Is Proof of Presence

Every rep is a receipt. It says, "I showed up." Strength isn't about dominance; it's about dependability. You can't fake it, and you can't borrow it.

### Takeaway

Change doesn't begin with the plan. It begins with the pull. Start small. Start ugly. Start now. Motion — not motivation — is what saves you.

### Reflection Question

What's the smallest undeniable action you could take today to prove to yourself you've begun again?

# FOURTEEN
# THE 30-DAY REBOOT

"The cave you fear to enter turns out to be the source of what you are looking for. The damned thing in the cave that was so dreaded has become the labor." — Joseph Campbell [i]

Eighty-nine percent of men say they have clear goals. Yet barely a quarter act on them every day. [ii] Men are nearly 50% more likely than women to delay starting new habits, waiting for the "perfect system" before they take a step. [iii] Neuroscience shows the opposite: the smaller the win, the faster the adoption—habit formation spikes by over 300% in the first month when men start small instead of trying to overhaul everything at once. [iv]

The conference ballroom hummed with deals and futures. Men in blazers working their angles, their exits, their next big thing. I wore the mask well—firm handshake, easy laugh, the practiced lean-in that said I belonged. But when the elevator doors sealed shut and I keyed into my hotel room, the silence hit like cold water.

Stiff bed. Recycled air. That hotel carpet smell—part cleaning chemical, part trapped decades. I pulled open the bedside drawer: Gideon Bible on the left, overpriced chocolates on the right, void in between. The drawer was a reflection. Sacred text I wouldn't read, sugar I'd regret, and the hollow space where something real should live.

I'd flown across the country to be part of something that mattered. Instead, I lay on polyester sheets with my chest seized like someone had cinched a belt around my ribs, drowning in the kind of loneliness that has no language. Not alone lonely. The difference between empty and hollow.

This was my pattern. Day 1: fire in the belly, notebook fresh, plan bulletproof. Day 4: emails pile up, energy bleeds out. Day 7: notebook slides into the drawer with the others. Day 30: shame thick as tar.

It wasn't weakness. It was system failure. Trying to run tomorrow's software on yesterday's hardware. The operating system rejecting every update I tried to install.

The paralysis followed me everywhere. Morning after morning, I'd stand in Alan's garage. Five-thirty AM. Steel cold through my socks. Dust on the barbell so thick you could write your name. The steel smelled like rust and old sweat—evidence of work done by other men, not me. I'd stand there, arms crossed, chest shallow, telling myself: tomorrow, when the plan is perfect, when I know the right program.

Then came the back injury.

It wasn't a car crash or some heroic accident. It was a Tuesday morning, bending to tie my shoes before heading off for a cup of coffee. A white-hot knife shot through my lower spine and dropped me flat on the terrazzo floor. I couldn't move. Not inch by inch. Not without pain like vinegar and salt pushed into an open wound. I couldn't even reach for my phone in plain sight. I was stuck. I sobbed.

Weeks followed in slow humiliation. I shuffled like an old man from bed to bathroom. Sitting was agony. Driving impossible. Every step sent a pulse up my spine akin to stepping on a pin tack bare foot. At night, I'd barely sleep, no position or number of pillows help any relief beyond minutes.

Doctors gave me scans and scripts. "Bulging disc. Rest. Painkillers." Physio handed me a list of movements that felt laughable lying on the floor lifting my leg two inches like a toddler learning to crawl. I wanted to throw the sheet away. I was a man who had done pull ups with twice his weight, run sub-thirteen-minute five kilometers, built houses, rode downhill mountain bike and motocross. And now I couldn't carry a shopping bag without fear of collapse.

The rage and shame were worse than the pain. Rage that my body had betrayed me. Shame that I had betrayed it first—years of red-lining, numbing, neglect. Staring at my face, I didn't see a man. I saw a broken machine I didn't trust.

But the floor became my classroom. The toddler exercises became scripture. Ten minutes a day, then twenty. Bridges, bird dogs, stretches that felt beneath me—but slowly, almost invisibly, my body began to remember. Breath reached deeper. Shoulders softened. The knife-edge in my spine dulled to an ache, then to silence.

By month six, I wasn't sprinting up mountains. But I was slow jogging miles in the wilderness without fear. I was loading plates back on the barbell—not heavy, not impressive, but honest weight, moved with control. More than that, I was listening. I caught the warning signals before they screamed—tightness in the hips, heat in the low back, breath shortening. The machine was teaching me: maintenance or breakdown, there is no middle.

That injury stripped away my illusions. I had thought strength was in the weight lifted, the miles clocked, the exterior armor. The reality was harsher, simpler: strength lives in stewardship. Ignore the machine and it revolts. Tend to it and it carries you.

I came to realize this: once you're financially free, life narrows to two things worth guarding above all else — love and health. Lose either, or the rest collapses. Hold both, and almost anything is possible.

Personally, I'd add a third. Call it faith, call it purpose, call it simply the refusal to believe you're here for nothing. Without something bigger to lean into, you can distract yourself for a lifetime, but the emptiness will wait. Love, health, and that horizon beyond yourself — together they are the real wealth. With them, money becomes just energy, not master.

That lesson should have been enough. Love, health, faith—the real wealth. But collapse has more than one doorway. The body had forced me to listen; I thought stewardship learned. What I hadn't seen was how the same neglect had crept into my work. The garage became another cave. Not vertebrae snapping this time, but paralysis of purpose—plans stacked high, execution at zero. The same fear that wrecked my back now stalked my future.

My shoulders would burn from holding tension. Breath trapped high in my ribs. The dust gathered like an accusation.

My office told the same story. Whiteboards covered in systems. Notebooks stacked like monuments to good intentions. Hundreds of frameworks, thousands of arrows, zero movement. I called it research. Planning. Refinement. But it was fear wearing the costume of preparation. Fear of starting wrong. Fear of being seen trying. Fear that putting words into the world would prove what I suspected: I wasn't enough.

The book became my perfect paradox. The thing I said would free men was the cage I'd built for myself. Pages of outlines that never became chapters. Promises to readers I hadn't met because I was too scared to ship.

Then something cracked. Not dramatically. Quietly.

One morning, the shame got heavier than the fear. I didn't make another plan. I didn't draw another diagram. I got on the garage floor—that same cold concrete—and did five push-ups. Arms shaking. Form terrible. But done.

Then I opened my laptop and typed one sentence. Not the perfect opening. Not the killer hook. Just one true sentence about being afraid.

That was Day 1.

Day 2: Six push-ups. Two sentences.

Day 7: Still showing up, even when the sentences were garbage.

Day 14: The notebook stayed on the desk, not in the drawer.

Day 17: the crack. Momentum had been building; I felt almost bulletproof. Then came a call about a court date and heavy barrister fees for another mediation hearing.

Years earlier I had already liquidated assets, divided cash evenly, acted against legal advice. Still trying to be reasonable. Still trying to be liked. It's a common trap: confuse fairness with self-erasure.

In those months after separation, I had imagined a two-way street — two adults facing their part of the wreckage, each doing their work. What unfolded was a different road entirely. Long disclosure lists. Fragmented returns. Endless legal letters. What I'd mistaken for mutual accountability became a reflector held only one way.

That realization was brutal, but it forced something valuable: a forensic audit of my own patterns. Every memory thrown at me — accurate or distorted — became material for ruthless self-weeding. It was the first time I saw how people-pleasing had been my operating system. The upside of that flaw is that it accelerates change: when the spotlight turns on you, you adapt fast. It's not sustainable or noble — but at the time it helped me cut out what needed to go.

Old shame came flooding back like muscle memory. A wave of grief, the air sucked from my lungs. Years of financial and emotional cost stacked high. The legal expense was only the surface. The deeper toll was spiritual, physical, invisible.

That night, instead of writing, I sat in my car outside a bottle shop for forty minutes. Engine running. Hand on the gear shift. The neon OPEN sign bleeding green through the windshield. I could taste the Pinot Noir already — clean, numbing, familiar.

My phone lit up: a text from my son.

> "Dad, you up for a call?"

I drove home. Didn't drink. Didn't write. But I didn't disappear either.

The next morning, I didn't need a new system. I already had one. Five push-ups. One sentence. The ritual I'd built on the garage floor months before — still waiting, still working.

Day 18 began not as a restart but as proof: once you've built a rhythm from truth, you can fall out of time and still find the beat again.

By the third round I finally understood — thirty days isn't transformation. It's evidence. Evidence that micro-movement outlives mood. Evidence that failure only counts if you don't re-enter the fight. Evidence that progress beats perfection every time.

The notebooks never saved me. The practice did. The framework didn't need to be flawless. It just needed to run.

Planning is procrastination with a spreadsheet. Movement is the only cure.

Thirty days works because it's long enough for neural pathways to start carving new routes but short enough that your resistance doesn't have time to build a fortress. It's proof of concept for your own life. Not a magic number—just enough time to gather evidence that you're capable of change.

What starts as discipline becomes habit. What starts as habit becomes identity. What starts as "I have to" becomes "I am."

You don't rise to the level of your goals; you fall to the level of your systems. Time doesn't always make problems go away or take away the pain—it's an excuse for inaction. Face problems, see them as level-up opportunities to get stronger, hit them hard, hit them head-on, every time. That's how winners keep winning. Don't let good momentum fool you that continued effort is not required. That's why people lose.

Ultimately, operate as if you have no choice but to do this task in front of you. Rituals build the man, not motivation. Discipline is choosing what you want most over what you want now.

The reboot isn't the plan you perfect. It's the code you run.

## PRACTICES & DRILLS

### Reflection Prompt – Your Uninstalled Update

What knowledge or tool have you collected but never installed in your daily life?

### Exercise – The Micro-Install

Take that update and shrink it to the smallest daily action you could repeat for 30 days without fail.

### Drill – Visible Tracking

Choose one way to track your reboot—wall calendar, notebook tick, app reminder—and commit to it every day for the next month.

### Takeaway

The notebooks are coffins for good intentions. Movement is resurrection.

### Reflection Question

What single update would matter most if you committed to running it daily for the next 30 days?

# PART FOUR
# COHERE – LEAD FROM WHOLENESS

Live the truth that outlasts you.
This is where purpose stops being an idea and becomes the way you move through the world.
Coherence is success — not outcomes, but every part of you saying the same thing.
What you've built now teaches others how to stand.

**Call to action:**
Know your why. Live it daily. Leave something worth remembering.

# FIFTEEN
# INSTALLING PURPOSE

"The purpose of life is not to be happy. It is to be useful, to be honorable, to be compassionate — to have it make some difference that you have lived and lived well." — Leo Rosten [i]

"Your why becomes your way. Without it, you're just wandering with expensive equipment."

Performance addiction doesn't just burn us out in daylight —it stalks us when the world goes silent. When the applause fades and the house sleeps, the mask doesn't fall off; it tightens.

Three a.m. has its own geography. The ceiling becomes a map of every wrong turn. The darkness isn't outside — it's pooled in your chest, rising toward your throat like water in a sinking ship.

I know because I've been there. Several times.

The first was after the business collapsed. Partners turned predators. I lay there doing the math—monthly expenses, runway, how many years they'd be okay without me. The math was clean. Cleaner than continuing.

The house held that unnatural silence where even the walls seemed to hold their breath. Appliances kept breathing mechanically — proof the world goes on while you don't. My sons slept two rooms away. I could feel their trust through the plaster, believing Dad had answers. But I was doing division problems with my own existence.

The thought arrived so quietly I mistook it for logic: *They'd be better off with the money than the mess.*

That's the lie that kills men at 3 a.m. — not dramatic despair, but terrible arithmetic. You become a liability on your own balance sheet. Love gets reframed as burden. Presence turns into debt.

I got up. Walked to the bathroom. Looked at my hands gripping the sink. My father's hands — same thick thumbs, same veins. He'd made it to seventy-five, through his own financial vapor, his own 3 a.m. geographies.

If he could last, maybe I could too.

Every man eventually sees his father's ghost move through his own reflection.

That's when mortality stops being theory.

Another time was different. Success this round — money flowing, business thriving — but the marriage was dying in increments, and I couldn't name why. We had everything. We were nothing. I lay beside her, eight inches away, unreachable.

The ceiling asked different questions: *What if this is it? What if you've peaked? What if the rest is just maintenance until death?*

That's the other lie — that purpose must be climbing. That if you're not ascending, you're already buried.

At forty-seven, with twenty thousand nights behind me and maybe ten thousand ahead, the math turned existential — not about money but meaning. Not *can I survive?* but *why bother?*

Success without self feels like winning a game after everyone's left the stadium.

The third time was the worst because it was the quietest. No crisis. No loss. Just this slow recognition that I'd been performing my entire life. Every achievement, every relationship, every mirror — stages for a show no one asked for.

I wasn't suicidal. I was already dead; I just hadn't stopped moving yet.

At 3:17 a.m., staring at the clock, waiting for it to matter, a thought came clear as water: *You're not tired of living. You're tired of performing living.*

That was the click — small, almost mechanical — like a bone slipping back into socket.

I didn't need to die. I needed to stop performing life and start living it.

Purpose isn't what you build; it's what remains when you stop building. It's not your achievements stacked high — it's the ground they stand on.

And at 3 a.m., when the performance ends and the silence get honest, purpose is sometimes just this:

Men don't break because they're weak; they break because they've been taught worth through metrics.

The 3 a.m. crisis is the collapse of that equation.

It's not depression—it's miscalculated identity.

When the arithmetic fails, the only number left that matters is one: you, still breathing. I've met other men in that same dark hour — men who made it to the top only to find it empty.

One of them was **Graham.**

Large-scale studies show the same fracture men already feel in their bones. Adults with a high sense of purpose live longer, healthier lives; those without it face higher risk of early death. [ii] Purpose isn't just mood — it protects against depression and anxiety. [iii] It even predicts lower disability, higher well-being, and better health behaviors as we age. [iv] Yet most workers still report being disengaged at their jobs, doing tasks that feel empty of meaning. [v]

Success without purpose is like buying the latest smartphone — flawless screen, unlimited data, every feature working — and never installing an app. Everything functions, but for what?

Graham knew that emptiness. By fifty, he had a thriving financial advisory practice, a beautiful home, and respect in his field. His work paid well and challenged him. Yet, one Friday afternoon after another "successful" quarter, he sat in his office staring out the window. The numbers looked good. His calendar was full. But inside, he felt hollow, as if the machinery of achievement was still running after the driver had left the car.

"I had all the components of success," he told me later, "but they weren't connected to anything bigger. I was fully functional, but aimless."

That realization hit harder than any financial setback. Metrics had driven his career, but without purpose, they were just data points — activity without meaning.

I know that fracture. The house breathes only wind. The body's done, but the mind keeps grinding. The chest a clenched fist, holding everything that won't let go. I'd built companies, sold them, made money, lost money, collected the toys. But lying there in the dark, none of it held me. The question hammering: What's the point?

Success without purpose is just noise in the dark.

After the marriage ended, I walked out of the last place I'd renovated and felt the echo. Empty rooms. White walls. Just the hum of the fridge. The trophies and bank statements meant nothing. My kids weren't little anymore. The chapter was closed, but the absence was deafening. For the first time in my life, I saw I'd been running a 33-year operating system without ever asking if it had a purpose beyond survival — Dad's old code from Chapter 3, "provide and protect," but never asking what for.

Without purpose, freedom feels like exile.

Then came a different kind of lesson. For years, I painted as part of my own healing. Faces fascinated me — Wim Hof, Gabor Maté, Ken Wilber, Lewis Howes, the men whose work had kept me alive. Once, I'd given away a canvas at an art therapy charity auction — a boy staring at a Ferrari through a shop window. It sold for $5K. But that was transaction, not transformation.

*I Have a Dream - Ferrari, acrylic on canvas 100 × 100 cm (39 ⅜ × 39 ⅜ in)* — Lee Powell (Keny)

Later, another charity asked if I'd paint something new. I said yes, not for recognition, but because the people who ran it were divine and had been such a blessing to me. I painted a modern portrait of Mary — a simple act of blessing, nothing more. For weeks, I held that intention: no ego, no performance, just give.

When I arrived at the event, something strange happened. Even as I lifted the canvas from the back of the car, people stopped. They stared. By the time I set it on the easel, a crowd had formed. Men and women, young and old. Not just women, though it was a feminine painting. Men too. Drawn in, silent, present. Phones lowered. Conversations halted mid-sentence. One woman's hand went to her chest. A man in his seventies removed his cap.

The winning bid came from a 22-year-old man — $8K for a painting no one expected him to want. That day taught me more about purpose than any seminar. Purpose wasn't in the brushstrokes. It wasn't in the applause. It was in the atmosphere created when intention was pure.

**Mary** — *Acrylic on canvas, 100 × 100 cm (39 ⅜ × 39 ⅜ in). Painted and donated by Lee Powell (Keny). Sold at charity auction for $8 000 to a 22-year-old man.* Proof that pure intention is magnetic across age and gender.
(Photograph: Lee with buyer and his brothers.)

I was asked to speak that day without prior notice. And as I looked at the crowd, I understood purpose isn't the empire you build. It's the atmosphere you create. When you do something with a pure heart, not for gain, it becomes magnetic. People feel it. They gather around it. They carry it away.

People don't remember what you built — they remember how you made them feel while building it.

That's not sentiment. It's science. Research in emotional contagion shows that our intentions alter the emotional states of those around us. [vi] People in shared moments often exhibit physiological synchrony — their bodies literally "tune" to each other. [vii] The crowd didn't just see a painting. They felt the intention behind it.

That painting changed how I paint. It changed how I write. It changed this book. Because I understood, finally: the point isn't to impress. The point is to bless.

I remember one of my sons asking me, years ago, "Dad, why do you work so much?" I told him it was for the family. For him. For security. But the question stuck like a thorn. I worked so much because I didn't know who I was without it. My shoulders hunched over screens, teeth welded, eyes burning from blue light. The gap widened between us, and the realization landed slow and cruel — he wasn't asking for more provision. He was asking for me.

He wasn't asking what I did. He was asking how I made him feel.

I once thought purpose would be found in the chase. Build the company, sell the company, buy the freedom. But when I finally stepped away, the freedom felt like exile. I had time, but no mission. Days blurred together. I'd tinker with ideas, start a project, walk away. I'd scroll social media, watching other men lead movements, build revolutions. One morning I saw a post from a guy I'd gone to school with — he'd started a foundation teaching woodwork to troubled teens. 6K likes. Not because of the craft, but because of the clarity. The acid burn of envy wasn't because I wanted their lives — but because I could see they had a purpose.

You can have every tool, every resource, every credential — but without purpose you're still just drifting.

The epiphany was a whisper. One morning, I sat with a notebook, weighed down by the static of my own life, and wrote a question: What will still matter in ten years if everything else collapses?

The pen felt heavy in my hand, dragging across the page like resistance itself. Ink bled through the paper, smudging my thumb as if my body was desperate to leave a mark. The air in the room was stale; windows sealed against the cold. But with each line, something shifted — oxygen returning, faint but undeniable.

The answer wasn't money. It wasn't titles. It wasn't recognition. It was my sons. It was Carolina. It was the work I knew I was born to do — helping men not burn their lives down the way I almost did. That was the pivot. Purpose wasn't out there. It was in the marrow of what I already carried.

Purpose isn't out there — it's what still matters when everything else burns down.

If you can't name it, you'll numb it. The vodka, the lozenges, the endless scrolling — they're not the problem. They're the anesthetic for a life without direction.

Purpose doesn't live in abstract nouns; it lives in what your attention returns to when you're honest. If you flood your day with noise, your subconscious learns to predict more noise. If you seed your day with signals tied to what still matters in ten years, your system will start surfacing those paths without you forcing it.

Your subconscious isn't passive. It's an algorithm that learns from your focus. What you stare at is what it starts serving you. Repetition rewires priority. When your attention keeps returning to the same signals, your system learns to predict more of them.

Tiny protocol: pick one Purpose Signal you can't miss (a phone lock-screen line, a values card on your keyboard, a timer titled "Be the calm he trusts"). See it 10–20×/day. That's not cute —

it's conditioning. You're teaching your prediction engine what "normal" is. If your head has been running on dark, doubtful loops, saturate your day with the opposite. Over time, the unsolicited thoughts you assumed were "just you" start to shift — steadier, hopeful, proactive — because you trained what your mind expects to find. [viii] [ix] [x] [xi] [xii]

The morning, I started the portrait of Mary, the house smelled like linseed oil and coffee. I wrote one line on masking tape and stuck it to the easel: Bless, don't perform. Every time my hand reached for the brush, I saw it. The hours weren't loud — they were steady. Paint on my knuckles, back aching from standing, but mind clear. When I carried the canvas into the charity hall and strangers stopped mid-sentence, it clicked: intention had shaped attention; attention had shaped the work; the work shaped how people felt. That's purpose made visible, not performed.

Most purpose failure is input failure. Change the inputs, and your subconscious will do most of the heavy lifting overnight.

When I finally aligned my daily actions to that — training my body, writing *ManOS*, painting, leading men in conversation — the static cleared. Setbacks became recalibrations, not collapses. Every morning rep, every page, every hard talk stitched itself into a larger story. For the first time, I wasn't just aligned. I was coherent. Whole.

Alignment keeps you balanced. Purpose makes you whole.

Most men wait for purpose like weather. They think it arrives from the outside, a storm that suddenly hits. It doesn't. Purpose is proved, not found. You prove it every time you take one of your values and make it real for another human being.

Pick one of your own values for the week. Not a slogan, not a noble word that sounds good in a workshop. A value you've already named in Chapter 5. Write down one person in your life who could feel that value if you lived it out—your partner, your son, a mate at work. Then make a single sentence promise:

*Because I stand for [value], I will help [person] move from [current struggle] to [desired state] in [timeframe] without [fear].*

Keep it one line. If you can't compress it into that, it usually means you don't yet know what you're promising. The line forces clarity. And clarity is where purpose begins.

For me, one of those lines looked like this:

*Because I stand for presence, when I call my sons I will shut the laptop, stop moving, and simply listen instead of filling the silence with advice.*

They're grown men, 27 and 29, living in another state. For years I'd catch myself half-distracted scrolling, tapping at the keyboard, or turning the call into an unsolicited coaching session. Presence for me isn't about being in the same room. It's about refusing to make them background noise. One clear line forced me to notice: am I listening, or just waiting to talk?

Now test it. Why you? What scar, skill, or access makes you the right man to carry it? Take the rep within seventy-two hours. One action. A phone call, a note, a hard truth, an invitation. Small, visible, undeniable.

Then check yourself. Courage—did I step in? Honesty—did I tell the truth? Self-Reliance—did I carry it through?

Do these enough times and purpose stops being poetry. It becomes a pattern. Others feel it. They trust it.

You've already seen this in paint. In The Crooked Line, the first line you drew was off-ratio — inherited, misaligned. You didn't erase it. You let the echo remain, then laid down a truer line. That canvas became the Presence painting: proof that wholeness doesn't come from erasing the old code, but from writing a truer one over it. Purpose works the same way. You don't erase the man you were. You prove the man you are, line by line, action by action, until others can feel the difference.

Purpose defined this way is more than sentiment. It's consistent with the research. Men who frame their purpose in terms of contribution and service to others show greater well-being and resilience.[See iv] Longitudinal studies confirm that a clear sense of life purpose predicts lower risk of early death.[See ii] Meta-analyses link higher purpose with reduced depression and anxiety, and better stress regulation.[See iii] And neuroscience shows that intention is socially contagious: emotions spread through groups, and even physiology begins to synchronize when people share meaningful moments.[See vi & vii]

## PRACTICES & DRILLS

### Reflection Prompt — Your Vector at 3 A.M.

When the ceiling stares back and nothing feels real, write down one thing that would still matter to you ten years from now, even if everything else collapsed. This is your true north when the map burns.

### Exercise — Map Your Assets in the Dark

List three skills, three relationships, and three resources you already have that could support that one thing.

These are your handholds in the blackout — proof that you're not starting from zero, only from silence.

### Drill — 72-Hour Proof of Life

Choose one of your values. Name one person. Write one clear sentence of promise.

Deliver the proof within seventy-two hours. No drama, no waffle — just evidence that your value creates value for someone else.

At 3 a.m., the question isn't "What's my purpose?"

It's "Can I turn one value into breath for another human being before the sun comes up?"

### Grounding Protocol — Five Alive

If the darkness returns: sit up, feet on the floor, name five things that still exist.

Presence interrupts the algorithm. Reality is never as gone as your mind claims.

**Reframe**

You are not failing; you are re-entering reality. The system reboot feels like collapse only because the old code is dying.

**Takeaway**

Purpose is both construction and continuance. It's built in daylight and proven in darkness.

Without it, the operating system runs but delivers nothing that matters. With it, even collapse becomes calibration. People don't remember what you built — they remember how your presence felt while everything was being rebuilt.

**Reflection Question**

If your current success vanished tomorrow, what part of you would still feel worth living — and why?

Then answer the deeper one:

When the silence returns tonight, will you choose to perform life or to live it?

Complete the A10B. Purpose Integration Worksheet and review A10. Purpose Statements from Real Men for examples.

When a man lives his purpose instead of performing it, the dawn doesn't just arrive — he becomes it.

# SIXTEEN
# LEADING BY EXAMPLE, NOT TITLE

---

"Example is not the main thing in influencing others. It is the only thing." – Albert Schweitzer.[i]

---

The holiday table was set, plates steaming, the smell of garlic bread and roast meat hanging in the air. I heard the buzz of my phone against the wood. Without thinking, I picked it up. The glow from the screen cut across the dishes. My twelve-year-old son didn't look away. He didn't sulk or roll his eyes. He just stared straight through me with a gaze sharper than his years.

"Dad, can you put the phone away?"

I half-laughed, defensive. "I've got responsibilities as a boss. This is important."

He didn't blink. He didn't soften. He just delivered the line that cracked the mask I was hiding behind: "Dad, you're the boss with everyone else... why not with us?"

The fork stopped halfway to my mouth. My chest caved like someone had punched through it. In twelve words, my son had dismantled every illusion I carried about leadership. I wasn't leading. I was performing. Authority without presence is just noise with a title.

In the rearview, I wasn't absent. I was in the house every day. But I didn't lead.

My father had his own shadows. He needed attention, admiration, an audience. Sometimes that meant keeping me or my brother sitting there while he held court — even from the toilet, pants around his ankles, monologuing while we waited outside. At the time, I didn't even register it as strange. That's the thing about growing up inside distortion: you don't know the water's dirty until someone pulls you out of it.

To be fair, he worked hard. We never went without. He got us out of council housing when no one in our family had ever owned property. He bought a house outright in the country, the first in his bloodline to do so. I'm grateful for that. Life could've gone very differently — if not for that escape route, I probably would've done a stint in jail. His drive changed the trajectory of our lives.

But his way of leading left a scar. The lesson I took wasn't strength, it was survival: don't provoke, don't contradict, keep the peace. And here's the irony: he led by taking all the air out of the room, and I repeated it by giving all the air away. Overt control became covert appeasement. His certainty turned into my silence. Two sides of the same coin — both teaching the boys that someone else's moods ran the house.

He'd say he was "playing devil's advocate, for your own good." I'd say I was "keeping the peace." Both were lies. His tore through with force; mine with absence. Neither protected the people who needed it most.

That wasn't leadership. That was surrender dressed as patience. And it left my sons carrying weight that should have been mine. And in staying longer than I should have during that marriage, I modeled the wrong code to my sons: that endurance equals virtue, that silence equals love, that disappearing is moral. That's how men unknowingly pass down weakness — through the examples they never question.

I thought I was protecting them by staying. I was teaching them to abandon themselves. Now my boys know. Because I've told them the truth, not the performance. They've seen the cracks, heard the apologies, felt me present without the mask. We sat together, raw, and said it out loud: it ends with us.

That's the power of even clunky, late leadership. You don't have to get it perfect. You don't have to undo every scar. But if you face it, own it, and lead different — even with trembling hands — you can stop the cycle. You can hand your sons a different code.

That's not theory. That's the real inheritance. My father's volume. My silence. Their freedom. Leadership isn't flawless. It's honest enough to end what should never repeat.

Trauma research calls it repetition compulsion — gravitating back to what's familiar, even if it harms us, until the cycle finally becomes conscious. [ii] I didn't see it then. I just knew it felt familiar. Familiarity has gravity. But silence and surrender only replicated the very wound I swore I'd never pass on.

Now my boys know. Because I've told them the truth, not the performance. They've seen the cracks, heard the apologies, felt me present without the mask. We sat together, raw, and said it out loud: it ends with us.

That's the power of even clunky, late leadership. You don't have to get it perfect. You don't have to undo every scar. But if you face it, own it, and lead different — even with trembling hands — you can stop the cycle. You can hand your sons a different code.

That's not theory. That's the real inheritance. My father's volume. My silence. Their freedom.

Leadership isn't flawless. It's honest enough to end what should never repeat.

Leadership isn't what you command. It's what people choose when choice is all they have.

I carried the same blindness into brotherhood. Thursday nights, a circle of folding chairs in a church basement. The air thick with stale coffee and unspoken weight. Men would sit, wrestling with words that wouldn't come, silence expanding like a bruise. I couldn't bear it. Every pause felt like failure. So, I filled it. I rescued them with my voice, my stories, my wisdom.

They learned something from me, but not what I intended. They learned to wait me out. They learned that if they sat quietly long enough, I would carry the weight they were too afraid to lift. I thought I was modeling strength. I was teaching dependence. What looked like support was sabotage.

When you rescue men from their silence, you rob them of their voice.

It happened at work too. A project worth hundreds of millions. The conference room smelled like burnt coffee and anxiety sweat. My boss sat at the head of the table, waiting. A question came that I didn't fully know the answer to. My chest tightened. My pulse hammered in my neck.

Instead of pausing, I bulldozed. Words spilled out, over-explaining, manufacturing certainty from vapor. I thought I was proving I belonged in that room. What I proved instead was that I didn't trust anyone else there. By filling every gap, I made them smaller. They would comply, but they wouldn't commit. They'd execute the tasks, but none of them would follow me through fire.

The man who must prove he's the smartest in the room ensures he's surrounded by men who've learned to play dumb. I was still trying to control every narrative, manage every outcome. That delusion followed me straight through the divorce.

I liquidated everything. Not threw away—deliberately dismantled. Thirty years of building, gone. The cash-flow businesses that printed money. The properties that built wealth. Every piece of clothing from that life, dumped in charity bins like shedding dead skin. I split it all fifty-fifty, exactly down the middle, against every lawyer's advice.

"You're insane," they said. "You'll regret this."

But I needed the cut clean. No monthly payments binding me to the past. No financial tentacles keeping us entangled.

I came home one day to find my beach house stripped. We'd been living apart for some time—six and a half hours of freeway between us. It worked.

She'd come without telling me, sold what was there. A jar on the kitchen counter: just over $1,000 cash—my fifty percent. The Miele washing machine and memory foam bed I couldn't move became someone else's fresh start through the agent's charity. Everything else fit in a camper van.

Driving away in that camper van, I felt both hollowed out and weightless. Like I'd been carrying stones in my pockets for decades and finally emptied them into the sea.

I used to joke passive-aggressively about being an ATM—a machine that dispensed cash in $20K lots. The joke wasn't wrong. It was the only truth I'd let myself speak for decades. And here I was, dispensed down to pocket change.

The irony burned. My possessions returned that pocket change, yet for years after, I'd bend over for financial colonoscopies—this account, that statement, credit card histories, business records. Millions supposedly hidden while she built her practice as a "conscious uncoupling coach." My lawyer called it something else: "Divorce Coach." We laughed at that—gallows humor between subpoenas. She taught conscious separation while practicing conscious extraction. Preached peaceful uncoupling while perfecting tactical decoupling. The joke wrote itself, but the punchline came with six-figure legal bills.

You learn to cauterize. No longer grant access to your nervous system. Give wide berth to the wreckage. Not bitter—just done bleeding. The legal exchanges tell their own story now, filed away with the court documents. Facts on paper, no longer flesh wounds. That's the final lesson: some people teach you boundaries by crossing every one you had.

But I kept my word. Never poisoned the well. When the boys asked what happened, I opened a shared drive. "Legal documents are in there. Read them or don't." Then I'd change the subject.

And here's what surprised me: the quiet satisfaction that followed. Not moral victory. Not performance. Just the deep calm that comes from knowing you didn't add toxin to an already dirty river.

You don't stay quiet because nothing is at stake—you stay clean because doubling the rot only contaminates the people you're trying to protect. You don't need to justify or correct the narrative. You just need to know you didn't contribute to the decay.

That's the strange power of self-respect: it's internal, private, immovable. People can distort your name, rewrite your motives, weaponize your silence—but inside, you know how you showed up. Gaslighting tries to take that from you, to corrode the last place you feel real. When you've lived in that long enough, reclaiming inner clarity feels like a fish discovering water for the first time—or like a prisoner born inside the walls finally stepping into air. Once you taste that clarity, you guard it like oxygen.

And no, it isn't about becoming "self-sustaining." Humans aren't built as closed systems. We live in community, in relationship, in the quiet exchange of presence and weight. What this work gives you is wholeness. Enough internal alignment that you stop draining the people you love. Enough stability that you can offer presence instead of pulling energy from every room you enter. Enough clarity that you expand the emotional space around you instead of contracting it.

Wholeness isn't independence—it's becoming a man who can add rather than extract.

They figured it out. Not because I told them, but because paper doesn't lie. Court documents don't need commentary. Facts have their own weight.

I'd watched other men vomit vitriol after divorce. Saw them feed on victimhood until everyone—kids included—got exhausted from the stench. The kids always work it out eventually. Sometimes it takes decades, especially when one parent weaponizes them. But truth has patience.

The propaganda was harsh. When your kids parrot words that aren't theirs—words designed to cut—you stand there and take it. Not for her. For them. They're watching how you hold yourself when the world tilts unfair. That's the only sermon that matters—the one you live, not speak.

Love builds. Lesser energies tear down—they need destruction to justify their existence, need something to break to prove they're real. Love proves itself through what it creates. That's the difference: destruction needs a target; creation needs nothing but itself. The parasitic feeds on the living. The living doesn't need the parasitic for anything. Your kids will remember who stayed building when everyone else was burning. Mine did. Through it all, my sons watched.

Through it all, my sons watched. Not the boy from the dinner table anymore—grown men now, twenty-seven and twenty-nine. For the first time, I stopped performing for others and for them. No polish. No speeches. Just the raw truth bleeding through:

"I'm struggling."

"I don't know how to rebuild."

"Some days I can barely stand."

I thought vulnerability would cost me their respect. Instead, it multiplied it. They leaned in. Asked real questions. Shared their own fractures—wounds I hadn't known they carried. How they'd learned to stay quiet to keep peace. How they'd swallowed their voice when conflict rose. How they'd watched me disappear into work while their mother's emotions filled every room.

We cried together. I apologized for not showing them what a real man looks like in relationship. For not protecting them from the dynamics they absorbed. For teaching them, through my silence, that love meant self-erasure.

The map redrew itself and respect became friendship. And friendship became the only leadership that matters. Leadership is measured not by how many obey you, but by how many become stronger because they knew you.

The data confirms what my son already knew. Seventy percent of managers admit they feel like frauds with titles.[iii] Two-thirds of young men report having zero positive male leadership models—not one man they'd follow by choice.[iv] More than half confess they lead differently at work than at home, wearing masks that change with context. Fewer than one in four feel confident developing others instead of just directing them.[v]

We've confused the costume with the man. The title with the truth. Authority with influence. But leadership isn't the nameplate on your desk or the corner office. It's the weight of your life when the room empties and no one's required to listen anymore.

I once ran teams, led men's groups, built companies. But none of it taught me more about leadership than my son's twelve words across a holiday table. Then the silence I smothered in that circle of chairs. Then the bluff I sold in that conference room. Then the unvarnished truth I finally spoke to my sons when the masks came off.

If you can't lead in your own kitchen, with your own blood, when no one's keeping score—you're not leading anywhere else either. You're just management in a man costume.

I don't miss any of it. Not the houses, the businesses, the suits, the status. Just my boys. That used to make me feel guilty—shouldn't I grieve the life I built? But the emptiness of that grief tells its own truth. I found real love after the wreckage. Not the word. Not the performance. The thing itself—love that asks nothing but presence, that gives without keeping score, that stays when there's nothing left to take. With myself first, then with someone who loves without an invoice. When you find that, you want it for everyone. Even the ones who taught you, through pain, what love isn't.

The phone stays face-down at dinner now. Every time.

## PRACTICES & DRILLS

### Reflection Prompt – The Kitchen Table Test

Write down the three people who matter most to you. Ask: Would they follow me if they didn't have to? If I had no title, no money, no leverage—would they still choose my direction? Sit with whatever rises.

### Drill – Hold the Silence

Next conversation, meeting, or group—when silence falls, don't fill it. Count to ten. Watch what emerges when you don't rescue the room from its own weight.

### Exercise – The Crux Question

Tonight, ask: Where am I performing leadership instead of living it? Write one true sentence about the gap. No decoration. Just the truth.

### Gratitude Reframe – Name Your Teachers

Think of someone who led you without a title. A grandfather, a coach, a friend. What did they model that no position could have taught? Thank them, even if only in your mind.

### Takeaway

Authority commands the room. Example changes it. Leadership without presence is just noise with a nameplate.

### Reflection Question

Who in your life sees through your performance—and what truth are they trying to show you?

# SEVENTEEN
# WHAT YOUR KIDS WILL REMEMBER

Men die by suicide at four times the rate of women. [i] Barely one in five younger men ever step into treatment when they need it. [ii] Fifteen percent of men say they have no close friends at all, compared to ten percent of women. [iii] A whole generation is slipping out of the workforce — male participation down from 96% in the 1950s to 86% today. [iv] [v]

The numbers tell a story, but not the one your kids will remember.

---

"Your children need your presence more than your presents." — Jesse Jackson [vi]

---

The night my son almost didn't come home, I learned what inheritance is.

It didn't happen in a résumé or a deal. It was on a beach, black as pitch, waves pounding like war drums, my breath torn out of me with every step.

Earlier that evening, I'd walked into his room. The music was ugly, distorted, a soundtrack for despair. A thought landed in me with the weight of certainty: He's not coming home.

A few minutes later, his mother burst into tears, saying the exact same words. Our boy had driven off. Eighteen years old. Brilliant, furious, living fast — too fast. Cars weren't toys to him. They were weapons, extensions of his body. If he wanted to end things, he knew exactly how.

She wanted to chase him in the car. I knew we'd never find him like that. No tracker. No GPS. He was gone.

So, I stepped onto the sand.

The beach stretched for three kilometers, no moon, no lamps, no people. Just me and the roar of water. The cold wind cut my face. My shoes sank into the sand, heavy as lead.

Halfway down, the terror hit. Not worry. Terror that felt alive. The sense of being surrounded — not by people, but by something darker. I could feel it pressing in, whispering that he was already gone, that I would never see him again. My chest clamped tight.

I reached for the only words I knew. The Lord's Prayer, muttered into the roar. Again. Again. Each line like a rope I was gripping in the dark.

Somewhere in me the thought came: If I can make it to the rock at the far end and touch it, he'll come home. Ridiculous. Irrational. But it gave me direction. One foot after the other. Sand dragging me down. Wind in my face.

When I reached the rock, I pressed both hands against it, forehead leaning on the stone, whispering the prayer like a man begging for breath.

Relief flooded through me, but the fight wasn't over. I turned back. The middle stretch was worst — the blackest part. The sense that I was being watched, hunted. My heart slammed in my chest. I could almost hear laughter in the wind. I kept praying, every word a weapon.

Finally, the house lights appeared faint on the horizon. I stumbled back up the driveway, shaking, exhausted.

And then I heard it — the low growl of his car engine. Headlights sweeping. He pulled in. Alive. I didn't save him. But I had fought for him. They don't inherit your control. They inherit your fight.


After that night I knew we needed a reset. Just him and me.

We flew to New Zealand. The North Island, mountain bikes, every downhill track we could find. For three days he was prickly, testing me, shutting me out. And then the thaw came. Laughter with strangers. Long rides together. For a moment I had my boy back.

On the last day, the organizers brought out a drone to film us. My ego surged. I launched down the "easy" trail, wide gravel, open run. My son shouted behind me to slow down. The drone whined overhead.

Then I saw it. Not a bend. A knife-edge. Hairpin slicked with water.

Time slowed. Gravel sprayed. My brakes screamed under my hands. The edge kept rushing closer.

I thought: *This is how I die. After all this, on the easy run.*

The bike tipped. The sky flipped. I remember my son's voice yelling my name, a bitter, iron tang spread across my tongue like blood I hadn't drawn, the sensation of floating before the world dropped out.

Impact. Silence. Cold. The smell of moss and wet dirt filling my nostrils. For a heartbeat I thought I was dead.

Then voices above me, frantic. A rope thrown down. I was wedged in the only outcrop for meters, just above a sheer drop. The crew shouted for me to leave the bike. I clung to it anyway. They hauled me up, both of us somehow unbroken.

That night we ended in a pub, laughing too loud, alive. Imperfect fatherhood. But real.

They don't remember your flawless fatherhood.

They remember that you stayed in the ride.

A different struggle.

He was top of his class in English, brilliant in everything he touched. I assumed he'd go to university. I couldn't picture anything else. So, when he said, "mechanic," something in me flinched. Not because I disrespected the trade — I'd mixed cement, carried bricks, done my share of labor — but because I imagined something safer, something bigger.

He wasn't thriving at school. Doing well, yes — but never fitting. The signs were all there. The dyed hair in protest.

The quiet misfit energy. He did the grades, but the environment wasn't built for him. His brother thrived there; he didn't. But back then I believed you couldn't send two boys to two different schools. Now I know the opposite is true — you build the world to fit the boy, not the boy to fit the world.

So, when he said "mechanic," I over-corrected. I went looking for something that *looked* like university but still felt practical. I found a design academy in Florence. Prestige on paper. A host family. A grandmother who cooked. A per-diem allowance — enough to live, not enough to get lost.

We went together in winter. Florence was cold, wet, stripped of tourists. Drains smelled faintly of sewage; the alleys echoed underfoot. I pointed at the Duomo like a promise. Told myself I was expanding his world when subconsciously I was dragging him into mine.

At dinner he barely spoke. Pushed pasta around the plate. In the studio he slumped, polite, glazed. Too well-mannered to rebel, but the truth was obvious: this wasn't his dream.

He asked to come home. I said yes — on one condition: complete an online mechanic's course first. It should've taken months. He finished it in two weeks, top marks. Then he came home, took an apprenticeship, and never looked back.

Within a year he was rebuilding Ferraris — still barely in his twenties, engine numbers memorized like scripture, the kind of craftsman other men learn from. Collectors asked for him by name. Two workshop owners — both running multi-million-dollar operations, both successful men simply ready to retire — offered him their businesses outright. He turned them both down. Not because he couldn't run them, but because he didn't want the headache. He liked being on the tools. Liked the craft. The purity of it.

Seven years later, health caught up with him — hands peeling raw from chemicals, wrists burning. So, he pivoted again.

He came to work with me. Learned programming the old way — C++ from first principles. I made him build a Space Invaders clone before he was allowed near anything modern. No drag-and-drop, no pre-built widgets. If he wanted a button, he had to *draw* the button — pixel by pixel, edge by edge. Then Asteroids. Then deeper. The good stuff. Hard, clean, conceptual thinking.

To his credit, he read everything I gave him. Even Bjarne Stroustrup — the full thousand-two-hundred-and-twenty-two-page C++ programming gospel that no sane human has ever finished willingly. That book is pure penance. A rite of suffering. I used it as fatherly "guidance," but truth is, I never made it past the middle chapters. He read the whole damn thing. We still laugh about it. Nothing humbles you faster than your son doing the homework you only pretended to finish. He even contributed code to some of the Scrivener authoring internals. Smart kid.

Those two years working side-by-side were some of the bests of my life. We built things together. We argued about pointers. We laughed at bugs. I gave him work to do and watched him rise. In my own way, I was retrofitting everything I should've installed earlier.

He eventually left IT. Saw the shape of the future before most. Pivoted again — light on his feet. And now he trades full-time with his brother, both self-taught, both carving their own path. Still loves his cars. Still knows who he is.

Any industry can pay if you commit to mastery. He could've run a workshop. Could've stayed in code. Could've done a hundred things. What mattered was that he kept choosing what fit his nature instead of inheriting mine. I learned that from him.

I do miss him. But I'm proud in a way that's hard to articulate — proud that he found a path that was his, not mine. Proud that he outgrew the story I tried to write for him.

It's important for a father to be firm and fair—to let his kids wrestle with hard things instead of rescuing every fall. Overprotective parenting is linked to diminished psychological resilience in adolescents; the brain's error-correction signals grow muted when mistakes are preemptively swept away. [vii]

Sometimes your job isn't to fix what's broken but to stand steady—say, *you've got this*—and let them build the muscle of struggle. Sit in the tension with them, stay calm, and let responsibility take root in their bones.

I over-corrected at times. Tried to wrap them in cotton wool, thinking they'd be spared what I endured. But every child will suffer—in ways you can't predict, in places you can't control. Your job isn't to stop that; it's to be the safe ground they return to. To be open when you fail them. To show what it looks like to own your errors instead of blaming. To model self-correction in real time.

Kids inherit the programs we run—ours, their mother's, their grandparents', their teachers'. Some of it you'll never see until years later. Don't fret. What matters is keeping the door open: to be the place they can lose their shit without fear, where secrets stay safe, where sometimes you lay down a hard line they hate—and that hard line is the most loving thing you could give them.

Reality check: if you don't let your children meet pain now, the world will. Better to help them build the muscle young than leave them soft for a world that isn't.

A father's love isn't in the steering. It's in the staying.

Another time, my youngest son wanted to learn trading. I didn't understand it, so I signed up with him. A full year. Sat beside him with my notepad, scribbling on candlestick charts, trading real money, pretending to keep up but just making sure he wasn't being led into a trap.

It started at one of those "entrepreneur conferences" they bait you into with a billionaire on the poster — Richard Branson's face blown up on the flyers, twenty minutes on stage at the very end of the day, then gone.

The build-up to those twenty minutes was an assembly line of pitches. Course sellers. Hustle-preachers. Dream merchants. The usual carousel.

Then came the self-proclaimed forex guy — really an IT guy in the business of selling courses, not trading. He strutted across the stage with the same tired formula: freedom, beaches, tennis courts, "helping my family thanks to this one simple strategy." The kind of pitch built by the lowest common denominator for the lowest common denominator.

And the mind boggles — if it were that easy, how is the entire planet not retired by Thursday? But my son lit up. And that mattered more than the noise.

Every instinct in me wanted to pull him aside, tell the salesman to cut the bullshit, and walk out. But one look at my son — really look — and I could see it. Curiosity. Hunger. Something alive. And it took every ounce of restraint not to kill that spark just because I'd seen the trick before.

So, I swallowed my cynicism and enrolled with him, just to keep him safe while he learned.

Years later he worked it out himself: that "big example trade" the instructor used to hook the room — twenty thousand pounds in seconds — wasn't expertise. It worked because he had a couple of million pounds of leveraged exposure behind the button. Not because he moved the market — he didn't. Because with that account size, a tiny flick at market open — a couple of points — explodes into eye-watering profit or loss. A parlor trick. A coin toss dressed up as mastery.

He could've made twenty grand or lost twenty grand just as fast — a 50–50 wrapped in a sales pitch. The average bloke in the room couldn't replicate it because the average bloke didn't have seven figures sitting in an account waiting to be lit on fire.

We still laugh about it. The math's was obvious once he had real skill. But that wasn't the point. The point was presence.

He remembers that I sat beside him. Not my competence. Not my notes. Not the trades. Just that I was there — shoulder to shoulder — while he tried to build something that lit him up.

And that's what kids carry. Not whether you mastered the thing. But whether you stood beside them while they tried.

Late in life I learned to tell my kids: watch what people do when it costs them, not what they say when it's easy. Research shows our instincts aren't wrong — behavior under stress is a sharper predictor of truth than polished words. [viii] Children pick up the same code. They don't internalize what we preach; they internalize what we model. [ix] Trust is built — or broken — not by declarations, but by whether we live congruently when the pressures on. [x]

Actions don't lie.

And there are the smaller scars.

Answering their calls while typing, pretending I could do both. The sigh at the other end of the line when they realized I wasn't there. The scrape of a chair, the silence stretched thin.

The running joke — "Dad, you're doing it again." Laughter on the surface, but a sharp edge underneath. It's hard as a father not to flood the room with advice or to split your attention, but the research is brutal: even the silent presence of a phone on the table is enough to fracture trust and empathy. [xi] Studies show that when parents divide themselves with devices, their responsiveness drops and kids act out more in return. [xii] In families and marriages alike, "phubbing" — phone snubbing — erodes closeness, leaving relationships thinner and more brittle. [xiii]

Presence isn't proven once.

It's tested in the tiny moments.

They can survive your failure.

They can't survive your absence.

. . .

What they inherit is not your provision but your presence. Not your plans but your scars. Not the control you thought you had, but the way you fought, stayed, and listened.

They don't remember your titles. They remember your tone.

They don't remember your wealth. They remember your weight beside them.

They don't remember your control. They remember your fight.

Presence is the only inheritance that cannot be spent.

But presence only becomes urgent when time becomes visible. Marcus learned this at fifty-one. Tuesday morning. Reached for his coffee cup. His back said no.

Not pain—complete refusal. A full system lock from L4 to L5. He dropped to his knees, not from agony but from betrayal. This body that had carried him through everything—rugby, marathons, mergers—suddenly couldn't perform a coffee pour.

He crawled to the couch. Literally. A grown man, successful, strong three days ago, now moving across carpet like something wounded. His youngest found him there. "Dad, you, okay?"

What do you tell a sixteen-year-old when your body publicly admits mortality?

Three weeks of recovery. Three weeks of watching his father's walk emerge in his own reflection. The shuffle. The careful descent into chairs. The grunt when standing.

His father had lost most of his right foot to diabetes—toes first, then the rest, piece by piece like territory surrendered in a war. Still alive at seventy-eight, still fighting, but diminished. Marcus saw it now in his own morning struggle—not the diabetes, but the pattern. The slow retreat from capability to compensation.

But worse was the mental shift. Every project suddenly had a timeline. Every goal got audited against actuarial tables. He'd built companies thinking he had forever. Now he had maybe twenty good years, optimistically.

The real terror wasn't death. It was watching himself fade from player to spectator to memory while still breathing.

Then he visited his father. Watched him navigate the kitchen on his partial foot, gripping counters, pivoting on his good leg. Still making his own coffee. Still refusing help.

"You know what I regret?" his father said, unprompted. "Not the foot. Not the pain. I regret all those Saturdays at the office when you were ten. All those bedtime stories I was too tired to read. The games I missed because of meetings that meant nothing."

He looked at Marcus. "I'm not afraid of running out of time. I'm afraid you'll remember me as someone who was always about to show up."

That's when Marcus understood. Legacy isn't what you build. It's what remains in the people who watched you build it.

His back healed. Mostly. He still feels the ghost of that lock most mornings—a small reminder that this machine has an expiration date. But now he knows what matters: not the years remaining, but the mornings where someone needs you to pour the coffee, even if it hurts.

One of his sons asked him months later, "Dad, why did you stop working weekends?"

"Because I finally understood that presence ages better than paychecks."

The transition from building to being isn't defeat. It's the final evolution.

You stop constructing monuments and start becoming one—weathered, imperfect, standing anyway.

Viktor Frankl called it logotherapy—the idea that man is not destroyed by suffering but by meaninglessness.

Every weight a man chooses consciously becomes bearable; every burden forced on him without purpose corrodes.

ManOS turns discipline into direction by giving the "why" back to his pain.

Freedom is not the absence of duty—it's choosing the duty that makes suffering worth it.

That's when I understood: presence isn't just what they need. It's all we must give. The transition from building to being isn't defeat. It's the final evolution.

## PRACTICES & DRILLS

### Reflection Prompt – The Missed Call

Think of one moment when you were with your child but not fully present scrolling, typing, half-listening etc. Write down what code that absence might have taught them. Sit with it without excuse.

### Drill – Phone Face Down

In your next conversation with your child, turn your phone face down or out of reach. Nothing divided. Give them your full face, your full weight.

### Exercise – One-to-One Reset

Plan a short trip or ritual with each child—just the two of you. No agenda. No lecture. Enter their world and let them lead the way.

### Gratitude Reframe – The Hard Line

Think of a time you laid down a boundary your child hated, but it shaped them. Instead of guilt, thank yourself for holding that line. See it as love in its hardest form.

### Takeaway

Your kids don't need you flawless. They need you present. And presence is the code they will inherit when you are gone.

### Reflection Question

When your children look back, what code will they remember you running in front of them?

# EIGHTEEN
# THIS IS THE MOMENT

*"Arrival is illusion. Movement is survival."*

When I finished my first serious rebuild, I thought I was done. Addictions gone. Body rebuilt. Direction restored. I remember telling a mate over coffee, "I think I've cracked it this time."

Three weeks later, I was telling myself that fifteen minutes on the treadmill counted as "maintenance." The barbell hadn't moved in fourteen days. I'd walk into the gym, do a few half-hearted sets, check my phone between every exercise, and leave before I'd even broken a sweat. Calling it efficiency. Calling it time management.

Looking back, it was uglier: I was negotiating with necessity. At forty-something, muscle doesn't stay by accident. Testosterone doesn't maintain itself. Bone density is use-it-or-lose-it. I knew the science. I knew that at my age, the gym wasn't optional—it was the difference between staying dangerous and becoming decorative. Between looking good in clothes and looking good without them. Between being a man who could protect and a man who needed protecting.

But knowing and doing live in different zip codes. I kept treating training like a sprint—binging for two weeks, then nothing for three. Hero sessions followed by ghost months. I hadn't learned the deeper code: vital men don't "go to" the gym. They ARE men who train. It's not an appointment. It's identity. Like brushing your teeth or breathing. You don't negotiate with it. You just do it because that's who you are.

That night, staring at my soft reflection, I saw that I was still treating maintenance like an event instead of essence. Still trying to "get back" to something instead of just being it. My legs felt heavy every morning, like I was dragging anchors. Sleep that should've restored left me more tired. The body keeping receipts for every skipped session.

Transformation isn't a single upgrade. It's maintenance. Like your phone, it doesn't matter how good the model is if you never install the updates.

I learned drift from watching my father's Yamaha 400 gather dust in our garage.

He'd grown up on mopeds—had a Lambretta he'd stripped down and rebuilt to be the fastest thing in his neighborhood. My mother told me stories about that bike, how she'd hold on tight as they tore through the streets, how free they felt. I was probably conceived on the heat of that freedom.

But the Yamaha barely moved. That beautiful machine, chrome pipes gleaming, just sat there while Dad left for work before dawn and came home after dark. Three times I remember him riding it. Once, he took me on the back. I was ten, terrified and thrilled as that deep engine roar shook my chest. "Lean into the corners," he said as I clung to him from behind, arms wrapped around his waist like my life depended on it. For twenty minutes, he was alive in a way I'd never seen.

Then back to the garage it went. Another year of dust.

He provided well. We never went without. Sunday mornings, he'd take my brother and me walking through fields before heading to the pub with Mum. They'd drink with friends for hours while we played in the garden out back, rain or shine. We'd get crisps and lemonade occasionally. It was enough. It was good.

But I'd catch him sometimes, standing in the garage, just looking at that bike. Not touching it. Not starting it. Just standing there like a man visiting his own grave.

That's one of the places I learned drift: a beautiful machine parked in a hard-working man's garage. Provision without pulse. Not "the origin story," just one of many echoes—how boys learn that being good means going still, that duty outranks aliveness, that the wild thing in your chest can wait "until later."

I got so good at being good that I forgot what it felt like to be free.

Forty years later, I was doing the same thing. Not with a bike, but with everything that made me feel alive. The barbell gathered dust while I told myself I was too busy providing. The journal was not opened—twenty-three days between entries, then forty-one, then nothing. The mountain bike hung in my garage like Dad's Yamaha—a monument to the man I used to be, or could have been, or might be someday when things slow down.

Drift is inherited. Passed down like a pocket watch, father to son, generation to generation of men who mistake sacrifice for love, who think providing means disappearing, who teach their boys that being good means being gone.

Drift doesn't announce itself. It whispers.

The same pattern infected my work. For years, I kept contracts on life support because I didn't want to rock the boat. $3M gone because I chose comfort over clarity. Another deal hemorrhaging while I told myself I was "maintaining trust." Reality? I was bleeding leverage one avoided conversation at a time. Neglect dressed as optimism. Drift wearing a suit.

And it showed up in the places that fed my soul. My mountain bike leaned against the garage wall, tires half-flat, chain stiff with rust. Eighteen months since I'd touched it. I told myself the trails would wait. I told myself I was busy building the business, being present for the kids. Every day I walked past that bike, the shame sharpened like a blade. That bike wasn't just exercise. It was where my body remembered it was alive bombing down single track, lungs burning, completely present. Neglecting it was neglecting the part of me that knew how to feel joy without thinking about it. Drift doesn't just steal fitness. It steals the things that make you whole.

The book nearly died the same death. Notebooks stacked like tombstones on my desk. Whiteboards covered in arrows pointing nowhere. Outlines labeled "final draft v7." I called it refinement. It was paralysis. Every day I didn't write, the weight doubled. The voice in my head got louder: Who are you to write this? You're just another broken man pretending to have answers. By month six, opening the document felt like lifting a car.

Drift wears different masks—barbell, masturbation, bike, blank page—but the physics are always the same: entropy wins unless you resist. Drift feels like heavy legs at sunrise, a jaw that won't unclench, sleep that doesn't restore, a heart that idles high for no reason, and a browser history that hides the thing you're avoiding.

Here's how it didn't roar. Here's how it whispered.

Two years after 75 Hard, I still looked carved — body lit like sculpture, mornings locked in ritual: cold rinse, journal, walk, lift. From the outside, it looked like order. Inside, legal bills mounted, letters arrived in capitals. The divorce machinery ground on — endless, expensive, exhausting.

Work in the traditional sense was gone. I was healing, writing fragments of *ManOS*, building AI models to teach myself coding, mentoring a handful of men—as much for my own learning as theirs. When you've built your life on momentum, stillness feels like failure. The gym was still there, but the spirit behind it wasn't. The barbell moved, but I didn't.

Evenings became the danger hour — 6:30 p.m., that low hum in the nervous system. My fingers started their twitch—muscle memory from a year of evening edges I'd bridged with wine. But I was past that now. Months clean. System running. Carolina cooking, garlic and music in the room.

"Just one," I said, pulling the Pinot from the rack. "We'll celebrate a year together." She looked up — not at my words, at my frequency. Women read frequency, not language. "Okay," she said. But her okay carried a question.

One glass became the new protocol. Not every night—that would be a pattern. Just Thursdays. Then weekends. Then any day that needed an edge softened. The mind's genius for self-legislation: I'm not numbing, I'm navigating. I'm not escaping, I'm transitioning. This isn't collapse, it's controlled descent.

Three weeks later the pages thinned, the water cooled, the walks slipped to "later." The lifts stayed, but something left — the pulse, the prayer inside the movement. The story in my head: I'm aware now; I can hold both discipline and ease. The truth in my body: I'm drifting, narrating the fall in slow motion, mistaking awareness for mastery.

Here's what I was doing: running my own code in debug mode, watching myself fall in slow motion, narrating the descent like a nature documentary. Watch as the male specimen constructs elaborate permission structures to avoid feeling what he's feeling.

The wine wasn't the problem; the permission was. I'd turned tenderness into something I could only access through a chemical password. Every glass was a vote that said: I can't access gentleness sober. I need a chemical bridge between armor and rest.

Six weeks in, Carolina said softly, "You're here, but you're not here." It landed because it was true. A millimeter of glass between me and the world.

That night I wrote it out—the full post-mortem:

*Hubris*: Thought I'd transcended the pattern.

*Trigger*: Exhaustion disguised as celebration.

*Act*: Nightly permission slips to numb.

*Cost*: Presence, morning practices, truth with Carolina.

*Boundary*: No alcohol when the ground is shaking.

Next morning: cold water, deep breath, three pages. Not redemption — return. Three days, then a week, then I stopped counting because counting made it heroic again. This wasn't a comeback story; it was maintenance. Carolina noticed before I said anything. "You're back," she said. I hadn't gone anywhere. But I hadn't been anywhere either.

The lesson wasn't about alcohol. It was about avoidance dressed as self-care. Every man has his bridge — wine, porn, scrolling, work, control — ways to cross the river without feeling the water. The trap isn't the substance; it's the belief that you need permission to be human.

My lie was that I needed wine to access softness. Another man's lie might be that he needs anger for strength, or achievement for worth. Same code, different syntax. Repair isn't abstinence; it's agency. Not I can't. I choose not to.

Now, when the fingers twitch, I light a candle instead. Same ritual, different bridge. Ceremony intact, substance changed. Every relapse writes new software, if you're willing to read the error report. Drift doesn't need a crisis; it only needs a permission slip.

## THE MAINTENANCE STACK

- Morning Reset (30 minutes) — Cold rinse (2–3 min): "Stand where I said I would." Journal (10 min): Trigger? Lie? One clean move today. Movement (15 min): no heroics.

- Evening Shutdown (15 minutes) — One-line audit: Where did I tell the truth slower than I could have? Substitute ritual (tea/breath/stretch). Phone down; lights low.
- On-Trigger Protocol (3 minutes) — Name it ("outrage born of grief"), breathe 4-4-8 ×3, unclench jaw, text a brother: "Spike. Not acting. Reset." Delay all righteous messages 24h.
- Weekly — One brotherhood call (permission to call your BS). One 60-min money block, then close the laptop.
- Monthly — What slipped? What boundary bent? What one repair restores 80%? Calendar it with a person attached.
- Relapse Protocol (real 9/10) — Same-day confession (partner + brother). Three-day strict reset. Written post-mortem: Hubris → Trigger → Act → Cost → Boundary. File it. Teach from it.

Sebastian, one of the men I worked with, learned this the hard way. He crushed his first thirty days—journaling every morning at 5:30 a.m., checking in with his wife before bed, training three times a week. His eyes were clear. His kids noticed. His wife said he felt like the man she married. He felt alive.

Then a deadline hit. The journal stayed closed one morning. Just this once. One day became three. The gym bag stayed in the trunk. By week six, he was back in the loop: Netflix until midnight, avoiding his wife's questions, snapping at the kids. When I asked what happened, he didn't blame the deadline or the stress. He said five words that contained everything: "I stopped using the tools."

No catastrophe. No crisis. Just neglect. And neglect is how men lose everything they've built, one skipped day at a time.

But James—another man in the same cohort—took a different path. Same initial thirty days, same commitment. But when his daughter got sick and the routine fell apart, he refused the all-or-nothing reflex: five push-ups beside the crib, a 60-second breath reset, two honest sentences to his wife instead of a shutdown. No heroics. Just identity: I'm a man who trains. I'm a man who tells the truth. I'm a man who checks in. Six months in, there was no drama to report—only evidence. Resting heart rate dropped from 72 to 58. Deadlift went from struggling with 135 pounds to pulling 315 clean. Bloodwork steadied. Temper cooled. His wife's shoulders dropped when he walked in. Tools don't change you in a weekend; they compound in silence.

Your kids won't inherit your victories. They'll inherit your daily code.

The only antidote to drift isn't dramatic. It's boring: maintenance. The ordinary daily reps.

I remember a Tuesday night. Kids asleep. House quiet. Shame rising in my throat like acid. Everything in me wanted to pour a drink, scroll, disappear. Instead, I reached for the journal. Not because I felt like it—because it was Tuesday, and Tuesday was journal night.

The first line was trash: I don't know what I'm doing and I'm tired of pretending I do. By the third paragraph, something loosened. The urge to numb backed off. The journal didn't fix anything, but it gave me ten minutes of truth instead of three hours of regret. Ten minutes was enough to break the pattern.

Another night, my oldest son came to me, torn between the safety of his job and a risk that lit him up. Old me would've delivered a lecture—either chase your dreams or play it safe. Instead, I pulled out the black foam dice from my desk drawer, gold letters etched into each side. Values dice. I rolled it. It landed on Courage.

I handed it to him. Said nothing.

He turned it over in his hand, stared for half a minute. Then he said quietly, "I already know what courage looks like here." The dice did what words never could — it made my voice land instead of echo.

I got a call from Tom. No agenda, no setup—just, "Mate, how are you truly doing?"

I hesitated. I wasn't hungover, just foggy from three glasses of wine the night before. Enough to blur the edges. I almost gave him the default: I'm fine. Busy, you know how it is.

Instead, something cracked. I told him the truth. Not all of it—just one line that had been clawing at my throat: I don't know how much longer I can keep this up.

Silence on the line. Then his voice, steady: "That's the first honest thing you've said in months."

Tools don't fail. We just stop picking them up. Maintenance keeps you alive. Momentum makes you dangerous again. When the drama dies, discipline takes over. Momentum doesn't start with motivation; it starts with an ordinary rep that says: *I'm back in motion because motion itself is sacred.* The men who stay lost wait for inspiration. The men who rise build rhythm instead. Momentum is peace in motion — no crisis required.

None of photographs well for Instagram. Beat-up journals with coffee stains. Foam dice that look like they came from a board game. A text thread with three men who check in every Sunday night. A barbell in a garage. The monthly values audit—just a piece of paper where I check: did my calendar match my claimed values? Did my spending align? Did my attention? Boring as hell. Essential as breath. These tools are anchors. Without them, drift wins.

Like that crooked line on the canvas from the beginning—the one I tried to fix, tried to make perfect, only to realize the flaw was the point. The crack where the light enters. The imperfection that makes it real. Maintenance isn't about perfection. It's about showing up to the mess, repeatedly, until the mess becomes the method.

Maintenance is what your kids will remember. Not the speech you gave them about values, but the journal they saw you write in every morning. Not the success you achieved, but the workout you didn't skip when everything was falling apart. What you repeat becomes their inheritance.

It's the same as the painting: you don't sand the old line off the canvas—you draw the true one every day until It's the line everyone sees.

And here's the brutal accounting: the operating system is already installed. You're already running code.

For most men, it's borrowed silence from fathers who never learned to speak, stoicism from grandfathers who came back from wars with locked jaws, provision without presence, strength without tenderness. That's the factory settings. And the factory settings are killing us.

We've already seen what the numbers say in *Brotherhood*: men are breaking in silence. Four times more likely to end their lives than women, twice as likely to report deep loneliness, and spending less time in meaningful connection than any generation before. The data doesn't need repeating; the pattern does.

The code is still broken.

What those statistics reveal isn't just social decline—it's a spiritual disconnection. The modern man is data-rich and meaning-poor, surrounded by information yet starved for integration. The collapse isn't happening in headlines; it's happening in kitchens, bedrooms, and quiet commutes, where men live as though their usefulness expired with their last achievement. Until the code is rewritten—from performance to presence, from metrics to meaning—those numbers will stay the same.

Meanwhile, studies show women are twice as likely to recognize and name their emotions accurately—not because they're naturally better at it, but because they've been given permission to practice while men were told to shut it down.[i] The code is broken.

*ManOS* is the rewrite.

Not a fantasy. Not a motivational poster. Not another productivity hack for optimizing your morning routine. A system. A framework you install and run daily so you don't drift into the man you swore you'd never become.

The reality is simple: men are behind. Women have been forced into wholeness by necessity—earning, leading, nurturing, advocating. Over recent years, women have outpaced men in college degree completion: 47% of U.S. women ages 25-34 hold a bachelor's degree, versus 37% of men._ii Women also now comprise much of the college-educated labor force (holders of bachelor's or higher) among adults 25 and older._iii In Australia, for example, ~37% of women aged 15-74 hold a bachelor's degree or higher compared to ~30% of men; Women now make up ~59% of domestic university students. iv In the UK, women occupy ~43% of board seats in FTSE350 companies, though only ~35% of senior leadership roles, and the full-time pay gap still hovers around 7%. v These gains haven't been optional—they required emotional literacy, resilience, connection, decision-making. Men who coasted on a single dimension now find that no dimension can be ignored. Wholeness isn't optional; it's table stakes.

We're behind not because men can't adapt, but because many of us haven't had to. Wholeness isn't optional; it's table stakes.

*ManOS* runs in sequence:

- Debug the inherited code. Notice the phrases that exit your mouth in your father's voice. The anger that flares exactly like his did. The silence you retreat into just like he taught you. Chapter 3. See the ghost code.
- Install the dashboard. Your body is trying to tell you everything—tight chest means pressure building, shallow breath means you're in survival mode, locked jaw means there's truth you're not saying. Chapter 4. Read the instruments or crash.
- Choose your values. Not the ones on the company website. Not the ones your dad preached but didn't live. Your actual values, proven in Tuesday choices.
- Map your wounds. Every man sees reality through the smoke of his not yet healed past. Your wounds aren't

weaknesses—they're the distortion field you need to account for. Chapter 6. When you know how you're bent, you can straighten.
- Learn to connect. Stop the performance. Stop the monologues. Real connection is a circuit: speak, listen, return. Chapter 8. Without it, you're alone in a crowd.
- Build brotherhood. Find two men who will call you on your masks. Not drinking buddies. Not business network. Men who know your real name. Chapter 9. Alone, you're prey.
- Maintain daily. Drift is physics. Entropy is real. The tools are boring—journals, workouts, values checks, brother texts. Chapter 17. Use them or drift.
- Write new code. Your children inherit your patterns, not your promises. Every time you choose presence over performance, truth over comfort, maintenance over drift, you're coding their future. Chapter 16. Legacy is daily.

This is the full system. Not fragments. Not tips. Architecture.

Because mediocrity isn't neutral. It's toxic. Every man who drifts takes his family with him. Every father who won't face his wounds passes them to his sons. Every leader who runs on autopilot creates organizations of sleepwalkers.

Nature doesn't do mediocrity. A redwood doesn't "try" to be tall—it grows or it dies. The ocean doesn't "work on" being powerful—it moves or it stagnates. Fire doesn't negotiate with what it will burn. Men were built for the same physics: collapse and rebuild, death and resurrection, the endless cycle of becoming.

When a man learns to run his operating system consciously—when he stops being passenger and starts being programmer—everything changes. Not overnight. Not dramatically. But irreversibly.

That's why this isn't optional. The world doesn't need more high performers burning out at fifty. It needs men who know how to fall apart and rebuild. Men who can hold paradox—strong enough to protect, soft enough to connect. Men who treat their wounds as teachers, not shame. Men who show their sons that strength includes tears, that leadership includes not knowing, that love includes staying present when everything in you wants to run.

The central lie we've been sold is that accomplishment creates satisfaction. That the next promotion, the next $1M, the next achievement will finally fill the void. But we're built for both—inner depth and outer impact, humility and pride, success and failure. The tension between them isn't a problem to solve. It's the engine of becoming.

Stop comparing your chapter 3 to someone else's chapter 20. Comparison is the killer of all joy, all hope, all progress. The life you have is the life you created—own it. Every choice, every drift, every comeback. Self-education is the only real freedom. Break free from inherited narratives. Take responsibility for what you've built and what you've broken.

The prescription is simple: Change yourself first. Debug your code. Install your values. Build your brotherhood. Maintain your tools. Then you'll have something real to offer.

The world is waiting. Your son is watching. Your partner is hoping. Your community needs what you could become if you stop drifting and start building.

This is the moment. Not tomorrow. Not after the next crisis. Not when you feel ready.

Now. Today. This breath. This choice.

Pick up the tool. Open the journal and write three sentences starting with 'I feel...'. Send the text. Lift the weight. Tell the truth. Choose presence. Break the drift.

The man you become is the code the world will run.

The morning light over Avoca looked different the day I went back.

Same beach. Same shelf where the water dropped off into dark blue.

But this time, I walked straight in.

The cold hit like it always did — that first electric slap that forces you to breathe or break.

I stood in the shallows, chest high, letting the salt sting wake every nerve. The rhythm was familiar — breath, brace, release.

Behind me, on the sand, two men were drying off. Younger, louder — not the old crew, but the next wave. One was talking fast, the other listening the way men do when they're holding something heavier than the words.

Through the hiss of the surf, I caught fragments: *the TABLE... BRIC... brotherhood.*

A pause. Then laughter that didn't quite hide the ache beneath it.

The listener didn't interrupt. Just let the silence breathe between them.

I turned back toward the horizon and smiled. The rhythm was still alive.

Not my system — *our system*. The one that's older than all of us. Men staying when it's hard.

The tide rose to my ribs. I closed my eyes, let the water carry my weight.

Not rebirth. Not redemption. Just rhythm.

The kind you don't negotiate with. The kind that keeps you human.


When I opened my eyes, the horizon was a thin gold line — not promise, not perfection, just proof.

Of motion.

Of breath.

Of life moving forward.

That's the whole code.

You keep showing up.

You keep moving toward the light.

You stay.

When the tide reached my ribs, I thought of that old Yamaha gathering dust in Dad's garage—chrome dulled, engine waiting. Different water, same lesson: motion keeps you alive. I stood there, salt on my tongue, paint still under my nails from yesterday's canvas, breath syncing with the swell. Nothing mystical—just maintenance.

A few years after I'd rebuilt — sober, strong, back in motion — I got invited to a charity event for the Fred Luizzi Foundation. I'd never met Fred. I didn't know what he was like day to day. But I met his people — two sons, two daughters, their partners, the grandkids — and you could feel him in the room. You know that? When a man's gone but his frequency is still in the family's eyes. Firm and fair, they said. Helpful for no reason. Just a good man.

What hit me wasn't the speeches. It was the atmosphere. Men and women both — all a little teary, all a little proud. That's when I clocked it: whatever Fred spent his life on was still working after he stopped breathing. That's wealth.

By that point my own life was good. I'd healed. I'd met the love of my life — somehow manifested her on a mountain in Tasmania. I was in great shape, mid-fifties and still rocking a six-pack, which — I'll admit — felt nice to run a hand over under my shirt and jacket. No tie. I don't do ties. The point is: body was home again, money was steady enough, love was overflowing.

And yet there was that ache. Not the old panic — just a small hollowness behind the ribs. Sitting there listening to people talk about Fred's impact, I realized what it was: my rebuild was mostly about **me**. My health, my relationship, my nervous system, my provision. All good, all necessary. But it was still... contained.

That afternoon I saw the next layer: *alignment is you with you; coherence is you with the world.* When your thoughts, words, money, time, and presence all point in the same direction — toward blessing somebody else — that's when the ache shuts up.

I remember thinking: *I've got love. I've got health. I've got enough coin to get to the end. So why do I still feel like something's missing?*

Answer: because it's a very small life if it ends with you. Providing for your family is noble. But if that's the whole project, it gets self-referential fast. Maslow will let you camp at "safety" for a decade, but your soul won't.

That's where ManOS crystalized — not from "I should write a book," but from sitting in a room full of a dead man's people and thinking, *I want that. I want my sons, the men I've worked with, the women who've waited for us to grow up, the world we leave — all of them to be steadier because I was here.*

Legacy isn't a statue. It's a *frequency* your family can still tune to when you're gone.

And here's the other piece I saw that day: I wasn't "done." I still had some mojo. I was just at the stage where the rebuild had worked, and now what was left was ongoing maintenance — which, is the whole game. You don't finish this and frame the certificate. You keep updating the code so the people watching you don't inherit your old bugs.

That's coherence. That's the Why that holds.

That's what this whole book distills to — a daily run sequence you can live: -

*Morning* — Cold rinse (2 min): *Stand where you said you would*. Three-line journal ("*I feel ...*"). Fifteen minutes of movement.

*Midday* — Quick values check: *Did my actions match my code?* One integrity audit.

**Evening** — Write one line in your journal: *"Today I delayed truth when..."* Name the moment in five words or fewer.

*Weekly* — Message one brother: *"All good or under pressure?"* No fix, no advice. Just presence. One Table (check-in call). 60-minute money block, then close the device.

*Monthly* — Repair one boundary. Teach one lesson forward.

That's the maintenance loop. The proof you're still in motion.

## PRACTICES & DRILLS

### Reflection Prompt — The Daily Debug

At the end of every day, open your journal and write one line only:

*"Where did I tell the truth slower than I could have?"*

That single audit will reveal every place drift begins.

### Drill — The Maintenance Loop

- **Morning Reset:** Cold rinse (2 min) → Three-line journal ("I feel …") → 15 min movement.
- **Midday Check:** Ask, *did my actions match my values?* Do one small repair if they didn't.
- **Evening Shutdown:** Write one honest line. Replace escape with ritual—tea, breath, stretch.
- **Weekly Proof:** Message one brother: "All good or under pressure?" No fixing, just presence.
- **Monthly Audit:** What boundary bent? What repair restores 80 percent? Calendar it.

These are not motivational habits; they're the software updates that keep the system alive.

### Exercise — Teach It Forward

Show your son, student, or brother one of these tools this week.

Not the lecture—just the act. Let him see the maintenance, not the myth.

### Reframe

Legacy isn't a story you tell when you're old; it's the rhythm you keep while you're still breathing.

**Takeaway**

The man you become is the code the world will run.

**Reflection Question**

What code are you writing today that your children, your culture, and your century will inherit tomorrow?

# THE MANOS FIELDKIT

## A COMPLETE TOOLKIT FOR COHERENCE

Every man's life runs on code. Some of it you chose. Most of it you inherited. When that code crashes, philosophy alone won't reboot it. You need a field manual — something that converts awareness into action. That's what this section is for.

The ManOS Field-kit is the practical half of the book — the bridge from insight to implementation. Each tool here translates principle into practice so the man you're becoming can survive first contact with the real world.

Many men don't fall because they were reckless; they fall because the world they trained for disappeared beneath them. Automation, outsourcing, and AI have erased the straight ladders our fathers climbed. A man can wake up overqualified, under-valued, and ashamed to admit he no longer knows where he fits. That isn't a personal failure — it's a structural shift. ManOS names it so it stops masquerading as weakness.

Rebuilding order in money, purpose, and brotherhood is not ambition; it's mental-health hygiene.

Every Field-kit entry connects to one of the four BRIC domains — the same map introduced in *The Map*.

B — BARE: Strip back to truth. Face the crash and return to what's real.

R — REFORGE: Rebuild what matters. Restore trust, connection, and brotherhood.

I — INSTALL: Make truth actionable. Turn practice into pattern. Discipline becomes instinct.

C — COHERE: Live from wholeness. Lead, contribute, and transmit coherence into the world.

Together, they form the operating system of a man's life — a loop you'll walk through again and again, each time at a deeper level.

## HOW TO USE THIS FIELD-KIT

Start small. Pick one tool and complete it fully. Integrate it. Don't collect tools — embody them. Share it. The Field-kit is built for circles, partners, and mentors. Upgrade it. Future Field-kit releases appear at getmanos.com/Field-kit.

These tools are simple but not easy. They ask for follow-through, not perfection. If you treat them like a checklist, they'll change nothing. If you treat them like a discipline, they'll change everything.

## BARE — FACE THE CRASH

A1. Doctor Letter & Comprehensive Diagnostic Panel

Give your GP or health professional a clear, comprehensive request for bloodwork and baseline diagnostics.

**How to use:** Print it and take it to your appointment. Hand it over without apology. It lists hormones, inflammation markers, metabolic and vitamin panels most men never get tested for.

**Goal:** Stop guessing. Get data. Know your numbers before the crash.

A2. Communication Scripts — When Words Fail

Give you language for hard conversations when your mouth goes blank — conflict, apology, repair, boundary, and truth-telling.

**How to use:** Pick the scenario closest to what you're facing (partner, brotherhood, work). Read the pattern, not the exact sentence. Speak it in your own voice. Stay slow.

**Goal:** Replace shutdown and sarcasm with clear, masculine, non-dramatic language so you can stay in connection without performing.

## REFORGE — REBUILD WHAT MATTERS

A3. Values Inventory

Identify, rank, and commit to the five values your life will run on.

**How to use:** Read the full list. Circle ten. Cut to five. Rank them. Write one sentence on how each value must show up weekly.

**Goal:** Align daily decisions with the inner code that defines you.

A4. Emotional Maps

Decode what you feel through the body, so you stop calling everything "fine."

**How to use:** Start where it hurts (throat, chest, gut). Match the sensation to the emotion map. Name it out loud. Act from the named emotion, not the triggered one.

**Goal:** Build emotional literacy — not to be softer, but to be accurate.

A5. Brotherhood Field Guide

Blueprint for starting and running a men's Table — a container for truth, not a coffee club.

**How to use:** Follow the meeting flow, Covenant, and speaking order. Rotate leadership. Keep time. No fixing without permission.

**Goal:** Build local brotherhood that calls you up and keeps you honest.

A6. Partner's Letter — To The Woman Who Loves A Man Doing This Work

Explain to her what this work is, so she doesn't mistake your focus or silence for withdrawal.

**How to use:** Share it or read it to her. Invite questions. Own your part. Make it a bridge, not an excuse.

**Goal:** Replace confusion with understanding and build compassion on both sides.

A7. When You're Being Played — Toxic Patterns To Recognize

Help you spot relational patterns that drain you — manipulation, intermittent validation, threat of withdrawal, and manufactured chaos.

**How to use:** Read the list of patterns. Circle the ones you're experiencing. Document two or three real interactions from the last month. Hold them up against the patterns without self-blame.

**Goal:** End confusion. See games for what they are. Stop negotiating with dysfunction.

A8. When You're Loved — The Real Thing

Show you what healthy, adult, mutual love looks like — so you don't walk away from the real thing because it feels unfamiliar.

**How to use:** Compare current or past relationships to the markers listed (consistency, repair, truth, support without control). Note where you resist it because you're used to chaos.

**Goal:** Train your nervous system to receive love that's stable, not dramatic — love that matches the man you're becoming.

## INSTALL — MAKE IT HOLD

A9. Clean Money Protocol & Tracker

Create a clear, shame-free view of your money so it stops running in the background like a silent stress.

**How to use:** List every inflow and outflow. Tag it (essential, growth, debt, drift). Track weekly. Run the protocol monthly to clean up leaks and emotional spending.

**Goal:** Make money honest, visible, and aligned with your values — financial nervous system calmed.

A9B. Forge — The Five Fires Of Financial Freedom

Move from "I pay bills" to "I build wealth" using five simple buckets.

**How to use:** Allocate income across the Five Fires: Foundation, Opportunity, Refinement, Gratitude, Enjoyment. Adjust percentages to your season — this is a framework, not a cage.

**Goal:** Give your money a mission so it serves your life, family, and future instead of disappearing.

## COHERE — LEAD FROM WHOLENESS

A10. Purpose Statements From Real Men

Inspire and calibrate your own purpose line through real, lived examples.

**How to use:** Read through the statements. Notice the shape (service + people + cost you're willing to pay). Draft your own and cut it down until it's honest.

**Goal:** Write a purpose line you'd sign publicly and can live daily.

A10B. Purpose Integration Worksheet

Turn your purpose from words into calendar, habits, and relationships.

**How to use:** Start with your written purpose. List 3 weekly expressions of it (at home, at work, with men). Schedule them. Review monthly.

**Goal:** Move from clarity → consistency → contribution. Purpose that lives in rhythm, not in your head.

## DIGITAL EXTENSIONS (2026 AND BEYOND)

Every man builds differently. Some need words. Some need movement. Some need a map they can hold.

ManOS was never meant to stay bound in a book. It's a living system — one that grows as men do.

What you've read here is the field manual. What's coming next are the tools: interactive maps, emotional dashboards, brotherhood frameworks, and digital systems that track the work — not the performance.

Each tool exists for one reason: to help men operate with presence, power, and truth in the real world — with their families, in their bodies, in their work, and in the quiet hours no one sees.

Updates and future modules at getmanos.com/tools — where the operating system expands, one function, one man, one upgrade at a time.

## CLOSING LOOP — THE SYSTEM RUNS AS ONE

If you've reached this point, you've walked the full circuit of ManOS — from the crash to the climb, from philosophy to practice, from self to system.

## THE MANOS FIELDKIT

The Field-kit isn't an appendix. It's the codebase for the man you're rebuilding. Each BRIC quadrant is a function, each tool a subroutine. When they run together — Bare, Reforge, Install, Cohere — the system stabilizes.

Keep it live. Revisit what slips. Update what no longer fits. This is an operating system, not a monument. The man you're becoming is the update.

For tools, updates, and community, visit getmanos.com — the home of every future release.

One system. One brotherhood. One upgrade at a time.

# A1. DOCTOR LETTER & COMPREHENSIVE DIAGNOSTIC PANEL

*Introduction for Your Doctor:*

I understand that not all of these tests fall within standard Medicare/NHS/insurance guidelines. I am happy to pay privately for those that are outside the usual funded panels. I'm seeking a more comprehensive, preventive screen to better understand my health picture.

I respect that every doctor must work within medical standards and practice guidelines. This request is not meant to challenge those guidelines — only to ensure I'm covering areas of risk and prevention that matter to me personally. If some items cannot be ordered through you directly, I'd be grateful for your advice on the best pathway to obtain them (specialist referral, private lab, or other service).

## A1. DOCTOR LETTER & COMPREHENSIVE DIAGNOSTIC PAN...

Requested Laboratory Tests

Hormones

- Testosterone (total and free)
- Estradiol (E2)
- SHBG (Sex Hormone Binding Globulin)

Thyroid Function

- TSH (Thyroid Stimulating Hormone)
- Free T4 (thyroxine)
- Free T3 (triiodothyronine)
- Reverse T3

Methylation & Nutrients

- Homocysteine
- Vitamin B12 with MMA (methylmalonic acid)
- Folate (5-MTHF)
- Vitamin B6

Energy & Inflammation

- 25-Hydroxy Vitamin D
- Fasting insulin
- HbA1c
- hs-CRP (high-sensitivity C-reactive protein)

Minerals & Toxins

- Ferritin
- Zinc

- Selenium
- Magnesium
- Heavy metals panel (if indicated by history/symptoms)

Genetic Flags (if available privately)

- MTHFR polymorphisms
- COMT variants

Note to Patient: If your GP cannot order all of these, consider referral to an integrative, functional, or preventive medicine specialist. In some countries (Australia, UK), not all are Medicare/NHS-funded even if ordered. Private labs and online health services sometimes offer panels you can take to a qualified practitioner for interpretation. Always seek follow-up with a licensed professional to integrate results into a safe, personalized plan.

# A2. COMMUNICATION SCRIPTS — WHEN WORDS FAIL

I used to think communication was about being right. Getting my point across. Winning. Then my marriage ended. My kids stopped talking. My business partnerships exploded. All because I never learned to ask the simplest question: *"What do you need from me right now?"*

That question changes everything.

## THE QUESTION THAT SAVES RELATIONSHIPS

Your partner starts talking. Your brain immediately starts solving. Stop.

Ask first: "What do you need from me—just an ear, feedback, or help solving this?"

She'll tell you. Usually, it's the ear. Sometimes it's validation. Rarely is it the solution your brain already mapped out.

During my first marriage, I heard, "You're a terrible listener but a great problem solver. I didn't marry a consultant. I married a witness."

That landed like a brick.

## THE 24-HOUR RULE

When I need space, I get maximum 24 hours. Not to punish. To process.

But here's what I learned after blowing this sixteen times: You have to say when you're coming back.

"I need until tomorrow at 7 PM to process this."

Then you show up at 7 PM. Not 7:15. Not "sorry, got held up." Seven. Your word becomes worthless the moment you break this promise. She's not tracking your logic. She's tracking your reliability.

I once disappeared for three days after a fight. Came back ready to talk. She'd already started grieving the marriage. Some bridges burn while you're "processing."

## THE POISON WORDS

These words are relationship napalm. I know because I've used them all:

"You always..." (Makes her the villain of your story) "You never..." (Erases every good thing she's done) "Whatever" (Passive-aggressive surrender) "Calm down" (Gasoline on fire) "You're just like your mother" (Nuclear option)

Here's what works instead:

## A2. COMMUNICATION SCRIPTS — WHEN WORDS FAIL

"You always" becomes → "I've noticed when X happens, I feel..."

Not "You always interrupt me" but "When I get cut off mid-sentence, I shut down."

See the difference? One attacks. One reveals.

## THE APOLOGY THAT REPAIRS

"Sorry" is a dead word. I must have said it ten thousand times. Changed nothing.

Real apology has anatomy. I learned this after my son stopped speaking to me for three months:

1. What you did: "I yelled at you about your grades in front of your friends." 2. The impact: "That humiliated you and broke trust." 3. No excuse: (Skip the "I was stressed about work") 4. The change: "I'm seeing someone about my anger." 5. The witness: "Will you tell me how that landed on you?"

The moment you add "but" anywhere, you've killed it. "But" is the eraser word.

## MID-FIGHT CONNECTION

Three years ago, mid-screaming match with my partner, I did something insane. Put my hand on my heart, then reached it toward her. No words. Just that gesture.

She stopped mid-sentence. "What are you doing?"

"Reminding both of us that I love you even while we're in this."

Now we have a stone—smooth, black, fits in a palm. When fights escalate, one of us places it between us. It means: *This is temporary. We are permanent.*

Sounds soft? Maybe. But it's kept us together through things that would have broken us before.

## THE SHIT SANDWICH THAT WORKS

Nobody wants feedback. Everyone needs it. Here's how to give it without starting war:

Layer 1 (True appreciation): "The way you handled the kids' meltdown yesterday was masterful." Layer 2 (The actual issue): "When you commit us to plans without checking, I feel steamrolled." Layer 3 (The partnership): "I want us both to feel heard in decisions."

My business partner taught me this after I'd been doing it wrong for years—just hammering people with what they did wrong, wondering why they got defensive.

## WHEN YOUR KIDS DESTROY YOU

My teenager said, "You only care about looking like a good dad, not being one."

## A2. COMMUNICATION SCRIPTS — WHEN WORDS FAIL

My chest caved in. Wanted to defend, list everything I'd done, the sacrifices, the money spent. Instead:

"You're probably right. Tell me what a good dad would look like to you."

Then I shut up for seventeen minutes while he unloaded years of built-up truth. Hardest seventeen minutes of my life. Changed everything.

## THE FEELING WORDS THAT UNLOCK HER

For thirty years, my emotional vocabulary was: fine, good, pissed, tired.

My partner gave me a list. "Try one of these instead of 'fine.'"

- Depleted
- Restless
- Heavy
- Hollow
- Fragile
- Raw

First time I said, "I feel hollow," she moved closer instead of away. Specificity creates intimacy.

When angry, try:

- Frustrated (goal blocked)
- Disappointed (expectation unmet)
- Hurt (love meeting pain)

"I'm disappointed" lands different than "I'm pissed." One invites conversation. The other starts war.

## EMERGENCY PROTOCOL

About to say something nuclear?

"I need to stop before I say something I can't take back."

Then leave. Not storm out. Leave clean.

My protocol:

- 10 deep breaths in the garage
- Cold water on wrists
- Walk the block
- Text: "I love you. Need 30. Will be back."

That text is crucial. It says: I'm regulating, not abandoning.

## THE UNIVERSAL TRUTH

Every fight is the same fight. It's never about dishes, money, sex, kids. It's about:

*Do you see me? Do you choose me? Am I safe with you? Do I matter?*

Answer those four questions in how you show up, not what you say.

Your body talks louder than your words. If your chest is tight, jaw clenched, breathing shallow—she knows. She's reading your nervous system, not your vocabulary.

Get your body calm first. Then speak.

## THE THING NOBODY TELLS YOU

The script that works best?

"I don't know what to say right now, but I'm not going anywhere."

I've used every technique, every tool, every framework. But that sentence—said while staying physically present—has saved more moments than all the others combined.

Sometimes the most powerful thing you can say is that you don't know what to say, but you're staying anyway.

That's not weakness. That's love with its sleeves rolled up.

Remember: These aren't performance scripts. They're pattern breakers. Every time you use one instead of running your father's program, you're rewriting generational code.

The words matter less than choosing presence over the old pattern.

That's the upgrade.

# A3. VALUES INVENTORY

The following pages contain the fifty-two core values that power *ManOS*. Each value is described in plain language: what it means, what it isn't, and the question it asks of a man. Together they form the foundation of the Triadic Engines—clusters of three values that generate movement and balance inside the system. These are not ideals to perform but coordinates to navigate by.

ACCOUNTABILITY — Taking ownership for your actions, impacts, and commitments. It means answering for your role in outcomes, not blaming or deflecting. Core question: What part is mine to own? Triad: Accountability → Responsibility → Stewardship (Owns specific actions).

ADAPTABILITY — Flexibly adjusting mindset and behavior as circumstances change. It means responding with presence instead of rigidity. Core question: How can I meet this moment freshly? Triad: Patience → Adaptability → Growth (Adjusts to what emerges).

## A3. VALUES INVENTORY

AUTHENTICITY — Living and speaking from what's real, not rehearsed. It means alignment between inner truth and outer word. Core question: Am I being true or performing? Triad: Self-Awareness → Authenticity → Integrity (Truth lived out loud).

BALANCE — Holding multiple demands without losing labor. It means rhythm, not perfection. Core question: Where am I over-weighted? Triad: Discipline → Balance → Peace (Order without rigidity).

BEAUTY — Seeing and creating harmony in form, thought, and feeling. It means noticing what uplifts the spirit. Core question: What is worth honoring here? Triad: Clarity → Beauty → Gratitude (Sees and amplifies the good).

CITIZENSHIP — Contributing to something larger than self. It means participating, not spectating. Core question: How do I serve my community today? Triad: Responsibility → Citizenship → Service (Acts for the whole).

CLARITY — Seeing things as they are, not as feared or desired. It means cutting through noise to truth. Core question: What's true right now? Triad: Curiosity → Clarity → Wisdom (Discerns without illusion).

COMPASSION — Meeting pain with understanding instead of judgment. It means strength with softness. Core question: Can I see his hurt without taking it on? Triad: Humility → Compassion → Forgiveness (Heart without weakness).

CONTRIBUTION — Giving what you have for the benefit of others. It means movement from surplus, not sacrifice. Core question: Where can my effort matter most now? Triad: Gratitude → Contribution → Service (Overflow into impact).

## A3. VALUES INVENTORY

COOPERATION — Working with others toward a shared end. It means respect for interdependence. Core question: Am I building with or against? Triad: Equality → Cooperation → Unity (Together moves further).

COURAGE — Acting despite fear. It means choosing truth over comfort. Core question: What would I do if fear wasn't the boss? Triad: Honesty → Courage → Integrity (Action aligned with truth).

CREATIVITY — Turning imagination into form. It means trusting inspiration enough to act on it. Core question: What wants to be made through me today? Triad: Curiosity → Creativity → Contribution (Expression as service).

CURIOSITY — Staying open to what you don't yet know. It means questions over conclusions. Core question: What else could this mean? Triad: Humility → Curiosity → Wisdom (Learning as lifestyle).

DISCIPLINE — Doing what matters when it's hard. It means devotion to consistency over mood. Core question: What deserves my energy today? Triad: Discipline → Perseverance → Self-Mastery (Effort becomes strength).

EMPOWERMENT — Owning your agency and helping others own theirs. It means lifting without rescuing. Core question: Am I leading from fear or freedom? Triad: Responsibility → Empowerment → Service (Power shared well).

ENTHUSIASM — Engaging life with energy and appreciation. It means full presence, not fake positivity. Core question: Where is my spark today? Triad: Gratitude → Enthusiasm → Vitality (Spirit in motion).

## A3. VALUES INVENTORY

EQUALITY — Recognizing the inherent worth of all. It means respect beyond hierarchy. Core question: Do I treat others as ends or means? Triad: Fairness → Equality → Justice (Honor across difference).

EQUANIMITY — Remaining steady through highs and lows. It means emotion felt, not ruled by. Core question: What's still true beneath the storm? Triad: Faith → Equanimity → Peace (Calm inside chaos).

FAIRNESS — Acting with impartiality and care. It means equal standards under pressure. Core question: Would I judge myself the same way? Triad: Integrity → Fairness → Justice (Balance in action).

FAITH — Trusting life even when you can't see the map. It means confidence in unseen order. Core question: Where do I need to trust again? Triad: Hope → Faith → Peace (Belief as stability).

FORGIVENESS — Releasing resentment without erasing boundaries. It means freeing yourself first. Core question: What am I still carrying that isn't mine? Triad: Compassion → Forgiveness → Freedom (Let go as power).

FREEDOM — Living self-directed and unchained by fear or false duty. It means choosing with awareness. Core question: Is this choice mine or inherited? Triad: Integrity → Freedom → Purpose (Choice in alignment).

GRATITUDE — Recognizing the good that already exists. It means attention over accumulation. Core question: What's already working? Triad: Beauty → Gratitude → Love (Appreciation as fuel).

## A3. VALUES INVENTORY

GROWTH — Expanding capacity through challenge. It means discomfort as teacher. Core question: Where am I resisting evolution? Triad: Adaptability → Growth → Wisdom (Stretch as path).

HONESTY — Speaking the unvarnished truth. It means clean communication, not cruelty. Core question: Am I telling the truth or managing perception? Triad: Honesty → Courage → Integrity (Truth embodied).

HOPE — Expecting goodness to return. It means refusing cynicism. Core question: What would hope do next? Triad: Gratitude → Hope → Faith (Belief in renewal).

HUMILITY — Seeing yourself accurately—no bigger, no smaller. It means grounded confidence. Core question: What can I learn from this? Triad: Humility → Curiosity → Wisdom (Openness as strength).

HUMOR — Remembering lightness even amid strain. It means perspective, not denial. Core question: Can I laugh without mocking? Triad: Humor → Joy → Vitality (Relief as resilience).

INCLUSIVITY — Creating spaces where difference belongs. It means invitation without dilution. Core question: Who's missing from the table? Triad: Equality → Inclusivity → Unity (Belonging as design).

INTEGRITY — Acting in line with your values even when unseen. It means wholeness over approval. Core question: What would I do if no one was watching? Triad: Authenticity → Integrity → Trust (Wholeness in action).

JOY — Feeling life's aliveness without permission. It means

allowing delight. Core question: What feels good because it's true? Triad: Gratitude → Joy → Love (Heart in motion).

JUSTICE — Upholding fairness and dignity. It means standing where it costs something. Core question: Whose voice needs mine? Triad: Fairness → Justice → Responsibility (Principle in action).

LOVE — Choosing connection over control. It means seeing the sacred in others. Core question: Where can I love better, not more? Triad: Compassion → Love → Unity (Heart as leader).

LOYALTY — Standing firm for those you've pledged to. It means presence through difficulty. Core question: Who needs me to stay? Triad: Trust → Loyalty → Responsibility (Commitment under pressure).

OPTIMISM — Expecting possibilities without ignoring reality. It means confidence in momentum. Core question: What could go right? Triad: Hope → Optimism → Faith (Positive realism).

PATIENCE — Allowing time to work its intelligence. It means steadiness, not passivity. Core question: What's ripening that I can't rush? Triad: Faith → Patience → Peace (Time as teacher).

PEACE — Inner stillness that doesn't depend on conditions. It means detachment from chaos. Core question: What can I release to rest? Triad: Equanimity → Peace → Presence (Still labor).

PERSEVERANCE — Continuing when comfort quits. It means endurance with purpose. Core question: What's worth suffering for? Triad: Discipline → Perseverance → Self-Mastery (Grit into growth).

## A3. VALUES INVENTORY

PRESENCE — Fully inhabiting the moment you're in. It means attention without agenda. Core question: Where am I now? Triad: Peace → Presence → Wisdom (Awareness as anchor).

PURPOSE — Living aligned to your deepest why. It means direction with devotion. Core question: What's the work that's mine alone? Triad: Freedom → Purpose → Service (Direction embodied).

RESPECT — Valuing boundaries and dignity in self and others. It means honor without fear. Core question: Do I treat others as sovereign? Triad: Responsibility → Respect → Justice (Honor in practice).

RESPONSIBILITY — Being answerable for your influence and choices. It means ownership before blame. Core question: What's mine to manage today? Triad: Accountability → Responsibility → Stewardship (Ownership matured).

SELF-AWARENESS — Knowing your motives, patterns, and impact. It means seeing yourself clearly. Core question: What drives me right now? Triad: Self-Awareness → Authenticity → Integrity (Conscious being).

SELF-MASTERY — Directing your impulses through discipline and choice. It means freedom through control. Core question: Who's driving — me or my habits? Triad: Discipline → Self-Mastery → Wisdom (Control as clarity).

SELF-RELIANCE — Depending on your own competence and inner resources. It means capability without arrogance. Core question: Can I back myself today? Triad: Responsibility → Self-Reliance → Freedom (Independence earned).

SERVICE — Offering time or skill for the benefit of others. It means contribution without ego. Core question: Where can I lighten someone's load today? Triad: Empowerment → Service → Stewardship (Giving with grace).

SIMPLICITY — Removing excess to reveal essence. It means focus, not deprivation. Core question: What matters here? Triad: Clarity → Simplicity → Peace (Less as strength).

SPIRITUALITY — Living in relationship with the unseen order of things. It means humility before mystery. Core question: What's the larger story I'm part of? Triad: Faith → Spirituality → Wisdom (Connection to source).

STEWARDSHIP — Caring for what's entrusted to you. It means service through guardianship. Core question: How do I leave this better than I found it? Triad: Responsibility → Stewardship → Service (Care in action).

TRUST — Relying on character proven over time. It means consistency between word and deed. Core question: Has he earned belief? Have I? Triad: Integrity → Trust → Loyalty (Belief through evidence).

UNITY — Acting as part of a greater whole. It means belonging without losing self. Core question: How can we move as one without erasing difference? Triad: Inclusivity → Unity → Love (Connection without collapse).

VITALITY — Energy flowing through body, mind, and purpose. It means aliveness, not frenzy. Core question: What keeps me alive today? Triad: Enthusiasm → Vitality → Joy (Life as fuel).

WISDOM — Understanding born of lived truth. It means clarity that has been tested. Core question: What lesson is life

## A3. VALUES INVENTORY

offering me now? Triad: Clarity → Wisdom → Peace (Knowledge tempered by grace).

# A4. EMOTIONAL MAPS

Emotions are coordinates, not commands. Each one marks where an old wound meets a current moment. These maps aren't for labelling weakness—they're for navigation. When you feel lost, trace the question that sits beneath the feeling. It will lead you back to movement, not management.

Most men don't start by feeling; they start by noticing. A tight jaw. A heavy chest. A gut that won't settle. We were trained to muscle through sensation instead of interpreting it, so our bodies became translators we never learned to read.

These pages exist to help you decode that language. Start with where it hurts or tightens. Trace it to an emotion. You're not diagnosing yourself; you're locating yourself. When you can name what you feel, you can work with it—not against it.

## PART I – SOMATIC INDEX: START WHERE IT HURTS

This is the entry point. Find the body zone that speaks loudest, then follow the trail to the emotions most often housed there. It's a map, not a verdict.

- Head or temples pounding → see *Frustrated, Confused, Overwhelmed.*
- Eyes burning or dry → see *Grieving, Resentful, Tired.*
- Jaw tight or aching → see *Anger, Control, Shame.*
- Throat constricted or sore → see *Unheard, Abandoned, Truth Suppressed.*
- Neck stiff → see *Burdened, Defensive, Fearful.*
- Shoulders heavy → see *Lonely, Overwhelmed, Responsible.*
- Chest tight or shallow → see *Anxious, Grieving, Hopeless.*
- Heart racing or dull → see *Fearful, Excited, Vulnerable.*
- Upper back burning → see *Resentful, Unsupported, Fatigued.*
- Mid-back tight → see *Pressure, Obligation, Lack of Support.*
- Lower back sore → see *Fear, Insecurity, Financial Stress.*
- Solar plexus buzzing or hollow → see *Guilt, Shame, Anxiety.*
- Stomach twisted → see *Fear, Regret, Intuition Ignored.*
- Gut heavy → see *Grief, Disgust, Powerlessness.*
- Hips locked → see *Control, Rigidity, Resistance to Change.*

## A4. EMOTIONAL MAPS

- Thighs tense → see *Drive, Competition, Anger Unspent.*
- Knees weak → see *Vulnerability, Surrender, Shame.*
- Calves cramping → see *Restlessness, Fear of Direction.*
- Feet cold or numb → see *Disconnection, Loss of Grounding.*
- Hands clenched or restless → see *Impatience, Anxiety, Readiness to Act.*
- Arms heavy → see *Resigned, Hopeless, Burdened.*
- Skin flushed or tingling → see *Embarrassed, Excited, Alert.*
- Whole body fatigued → see *Depressed, Overwhelmed, Depleted.*

Start where you feel it. Follow it to language. Then work it through the body again.

… A4. EMOTIONAL MAPS

# PART II – THE EMOTIONAL FAMILIES

## SADNESS FAMILY

LONELY — Born of early rejection, intensified by isolation. The drive beneath it is real connection, not performance. Left unchecked it slides toward withdrawal and self-pity. Felt in the chest, throat, and shoulders, the body curling around a missing presence. Practice: reach for proximity — a walk with a mate, a call, a shared task. Reset script: "Connection isn't found by waiting." Reflection: What am I craving right now, and who can meet it halfway? "Loneliness isn't weakness. It's longing waiting to be honored."

HOPELESS — Rooted in loss and futility, sharpened by repetition and failure. Its hidden drive is the will to believe again. The risk is paralysis dressed as calm. It drapes itself over the lower back, chest, and limbs like lead. Practice: move something small — your body, your space, your schedule. Reset script: "Hope is motion, not magic." Reflection: What might change if I believed progress was still possible? "Hope is not optimism. It's movement toward light."

GRIEVING — Born of love meeting loss, intensified by silence. The drive is to honor, not erase. The danger is numbing through control. It sits in the lungs, throat, and eyes. Practice: speak the name of what you lost aloud. Reset: "Love doesn't vanish; it transforms." Reflection: What do I want to remember without holding back? "Grief is love in its rawest form."

DISAPPOINTED — Formed by unmet ideals, stirred by perfectionism. The drive seeks integrity and justice. The risk is bitterness. It tightens the chest and diaphragm, bracing for the next let-down. Practice: separate hope from expectation. Reset:

## A4. EMOTIONAL MAPS

"Clarity without bitterness." Reflection: Was the hope wrong, or just the method? "Disappointment is clarity's uncomfortable cousin."

EMPTY — Born of depletion, intensified by endless output. It wants renewal, not escape. The risk is mistaking numbness for peace. It hums low in the gut and heart, a hollow under the ribs. Practice: rest without guilt, add what lights you up in small doses. Reset: "Nothing to prove, everything to feel." Reflection: Where did I last feel alive — and what drained it? "Feeling empty isn't failure; it's pause."

ABANDONED — Formed through broken attachment, intensified by distance. It drives toward safety through belonging. The risk is clinging or resentment. It drops weight behind the sternum. Practice: name who left and what part of you still waits. Reset: "They left; I remain." Reflection: Where do I still wait for someone who's gone? "You are your own return."

ASHAMED — Born of humiliation, intensified by exposure. It seeks to restore dignity. The risk is shrinking before judgment arrives. It burns in the neck and chest. Practice: tell the truth to a brother who won't flinch. Reset: "Shame loses power when spoken clean." Reflection: What would I say to a man I respected who felt this? "Shame fades when truth is spoken to it."

REGRETFUL — Born of moral failure, intensified by replay. Its drive is redemption through action. Risk: looping in guilt. It sits deep in the gut. Practice: make one repair. Reset: "Repair is proof of growth." Reflection: What did I learn, and how will I live it now? "Regret is past-tense responsibility. Honor it, then move."

GUILTY — Rooted in conscience, heightened by avoidance. It aims to restore order. The risk is endless self-punishment. Lives in the stomach, jaw, palms. Practice: apologize once, then stop re-sinning in your head. Reset: "I own it and move." Reflection: What's still mine to make right? "Guilt is a tool; use it to rebuild."

## SHAME FAMILY

DISMISSED — Born of invisibility, intensified by crowds or competition. The drive is to be seen without performing. The risk is overcompensation. Felt in chest, eyes, and jaw. Practice: ask directly for what you need. Reset: "Visibility without vanity." Reflection: Where am I hiding behind humor or charm? "Being seen begins with self-regard."

EMBARRASSED — Rooted in exposure, sharpened by scrutiny. The drive seeks acceptance. The risk is retreat. Shows up as flushed skin, shallow breath. Practice: stay present through the heat. Reset: "Stay in the room." Reflection: What story am I telling about how they see me? "Humility is courage that stayed."

INADEQUATE — Born of comparison, intensified by pressure. The drive is mastery. The risk is burnout. Lives in the shoulders and gut. Practice: define success for yourself. Reset: "Enough for today." Reflection: Who am I trying to impress, and why? "Competence grows quietly; comparison kills it."

UNWORTHY — Rooted in childhood rejection, reinforced by perfectionism. Drives toward proof through productivity. Risk: never resting. Carried in heart and solar plexus. Practice: affirm value without performance. Reset: "Worth is intrinsic." Reflec-

## A4. EMOTIONAL MAPS

tion: If I stopped producing, would I still be enough? "You were never required to earn your existence."

### SURPRISE FAMILY

STARTLED — Born of shock, sharpened by overstimulation. Drive is safety through control. Risk: hyper vigilance. Lives in the chest and neck. Practice: pause, breathe, ground your body. Reset: "I am safe right now." Reflection: What's the story I'm rehearsing that isn't true anymore? "Safety starts in the breath."

AMAZED — Rooted in wonder, intensified by humility. Drive: curiosity. Risk: losing awe through cynicism. Felt in the eyes and skin. Practice: pause to absorb beauty daily. Reset: "Stay astonished." Reflection: What have I stopped noticing? "Awe is the antidote to numbness."

CONFUSED — Born of contradiction, intensified by overload. The drive is clarity. Risk: paralysis. Lives in head and neck. Practice: simplify decisions to one next step. Reset: "Clarity follows action." Reflection: What question matters most right now? "Confusion means you're thinking honestly."

### TRUST FAMILY

RELIEVED — Born of release, intensified by tension broken. Drive: gratitude. Risk: dependency on relief. Felt through breath and shoulders. Practice: pause before filling the space again. Reset: "Rest inside the exhale." Reflection: Can I hold peace without rushing? "Relief is a small resurrection."

PEACEFUL — Rooted in acceptance, intensified by presence. Drive: harmony. Risk: avoidance. Found in heart and breath. Practice: sit in stillness daily. Reset: "Peace is practice, not gift."

## A4. EMOTIONAL MAPS

Reflection: Do I mistake quiet for growth? "Peace is earned by truth, not withdrawal."

GRATEFUL — Born of awareness, deepened by humility. Drive: appreciation. Risk: complacency. Lives in heart and hands. Practice: name three specifics aloud. Reset: "Gratitude widens what you see." Reflection: Where did I experience grace today? "Gratitude keeps the door open."

### FEAR FAMILY

ANXIOUS — Born of uncertainty, intensified by lack of control. Drive: prediction, safety. Risk: paralysis or control. Found in gut, chest, hands. Practice: name three things you can control now. Reset: "The body can't live in tomorrow." Reflection: What part of me needs reassurance, not results? "Anxiety is fear unanchored."

AFRAID — Rooted in threat, intensified by imagination. Drive: safety. Risk: avoidance. Felt in legs and spine. Practice: move the body until the mind follows. Reset: "Fear moves through motion." Reflection: What would courage look like here? "Fear is excitement without breath."

INSECURE — Born of comparison, reinforced by rejection. Drive: belonging. Risk: people-pleasing. Carried in jaw and stomach. Practice: state what's true without performance. Reset: "I belong where I stand." Reflection: What am I trying to prove? "Security begins when proof ends."

OVERWHELMED — Born of overload, intensified by speed. Drive: stability. Risk: shutdown. Felt in shoulders and lungs. Practice: slow the smallest task. Reset: "Do less, feel more." Reflection: What can I drop without consequence? "Overwhelm is attention spread too thin."

## A4. EMOTIONAL MAPS

## DISGUST FAMILY

REPULSED — Born of violation, intensified by betrayal. Drive: purity. Risk: judgment. Felt in gut and face. Practice: separate behavior from person. Reset: "Discern, don't damn." Reflection: What value was crossed? "Disgust protects integrity when balanced by compassion."

ASHAMED (moral) — Rooted in self-disgust, intensified by secrecy. Drive: moral repair. Risk: self-hatred. Felt in stomach and throat. Practice: confession to a safe witness. Reset: "Expose, don't hide." Reflection: What's the truth I most fear saying aloud? "Shame healed becomes integrity."

DISPLEASED — Born of unmet standards, intensified by expectation. Drive: correction. Risk: controlling others. Found in jaw and eyes. Practice: name disappointment without blame. Reset: "Adjust, don't attack." Reflection: What expectation is mine to release? "Grace begins where rigidity ends."

## ANTICIPATION FAMILY

CURIOUS — Born of wonder, intensified by openness. Drive: learning. Risk: distraction. Felt in eyes and fingertips. Practice: stay with one question. Reset: "Depth beats breadth." Reflection: What am I trying to understand? "Curiosity is reverence in motion."

EXCITED — Rooted in possibility, heightened by vision. Drive: creation. Risk: burnout. Heart races, breath quickens. Practice: ground enthusiasm with plan. Reset: "Direct the fire." Reflection: What structure will sustain this spark? "Excitement without direction burns out."

EAGER — Born of hunger, intensified by opportunity. Drive: achievement. Risk: impatience. Felt in chest and calves. Practice: pair action with patience. Reset: "Haste hides fear." Reflection: What am I afraid won't wait for me? "Eagerness needs aim."

## ANGER FAMILY

ANGRY — Born of boundary violation, intensified by disrespect. Drive: protection. Risk: aggression. Lives in jaw, fists, chest. Practice: express it cleanly — hit the bag, write, move. Reset: "Anger clarifies." Reflection: What boundary was crossed? "Anger is love's bodyguard."

RESENTFUL — Rooted in inequality, intensified by silence. Drive: justice. Risk: bitterness. Felt in shoulders and teeth. Practice: speak sooner next time. Reset: "Resentment is unpaid truth." Reflection: What truth went unsaid? "Bitterness is truth withheld too long."

## A4. EMOTIONAL MAPS

IRRITATED — Born of friction, intensified by fatigue. Drive: order. Risk: cruelty. Lives in temples and hands. Practice: pause before speech. Reset: "Tension seeks release, not war." Reflection: What am I resisting right now? "Irritation is tired control."

ENRAGED — Rooted in powerlessness, triggered by betrayal. Drive: restoration of agency. Risk: destruction. Rises through chest and throat. Practice: ground before confronting. Reset: "Channel, don't combust." Reflection: What power can I reclaim without harm? "Rage is truth without breath."

The body speaks first. Emotion is its language. Every sensation — the ache, the tightness, the throb — is an invitation back to presence. When you trace it to feeling, name it cleanly, and move it through the body, you return to coherence. That's emotional intelligence in its truest form: not therapy, not theory — embodiment. The man who can feel fully can live fully.

Cross-reference: See A3. Values Inventory to identify which values best balance your emotional patterns.

# A5. BROTHERHOOD FIELD KIT

Brotherhood doesn't happen by accident.

It happens when men decide to meet, stay, and speak the truth without flinching.

This is the operating system for that decision—built for men who already carry weight: fathers, leaders, builders.

Men who don't have time for endless talk but still need a place to tell the truth and be sharpened by it.

The Table isn't therapy. It's a forge.

## THE BROTHERHOOD FILTERS — WHO QUALIFIES

Brotherhood isn't built on enthusiasm but reliability.

A good man who's not ready can still break the frame.

Before you send an invite, test a man's weight.

- Keeps small promises. If he flakes on coffee, he'll flake when it counts.

- Holds tension without fixing. Rescuers breed dependence; witnesses build men.

- Tells on himself first. If he hides behind generalities, he's not ready.

- Guards your absent name. If he gossips with you, he'll gossip about you.

- Can disagree without exile. Brotherhood isn't a cult; it's a forge.

Real men stay. That's the only filter that truly matters.

## THE TABLE RITUAL — OPEN, MID, CLOSE

Every forge needs rhythm. This is the pulse that turns a group of men into a Brotherhood.

<u>How to Open</u>

Ask one line only: *"What's real for you right now?"*

No backstory. No warm-up. Just one honest sentence from each man.

The first answer sets the depth for the night.

This single line burns off performance faster than any icebreaker.

<u>Mid-Session Check</u>

When energy drifts or men slide into story, pause and ask: "Are we still in truth, or have we moved to story?"

## A5. BROTHERHOOD FIELD KIT

That question resets the current without blame.

Use it when conversation turns to commentary instead of confession.

<u>How to Close</u>

End with one line: "What truth are you taking home tonight?"

No feedback. No advice. Silence seals the night.

Let five quiet minutes close the room before any casual talk resumes.

<u>Duration</u>

Sixty to seventy-five minutes total.

Enough time for every man to be seen. Not long enough to hide.

This isn't catch-up. It's a calibration.

## THE COVENANT — READ ALOUD, THEN SIGN

Every forge needs boundaries. The Covenant is the contract that makes truth safe.

Read it aloud. Sign it in ink. Let silence seal the room.

1. Confidentiality or distance. What's said here, dies here.
2. No performance, no pity. We don't posture, and we don't patronize.
3. Truth before comfort. We tell the harder sentence kindly.
4. Ask before advice. "Do you want presence, questions, or strategy?"

5. We carry weight. If a brother reaches out, we make time—not every call, but every crisis.
6. Repair quickly. Conflict is friction; we polish, not punish.
7. Rotate the voice. No gurus. Every man leads a round.
8. How to use it: print it, sign it, re-sign when a new man joins.
9. No ceremony. Just ink and intent.

## THE 90-MINUTE FRAME

The Table works because it has limits. Structure creates safety, safety breeds depth.

Arrival (first five minutes): Phones off. Stand in silence. Breathe ten times together.

If a new brother joins, one man reads the Covenant aloud.

Silence resets the room; breath builds presence.

Opening Round (fifteen minutes): Ask each man, *"What's real for you right now?"* One sentence each. The first voice sets the truth level for the night.

S.A.L.T. Check-In (about twenty-five minutes):

Each man takes five minutes with the salt shaker in hand.

S.A.L.T. stands for State, Anchor, Load, and Traction.

<u>State</u>: How are you, truly?

<u>Anchor</u>: What's keeping you grounded right now?

<u>Load</u>: What pressure or weight are you carrying?

<u>Traction</u>: What one step will you take before the next Table?

## A5. BROTHERHOOD FIELD KIT

One man speaks at a time. No interruption, no advice. Just presence.

Deep Seat (about twenty minutes): Two men each take ten minutes in the Deep Seat.

They choose their mode before they begin.

Presence: Just sit with me; no words needed.

Questions: Help me see what I can't.

Strategy: Let's find a way forward.

The rest listen without fixing. Witnessing is the medicine.

Commitments (five minutes): Each man names one concrete action to complete before the next Table. The scribe writes every action in the log. Accountability turns talk into proof.

Closing Question (five minutes): Each man answers, *"What truth are you taking home tonight?"*

No commentary. No wrap-up talk.

When the final man speaks, breathe once, nod, and let silence close the night.

## FIELD NOTES – RUNNING THE TABLE

Every Table needs a keeper of rhythm—not a leader, but a timekeeper, anchor, and witness. His job is to protect the frame so the men inside it can drop their masks.

- Start on time. Respect is spelled punctuality. Once the hour begins, doors close. A late man joins silently.
- Pass the salt. The shaker isn't decoration—it's

permission. When a man holds it, he speaks. When he passes it, he yields.
- Hold silence. When a man finishes, don't rush to fill the air. Ten seconds of quiet lets truth land.
- Guard the minutes. A timer isn't tyranny—it's honor. Time is the only currency every man shares equally.
- Keep the ledger. The scribe records actions, attendance, and blessings. Don't archive emotion—log proof. Brotherhood is built on receipts, not vibes.
- Rotate the role. Every Table, a new keeper. Every man learns to hold the frame. No gurus. No hosts for life.
- End clean. When the clock hits time, breathe once, nod, and walk out lighter. No lingering downloads. No side therapy. The Table ends where silence begins.

## THE COVENANT IN PRACTICE

Signed paper means nothing without lived proof.

Brotherhood is measured in answered texts, kept appointments, and the way you speak about each other when no one's listening.

You're not expected to be on call every hour or do anything you didn't agree to.

You're expected to show up when it counts—and to make your word mean something again.

Dependability without drama. Accountability without weight.

That's how respect is rebuilt among men.

## SCRIPTS THAT WORK

<u>First Reach-Out</u>

"Brother, I'm building a small Table of men who don't leave.

One night a week. No performance. Real stakes. You in for a month's trial?"

<u>Boundary with Strength</u>

"I can give you presence tonight, not therapy.

You want me to sit, or help you find someone who can?"

<u>Repair After Heat</u>

"I overstepped last week with advice. That's on me.

I'm here to make it right—what would help?"

## BUILDING FROM ZERO

Brotherhood doesn't wait for permission.

If you're starting alone, build from the ground up.

- Pick a regular time and place—same café, same hour. Familiarity breeds trust.
- Join something that uses engagement, not small talk: boxing, breath work, service.
- Serve shoulder-to-shoulder. Sweat collapses distance faster than talk.
- Start a ledger of reliability. Show up early, text back, do what you say.

## A5. BROTHERHOOD FIELD KIT

Brotherhood begins with competence before chemistry.

## THE TWELVE TABLE SPRINT

Twelve weeks is enough to test rhythm, depth, and durability.

Each stage earns trust through proof and transitions strangers into brothers.

Table One — Invite Two Men. Make the calls. Book the first Table. Brotherhood starts with courage, not consensus.

Table Two — Write and Sign the Covenant. Words spoken aloud bind intent to action.

Table Three — Run the First Table. Time it tight—about seventy minutes. Discipline builds safety.

Table Four — Name One Behavior to Stop for Thirty Days. Accountability proves you're serious.

Table Five — Serve Shoulder-to-Shoulder. Move furniture, fix something, sweat together. Doing bonds deeper than talking.

Table Six — Skills Night. One man teaches something hard. Every man carries a gift, contribution fuels respect.

Table Seven — Cold Water or Hard Hike. Suffer on purpose. Shared discomfort is sacred glue.

Table Eight — Truth Night. Say the sentence you've avoided. The Table earns its depth when honesty costs you something.

Table Nine — Invite a Mentor Ten Years Ahead. Questions only. Perspective steadies pride.

Table Ten — Shared Meal. Optional family night. Integration keeps brotherhood human.

Table Eleven — Conflict Drill. Practice repair. Friction handled clean builds strength.

Table Twelve — Dawn Vow. Gather before sunrise. One minute of silence. Each man repeats: "I don't run."

It's not poetry. It's a declaration. When life gets hard, I stay.

Progress isn't a spreadsheet. Measure it by attendance, actions kept, and repair within forty-eight hours.

## WHEN THE TABLE CRACKS

Even with rhythm and good men, pressure finds the seams.

These are the most common cracks—and how to handle them cleanly.

## THE MONOLOGUE MAN

He dominates airtime—twenty minutes of story, no ownership. His tales circle the drain of blame.

Fix: use a timer and ask the single question that cuts through fog— "What's the next action you control?"

If he can't name one, the Table names it for him: "Pause."

## THE ADVICE FIREHOSE

He means well but floods every silence with strategy. His smarts become static.

Fix: before speaking, ask— "Do you want presence, questions, or strategy?"

It forces consent before counsel. If he can't help himself, rotate him into the Deep Seat next time so he learns stillness firsthand.

## THE LEAK

He breaks confidentiality—tells stories that aren't his to tell.

Leakage kills safety faster than betrayal because it breeds doubt.

Fix: warn once, directly and without venom— "Brother, that can't happen again."

If it happens twice, release him clean. No gossip, no smear— just clarity.

Brotherhood can forgive mistakes but not breaches.

## THE HIDDEN CRISIS

Addiction. Violence. Risk of harm.

When a man's behavior crosses into danger, the Table's job shifts.

You are brothers, not professionals. Support don't save.

Fix: name what you see with respect and firmness— "We're with you, but this is beyond us. Let's find the right help."

Stay connected but let trained hands take the lead.

The Table holds space; it doesn't become a rescue unit.

## JOIN, HOST, OR LEAD A TABLE

Visit getmanos.com/brotherhood to register as a Host, Leader, or Man Seeking a Table.

You'll find printable Covenants, step-by-step guides, and real stories from men building their own Tables across the world.

This is how we rebuild the network of men—one Table at a time.

# A6. PARTNER'S LETTER – TO THE WOMAN WHO LOVES A MAN DOING THIS WORK

## THE CORE LETTER

To the woman reading this,

Your man handed you this because he couldn't find the words himself. Not because he's weak. Because he's finally doing something brave looking at himself without the masks.

He's reading a book called ManOS. It's not about becoming someone new. It's about excavating who he was before the world told him to shut down, armor up, and perform instead of feel.

Here's what you need to know:

He's going to be different for a while. Not worse—just less predictable. Some days he'll be more present than he's been in years. Other days he'll be processing things he buried decades ago, and it'll look like he's somewhere else entirely.

He might cry. He might get angry at things that seem small. He might need to be alone more than usual. He might want to talk at unexpected times. None of this is about you, even when it affects you.

What's happening:

He's learning that the "strong, silent type" was killing him slowly. That providing financially doesn't equal being present. That saying "I'm fine" when he's drowning isn't protecting anyone. That the way his father did it—and his father's father—left out half the operating system.

He's not becoming soft. He's becoming whole.

What he needs from you:

Space without abandonment. When he goes quiet, he's not punishing you. He's sorting through decades of unprocessed truth. Let him go there but remind him you're still here.

Truth without attack. Tell him what you see, what you need, what hurts. But tell him like you're on the same team, not opposite sides.

## A6. PARTNER'S LETTER — TO THE WOMAN WHO LOVES A ...

Recognition without cheerleading. When you see him doing something different—being present with the kids, speaking his truth, showing up differently—acknowledge it simply: "I see you." Not a parade. Just recognition.

Your own boundaries. This work doesn't mean you accept unacceptable behavior. It means you both get clearer about what's real.

What might change:

He might quit the job that pays well but empties him

He might set boundaries with his family for the first time

He might admit struggles he's been hiding for years

He might want different things than he did before

This isn't him having a midlife crisis. This is him admitting the life he built isn't the life he wants. There's a difference.

The hard truth:

The man you get back might not be the one you married. He'll be the one you were supposed to marry—before he learned to perform instead of being present. Some women want their man to change until he does. Be honest about which one you are.

## A6. PARTNER'S LETTER — TO THE WOMAN WHO LOVES A ...

If you want the real him—not the performer, not the provider robot, not the "yes dear" guy—then this is the path. It's messy. It's non-linear. It's worth it.

He gave you this because he wants you on his team while he rebuilds. That's not weakness. That's the first sign he's remembering what real strength looks like.

He loves you enough to get real. That's everything.

## FOUR SCENARIO ADAPTATIONS

1. AFTER A FIGHT (Add this paragraph after "What's happening"):

We just had a fight that felt different. Probably because for the first time in years, I said what I felt instead of what would end it fastest. I'm not trying to win anymore. I'm trying to be real. That might mean messier fights before they get cleaner. I need you to know I'm not fighting you. I'm fighting to stay present instead of disappearing like I always have.

## A6. PARTNER'S LETTER — TO THE WOMAN WHO LOVES A ...

## 2. STARTING THE JOURNEY (Add to opening):

I bought this book because I'm tired of feeling empty while looking successful. You might not have known how bad it's been inside my head—I'm good at hiding. But I'm done pretending everything's fine. I'm 30 days into rebuilding, and I wanted you to know what's happening before you wonder why I'm different.

## 3. ROMANTIC RESET (Replace opening with):

I fell in love with you [time] ago. But somewhere along the way, I became a stranger—to myself and to you. I've been going through the motions, giving you my logistics but not my truth. This book is teaching me how to come back. Not just to you—to myself first, so I have something real to give you. I want you to know why I'm changing and where we're headed. I want us to win.

## A6. PARTNER'S LETTER — TO THE WOMAN WHO LOVES A …

**4. AFTER HITTING BOTTOM** (Add after first paragraph):

> You saw me hit bottom. The drinking/numbing/rage/silence finally broke something. Maybe you're the one who said 'enough.' Maybe you're still deciding whether to stay. I'm not asking you to trust me yet. I'm asking you to watch me rebuild. This book is the blueprint. This letter is me telling you I'm doing it this time — not just saying I will.

Delivery Ideas:

- Handwritten on real paper (not typed) with the book
- Read aloud during a calm moment, then hand it over
- Left on her pillow with a simple note: "This explains everything"
- After couples therapy as homework to share
- With flowers but not apology flowers—"beginning something new" flowers

The key: Don't over-explain. Let the letter do the work. Then shut up and let her process.

## A7. WHEN YOU'RE BEING PLAYED — TOXIC PATTERNS TO RECOGNIZE

*"All frustration comes from unmet expectation."* — Dr John Lund [i]

When I first heard Dr John Lund outline the twenty-one behavioral markers of toxicity, I stopped everything and took notes.

At the time, I'd been accused of being narcissistic and toxic — the kind of claim that can crush a reflective man.

Rather than react, I wanted data — not opinion. So, I turned to seasoned, clinical voices who studied behavior rather than projected it.

Lund's framework gave me what emotion couldn't: measurable, repeatable questions. Answering them honestly didn't just clear doubt; it offered peace. It reminded me that self-inquiry is strength, not guilt.

This assessment remains one of the cleanest tools I've found for men trying to verify their own relational integrity.

## A7. WHEN YOU'RE BEING PLAYED — TOXIC PATTERNS TO ...

*Credit: Dr John Lund, "How to Hug a Porcupine" (YouTube lecture 'Am I a Toxic Person?')* [ii]

# THE 21 QUESTIONS (ANSWER Y | N)

1. Have others accused you of being a perfectionist? Y | N

2. Have others accused you of being controlling? Y | N

3. Have others said you're highly critical? Y | N

4. Have others said no one is ever good enough for you? Y | N

5. Have others accused you of holding grudges for a long time? Y | N

6. Have others said you're stingy with compliments? Y | N

7. Do you often blame others? Y | N

8. Are you impossible to please? Y | N

9. Do you withhold love as punishment? Y | N

10. Do you add criticism to every compliment? Y | N

11. Are you easily offended? Y | N

12. Do you often contradict others? Y | N

13. Do you frequently complain about what isn't being done? Y | N

14. Do you frequently interrupt or correct others? Y | N

15. Do you "parent" equals — telling peers what they should, need, or ought to do? Y | N

16. Are you angry or upset much of the time? Y | N

## A7. WHEN YOU'RE BEING PLAYED — TOXIC PATTERNS TO ...

17. Do you react to others' non-compliance by yelling, swearing, or name-calling? Y | N

18. Do you threaten divorce, rejection, or abandonment? Y | N

19. Are you rude, curt, or dismissive of others' opinions? Y | N

20. Do you see yourself as more hardworking, responsible, or intelligent than others? Y | N

21. Do you rarely accept responsibility when things go wrong? Y | N

**Total Score ___ / 21**

### Interpretation (Dr Lund's Scale)

- 0–3 = Normal range (we all have rough edges).

- 4–7 = Critical and hard to live with.

- 8–12 = Highly critical and non-accepting — expectations exceed empathy.

- 13–16 = Toxic — damaging to others' self-worth.

- 17–19 = Headed for relational collapse (divorce, rebellion, conflict).

- 20–21 = Isolation — best suited to live alone until change begins.

## PRACTICE & DRILL

### Reflection Prompt - Take the quiz

Take the quiz once, then revisit it every twelve months. Not to judge yourself — to measure growth.

### Drill - Phone a friend

Run it in reverse. Ask a trusted friend or partner to rate you anonymously. Compare results.

**Reframe:** Honest measurement is not self-condemnation — it's maintenance.

**Exercise:** Keep your score written privately. If it rises, pause. If it falls, celebrate quietly.

### Takeaway

Reality testing is self-respect in motion. When you measure your behavior, you reclaim authorship of it.

### Reflection Question

When accusation meets evidence, which one do you trust — the noise or the data?

## FROM DATA TO LIVED EXPERIENCE

Before you assume you're the calm one in the storm, test it.

Once you've checked your own reflection and it comes back clean, you can start to see the patterns that almost broke you.

Here's what toxic looks like — not through psychology textbooks, but through scars.

## THE FALSE APOLOGY

*"I'm sorry you feel that way."*

That's not an apology. That's blame dressed in sympathy.

## A7. WHEN YOU'RE BEING PLAYED — TOXIC PATTERNS TO ...

They're saying your feelings are the problem, not their behavior.

Real version: "I'm sorry I said that."

Toxic version: "I'm sorry you took it that way."

See the difference? One owns. One deflects.

I spent decades hearing *I'm sorry you feel that way"* or *"I'm sorry you're so sensitive"*. I started believing maybe I was too sensitive.

Took therapy to realize feeling hurt when someone hurts you isn't sensitivity. It's human.

## THE REALITY REWRITE

*"That never happened." "You're remembering it wrong." "I never said that."*

You know what you heard. You know what happened.

But they're so certain, so convincing, you start doubting your own memory.

I started recording conversations on my phone. Not to use against her — to check my own sanity.

When I played one back and heard exactly what I remembered, the truth landed: I wasn't losing my mind. I was being deliberately confused.

If you're keeping receipts just to trust your own memory, you're not in communication problems.

You're in psychological warfare.

A7. WHEN YOU'RE BEING PLAYED — TOXIC PATTERNS TO ...

## THE FEELING OVERRIDE

*"You're not angry, you're just tired." "You don't mean that." "You're overreacting."*

Nobody gets to tell you what you feel. Period.

Someone once told me how I felt, then fought me for disagreeing.

*"You're not hurt; you're trying to manipulate me."*

I spent more time proving my pain was real than healing what caused it.

Your feelings are yours. If someone keeps telling you what you feel, they're not trying to understand you. They're trying to control the narrative.

## THE TRAP AND TRIGGER

This one's elegant in its cruelty:

- They stay impossibly calm while needling you.
- They find your exact trigger and press it.
- You finally explode.
- They point to your explosion: *"See? You're unstable / angry / abusive."*

Example: She'd bring up my father's abandonment during unrelated arguments.

Calm voice, surgical precision. When I'd finally snap, she'd say, "This is why nobody stays with you."

The setup is invisible. Your reaction is not. Now you look like the problem.

If someone consistently triggers you when you're calm then uses your reaction as evidence against you, that's not accident. That's strategy.

## THE COMPARISON WEAPON

*"Tom's husband brings her flowers every week." "David never forgets his wife's birthday."*

You're not competing with Tom, David, or any other man. You're in relationship with this person.

Comparisons aren't motivation. They're manipulation.

During one relationship, life was treated like a leaderboard — a friend's husband who made partner, a sister's husband who ran marathons, a coworker who remembered every coffee order.

I was competing without knowing there was a contest.

Here's the truth: If someone loved Tom's husband so much, they'd be with Tom's husband.

They're with you. The comparisons are about control, not improvement.

## THE ACCOUNTABILITY DODGE

When you bring up something they did:

- "Why are you attacking me?"
- "I can't do anything right."

- "You're always criticizing."
- "This is why I can't talk to you."

Suddenly you're apologizing for bringing it up.

The original issue vanishes. You're now comforting them for hurting you.

I once tried to discuss her spending our savings without discussion.

Ended with me apologizing for *"making her feel bad about herself."*

The money was never discussed again. Gone.

## THE HISTORY REVISION

- They change the story every time:
- Monday: "You said you'd handle it."
- Wednesday: "We agreed I would do it."
- Friday: "I never wanted this in the first place."

You start writing things down. Taking screenshots. Saving texts. Not because you're paranoid. Because you need proof of reality. If you need documentation to have a conversation, you're not in a relationship. You're in a courtroom.

## HOW TO KNOW YOU'RE IN IT

Your body knows first:

- Breath trapped high before they come home
- Rehearsing conversations in your head

- Relief when they're gone
- Exhausted after talking
- Confused about what just happened
- Apologizing constantly
- Not trusting your own memory

You find yourself thinking:

- "Maybe I am too sensitive."
- "Maybe I did remember it wrong."
- "Maybe I am the problem."
- "Nobody else would put up with me."

## THE EXTRACTION PROTOCOL

If you recognize these patterns:

1. Document everything. Not to win. To stay sane.
2. Stop defending reality. You know what happened. You don't need their agreement.
3. Find one trusted witness who can reflect reality back when yours gets distorted.
4. Set one boundary and hold it. Start small: "I won't discuss this while you're yelling." Then leave when they yell.
5. Get professional help. This isn't couples counseling territory. This is individual therapy territory.

## THE HARD TRUTH

These patterns don't get better. They escalate.

The person using them isn't confused about communication.

They're using sophisticated tools to destabilize you.

Love doesn't look like confusion. Love doesn't require you to doubt your sanity.

Love doesn't leave you exhausted from defending your own reality.

I stayed three years too long because I thought I was the problem.

Thought if I could just communicate better, be less sensitive, remember things correctly, it would work.

The day I left, my nervous system exhaled for the first time in years.

My kids said I looked different. Lighter.

That's what carrying someone else's distortions does — it literally changes how you hold your body.

## THE BOTTOM LINE

If you're reading this section and your chest is tightening because you recognize every pattern, you're not crazy.

You're not too sensitive. You're not the problem.

You're being systematically dismantled.

The communication tips earlier in this guide work with someone who's trying to connect.

They don't work with someone who's trying to control.

Know the difference. Your sanity depends on it.

A7. WHEN YOU'RE BEING PLAYED — TOXIC PATTERNS TO ...

Healthy conflict makes both people stronger.

Toxic patterns make one person smaller.

If you're shrinking, that's not love having a bad day.

That's something else wearing love's mask.

Trust your gut.

It knew before your head let you admit it.

## A8. WHEN YOU'RE ACTUALLY LOVED — THE REAL THING

After a lifetime of toxic patterns, real love feels suspicious. Too easy. Too calm. You keep waiting for the trap. There isn't one. Here's what love looks like when it's not wearing a mask.

### YOUR BODY RELAXES

When they walk in, your shoulders drop. Not brace.

I remember the first time my current partner came home and my chest didn't tighten. I noticed it—the absence of alarm. My nervous system wasn't preparing for combat. It was just... neutral. Calm.

That's what safety feels like. Your body knows you're loved before your brain believes it.

### THEY REMEMBER YOUR REALITY

When you bring up something from last week, last month, they remember it the same way. No revision. No denial.

## A8. WHEN YOU'RE ACTUALLY LOVED — THE REAL THING

"Remember when you said X?" "Yeah, I was wrong about that."

Simple. Clean. No fight about what was real.

My partner keeps notes about things I care about. Not to use against me. To remember. Found her notebook once—my favorite coffee, the book I mentioned wanting, the story about my grandfather. Evidence that I exist in her mind when I'm not there.

### YOUR FEELINGS ARE YOURS

When you say you're angry, hurt, frustrated, they don't argue with your emotions. They witness them.

"I'm pissed about this." "Tell me more."

Not "You shouldn't be." Not "You're overreacting." Just space for your truth.

She never tells me how I feel. She asks. And when I tell her, she believes me. Revolutionary after years of someone else narrating my internal life.

### CONFLICTS MAKE YOU CLOSER

After a fight, you understand each other better. Not less.

We had a massive argument about money. Ended with both of us understanding why money meant different things based on our histories. The fight became a doorway, not a wall.

When conflict creates more intimacy instead of more distance, you're loved.

### THEY CELEBRATE YOUR WINS

No competition. No minimizing. No "must be nice."

## A8. WHEN YOU'RE ACTUALLY LOVED — THE REAL THING

When I landed a big contract, she literally danced in the kitchen. When I started working out again, she said "I love seeing you take care of yourself." Not "about time" or "let's see how long this lasts."

Your wins are their wins. Your joy increases their joy. That's love.

### MISTAKES DON'T BECOME WEAPONS

When you screw up, they don't store it for later ammunition.

I forgot our anniversary. Completely spaced it. She was hurt, told me so, we worked through it. Six months later, during an unrelated discussion, it never came up. It was finished when we finished it.

Love doesn't keep score of wounds to use later.

### YOU STOP REHEARSING

You don't practice conversations in the shower. Don't preview your words for landmines. Don't edit yourself before speaking.

The first time I understood I'd stopped rehearsing, I was halfway through telling her about a work failure. Just telling it. Not managing her reaction. Not protecting myself. Just talking.

When you stop performing conversation and start having it, you're loved.

### THEY'RE CURIOUS, NOT CRITICAL

When you do something, they don't understand: "Help me understand why you..." not "Why would you..."

## A8. WHEN YOU'RE ACTUALLY LOVED — THE REAL THING

When I bought a motorcycle after swearing I never would, she didn't say I was having a midlife crisis. She asked what changed. Real curiosity. Found out together it was about freedom after feeling trapped for years.

Love asks why with genuine wonder, not judgment.

### YOUR GROWTH THREATENS NOTHING

When you change, evolve, level up—they adjust with you. Not threatened. Not left behind. Growing alongside.

Lost forty pounds, started dressing better, reading again. Some partners would get suspicious, insecure. She said, "I love watching you come back to life."

Your expansion expands them. Your rise raises them.

### THE SMALL STUFF

- They move your coffee cup to where you can reach it
- They lower their voice when you're overwhelmed
- They know which silence is processing and which is pain
- They touch you the way you need, not the way they need
- They remember the story about third grade
- They create space before you ask for it
- They say "tell me more" more than "you should"

### THE REAL TELL

You know you're loved when being yourself requires no courage.

## A8. WHEN YOU'RE ACTUALLY LOVED — THE REAL THING

Not your best self. Not your potential self. Your actual, Tuesday-morning, haven't-showered, failed-again, trying-anyway self.

When that person—that unedited version—feels safe to exist in their presence, you're loved.

## THE HARDEST PART

After toxic love, real love feels boring at first. No drama. No adrenaline. No trauma bonding. Just... steady.

Your nervous system might interpret calm as "not passionate" or safety as "no chemistry." That's the wound talking. Real love doesn't require your stress hormones. Doesn't need you activated to feel alive.

It feels like home. And if home was never safe, that feeling might take time to trust.

## THE BOTTOM LINE

Love makes you more yourself, not less.

You're not shrinking to fit. Not expanding to impress. Not performing to keep them. You're just... being. And that's enough. More than enough. It's everything.

If you're getting bigger, braver, calmer, clearer—you're loved. If you're getting smaller, quieter, more confused—you're not.

Trust the trajectory. Your growth tells you everything about whether the soil is poison or medicine.

Remember: Real love is so ordinary it feels extraordinary after toxic patterns. No pedestals. No pits. Just two humans choosing each other's growth over and over.

## A8. WHEN YOU'RE ACTUALLY LOVED — THE REAL THING

That's it. That's everything.

# A9. CLEAN MONEY PROTOCOL & TRACKER

Domain: Integration — Make It Work Daily

Bring consciousness and calm to how you earn, spend, and invest.

Money is emotion made visible. It tracks where your energy flows and what you believe about worth. Most men don't have a money problem; they have a *clarity* problem. They spend to escape feeling, not to build freedom.

The Clean Money Protocol rebuilds financial integrity from the ground up — not through tricks or apps, but through rhythm, awareness, and discipline. It's a system designed to outlast motivation.

## THE CLEAN MONEY PROTOCOL

1. Name the Flow.

For one month, write down every dollar that comes in and goes out. Not to judge — to see. If it feels confronting, good. Clarity precedes control.

2. Align the Spend.

Label each expense by value: *health, family, growth, peace, purpose,* or *vanity*. You'll see the truth fast. Some of your "needs" are just avoidance with better packaging.

3. Fix the Leak.

Cancel or reduce one recurring expense that doesn't serve your top five values. That single act — even a $10 leak — rewires your brain toward agency.

4. Build the Buffer.

Every pay cycle, automate one small act of stewardship: savings, debt repair, or contribution. Track it in the same place every time. You're not just saving money — you're building evidence of trust with yourself.

## THE BABYLON RULE — BUILD YOUR RESERVE

A man without reserve becomes a slave to circumstance. Every payday, before rent, debt, or indulgence, pay yourself first. Treat your future as a bill — non-negotiable, sacred, due immediately.

- Set aside 5–10% of every net pay. Automate it. No exceptions, no "once things settle."

- This is *not* spending money. It's a *reserve* — the muscle of foresight.
- Keep it separate: a savings or high-yield account you can't easily touch.
- Do it long enough and you'll feel it — not pride, but calm.
- The knowing that if the job disappears or life caves in, you still have *space to think*.
- Hold it until it equals at least three to twelve months of living costs.

You only break the seal for three reasons:

1. True emergency. Health, safety, or survival.
2. High-integrity investment. Something that expands your capability, not your image.
3. Compounding opportunity. A chance to build lasting independence — business, asset, or education.

Do this for twelve months at ten percent and you'll have roughly a year's income stored.

That's not theory — that's peace.

## WHY IT WORKS

Most men wait for more income before they start saving. The strong ones do it *backwards* — they save first, and the world reorganizes around that decision. Money is stored energy. When you hold it with integrity, it stops owning you. Wealth isn't a number — it's a nervous system that doesn't flinch when bills arrive.

## THE MANOS FINANCIAL CREED

1. Pay yourself first. Your future is your first creditor.
2. Spend by value, not mood. Emotion is the world's best salesman.
3. Never spend tomorrow's power today. Debt is a leash you volunteered for.
4. Use money to build margin, not identity. Freedom isn't found in things; it's felt in your breath.
5. Wealth is proof of discipline, not luck. Every saved dollar is a promise kept.

Goal: A calm nervous system, a clear ledger, and a reserve that lets you choose rather than chase.

Checkpoint:

If your shoulders tense when you open your banking app, you're not bad with money — you're out of alignment. Start small. Start honest. That's real wealth.

# A9B. FORGE — THE FIVE FIRES OF FINANCIAL FREEDOM

This Field-kit expands the money flow first introduced in A9. Clean Money Protocol & Tracker. Run A9 once to get your Stability Number; run this to move every dollar through a rhythm that buys freedom.

Money doesn't respond to moods; it responds to rhythm. You don't need a spreadsheet religion. You need a simple flow you can run on good days and bad. FORGE is that flow.

These are not commandments. They're rails. The percentages below are the ranges I tend to use; you'll jig them to fit your reality. The aim is freedom, not perfection.

The idea is that every dollar you earn moves through five fires. Each fire tempers a different part of your life. Starve one and the blade warps. Overheat one and you crack. Balance is what makes the steel ring true.

The five fires and what they do:

F — FOUNDATION (Essentials & Stability, ~50–60%)

This is rent or mortgage, food, utilities, transport, insurance, the non-negotiable that keep the lights on and you reliable to the people who count on you. Function: remove chaos. You can't build freedom on late notices and guesswork. If your Foundation regularly busts the top of this range, the system is telling you to cut, renegotiate, or relocate—painful, yes, but cheaper than chronic stress.

O — OPPORTUNITY (Savings & Capital, ~10–20%)

This is "pay yourself first." Treat your future like your first creditor. Automate transfers on payday so willpower isn't part of the loop. This pot builds your breathing room: emergency float, opportunity cash, the cushion that keeps you calm when the world tilts. Rule of thumb: march toward 3–12 months of Foundation covered. Touch it only for genuine shocks or true opportunities with asymmetric upside. If you don't know your real monthly cost yet, go back to **A9** and do the "Name Your Stability Number" and "Build Your Freedom Runway" drills first.

R — REFINEMENT (Growth & Mastery, ~10–15%)

Courses, licenses, tools, coaching, health upgrades, anything that sharpens the man and compounds your earning power. If it grows your capability or your capacity to sell it, it belongs here. Buy fewer status toys and more leverage.

G — GRATITUDE (Giving & Contribution, ~5–10%)

Gratitude isn't sentimentality — it's orientation. Neurologically, it shifts the brain from scarcity to possibility, rewiring the limbic system toward safety and openness. Studies from UCLA's Mindfulness Awareness Research Lab show that consistent gratitude practice strengthens neural pathways associated with optimism, empathy, and problem-solving — the same circuits that collapse under chronic stress. In plain terms: gratitude keeps the system online. It widens your field of vision when fear narrows it. It keeps you curious when life feels closed. A grateful man can still be ambitious, but he's no longer desperate. He stops hoarding opportunity and starts magnetizing it — because gratitude keeps the doors open, both in the world and in the nervous system.

E — ENJOYMENT (Play & Restoration, ~5–10%)

Travel, dates, art, sport, the fuel that keeps discipline from turning into resentment. You can white-knuckle your way to a number; you can't hate your life and call it wealth. Put a real number here and spend it guilt-free.

## WHY FORGE WORKS (AND WHY BUDGETS DON'T)

Budgets argue with desire. FORGE pre-decides desire. You still feel the pull, but the rails carry the flow. The buckets aren't just math — they reveal who you are:

Foundation = stability.

Opportunity = sovereignty.

Refinement = mastery.

Gratitude = meaning.

Enjoyment = vitality.

When your money aligns with your identity, you stop fighting yourself. Discipline stops being punishment and becomes design.

## HOW TO RUN FORGE THIS WEEK (NO DRAMA)

- Name your percentages for the next 90 days. Pick within the ranges above. They're dials, not laws.
- Automate the flow. Opportunity, Refinement, Gratitude, and Enjoyment should move automatically the moment income lands. Automation builds trust faster than willpower ever will.
- Split accounts (or sub-accounts) with nicknames: "FORGE-F, FORGE-O…" Seeing the label changes behavior.
- Do a 15-minute Friday check: balances, leaks, one adjustment. No shame, just steering.
- Quarterly recalibration: if life changes, your ranges change. Keep the model, move the numbers.

## A NOTE ON "PAY YOURSELF FIRST"

This sits inside Opportunity. If all you do for 12 months is skim 10% into O the minute your income lands, your nervous system will change. Margin is medicine. Start at 5% if you must. Walk it up. You're building breathing room and strike capital—cash that buys you time when hit and options when luck knocks.

Common snags (and clean fixes)

- Foundation always over 60%? You don't have a spending problem; you have a structure problem. Renegotiate the big rocks: housing, transport, subscriptions you've stopped seeing.
- Opportunity gets raided. Wrong tool for the job. Keep a tiny "Squeaks" buffer inside Foundation for

inevitable annoyances so you don't torch your future for a punctured tire.
- Refinement turns into retail therapy. Litmus test: does it raise your earning power or deepen your health? If not, it's probably Enjoyment pretending to be Growth.
- Guilt around Enjoyment? Put it in the plan, then spend it on purpose. Restoration is part of performance.
- No giving because 'I'll give when I'm rich'? You're practicing scarcity. Start at 1% if you have to. Train abundance now.

## FORGE + THE MANOS FINANCIAL CREED

a. Pay yourself first → lives in O.
b. Spend by value, not mood → the whole frame; Foundation + Enjoyment keep mood from running the shop.
c. Never spend tomorrow's power today → debt throttles O and R; keep the leash off your neck.
d. Use money to build margin, not identity → margin sits in O; identity sits in your values, not your purchases.
e. Wealth is proof of discipline → FORGE makes discipline visible.

# A9C. FIAT AND PROGRAMMABLE MONEY OVERVIEW

Every fiat currency in history has eventually lost all purchasing power — not always overnight, but through gradual debasement, replacement, or collapse. [i ii iii iv v vi]

That pattern isn't conspiracy. It's arithmetic. When governments print to cover deficits, inflate to fund wars, or manipulate rates to buy votes, the currency erodes. The Roman denarius was cut with base metals until it was worthless. The Chinese yuan of the 1400s — gone. The French *livre*, *assignat*, and *franc* — each replaced. The German mark before WWII — burned for heat. The British pound has lost over 99% of its value since 1900. The U.S. dollar, once backed by gold, now buys what a few cents did a century ago.

Even former Federal Reserve Chairman Alan Greenspan acknowledged that modern credit systems depend on perpetual expansion—new debt paying off old, liquidity feeding liquidity. Critics such as Bill Bonner, James Grant, and Murray Rothbard have argued that such a structure functions as a Ponzi scheme in all but name: sustainable only while confidence and credit continue to grow. [vii] [viii] [ix] [x]

That's not ideology — it's the mathematical reality of compounding debt within closed systems.

The system doesn't implode in a day. It decays through a thousand small permissions — quantitative easing, stimulus, bailouts, subsidies — each one framed as temporary. But the facts are simple: when money is no longer tethered to discipline, time, or labor, it becomes belief only. And belief always breaks.

That doesn't mean retreat from society or stack gold bars in a bunker. It means sovereignty — understanding that your stability can't depend on politicians, markets, or screens. Real wealth isn't digits. It's capability, community, integrity, and energy you control.

But sovereignty doesn't end with money. Most men trade their independence long before they lose a paycheck. They give it to systems that promise safety in exchange for surveillance. They hand it to convenience. They stop being citizens and start being users.

Privacy isn't paranoia — it's dignity. You don't take a shit in front of your coworkers or make love in front of your parents — not because you're hiding, but because some things are sacred. The same principle applies to your data, your money, your choices. When every click, action, or purchase is traceable, freedom becomes conditional. Scholars like Shoshana Zuboff have warned that this kind of one-way visibility transforms autonomy into data extraction—a dynamic echoed by the Cato Institute's recent report on financial privacy risks from CBDCs. [xi] [xii]

## A9C. FIAT AND PROGRAMMABLE MONEY OVERVIEW

Programmable money is programmable behavior. Remove cash and you remove the last untracked choice. A "central bank digital currency" may sound efficient, but efficiency is often just control in a nicer suit. You can't build sovereignty on permission.

Global studies warn of this risk: both the IMF and the Bank for International Settlements note that programmable CBDCs pose significant privacy and governance concerns. [xiii] [xiv]

A truly decentralized blockchain — the kind Bitcoin's creator, Satoshi Nakamoto, envisioned — was designed to remove single points of failure. [xv] The ledger is public, immutable, and distributed. No central authority can quietly rewrite history. That transparency is its integrity.

Transparency and privacy are not opposites; they're allies that protect different domains.

Transparency belongs to systems — it keeps the powerful accountable. Privacy belongs to people — it keeps the individual sovereign.

When systems are opaque, corruption breeds. When individuals are exposed, dignity dies. A healthy society demands both: transparent power, private citizens.

Centralized blockchains reintroduce the very disease decentralization was meant to cure. When one institution can validate, freeze, or rewrite, it's no longer a trust-less network — it's a database with better branding. Many so-called "digital currencies" promoted by banks or governments borrow blockchain's language but not its spirit. They keep the control, just move it behind new interfaces.

## A9C. FIAT AND PROGRAMMABLE MONEY OVERVIEW

That isn't conspiracy; it's arithmetic. When money creation and governance concentrate in a few hands, corruption isn't an accident — it's an inevitability.

Decentralization, properly done, is a design for honesty. When everyone can see the system's ledger, it becomes exponentially harder to cheat. When individuals can protect their own data, it becomes exponentially harder to be controlled. Power disperses outward, accountability scales upward. That's why systems built on transparency threaten those built on control — and why privacy for citizens is not secrecy, but self-respect.

History shows what happens when visibility flows only one way. Power justifies itself as protection — until it doesn't.

So, watch the laws that pass while the world is distracted. Follow the money, not the headlines. When every problem seems to have a digital solution, ask who wrote the code and what it collects.

The sovereign man doesn't live in rebellion. He lives in awareness. He knows where the lines are drawn, and which ones must never be crossed. Because once freedom is coded out of the system, you don't get it back with a password reset.

Freedom, like muscle, atrophies when unused. Train it. Defend it. Live it.

If this section raised your blood pressure, don't bunker — build margin. Go back to A9. Clean Money Protocol & Tracker to set your Stability Number, then run A9B. FORGE — The Five Fires of Financial Freedom to automate flow.

# A10. PURPOSE STATEMENTS FROM REAL MEN

Purpose isn't theory. It's biography written in real time. Every man below wrote his purpose in a single line — clear enough to survive pressure, simple enough to guide a lifetime. Use these as reflections, not templates. Let them provoke clarity, not comparison. When one lands in your chest, stop there. Ask why. That's your compass.

**The Builder** — "To create systems that make life lighter for others — because freedom should scale."

He left a high-paying job to build tools that cut wasted effort for small businesses. The sentence still guides every decision, from how he designs software to how he parents. His question each morning: *Did I build something that made someone's day easier?*

**The Father** — "To raise men who never have to recover from their childhood."

He came from violence and silence. His purpose is to end the inheritance. Every bedtime story, every boundary, every apology is part of that mission. Purpose became daily pattern — presence over performance.

**The Mentor** — "To turn pain into maps that shorten another man's suffering."

A recovering addict who now leads a men's program. His line isn't poetic — it's procedural. Each time he helps a man navigate relapse or rebuild self-trust, he's proving the sentence true.

**The Artisan** — "To make beauty that wakes people up to what they already have."

He paints abstract works shaped by meditation and music. His art isn't escape; it's a return — a way of seeing what's real. Success isn't measured in sales, but in the silence that follows a breath. Purpose became process, brushstroke by brushstroke.

**The Leader** — "To build companies that leave people braver than they arrived."

He runs a construction firm but sees it as a character forge. Apprentices learn craft and courage in equal parts. Purpose reframed the job: profits became a by-product of people growing.

**The Healer** — "To help men come home to their bodies so they can stay in their lives."

A physiotherapist who watched clients chase fitness while avoiding feeling. His sentence reminds him daily: the body isn't a project — it's a house. Every treatment is an invitation to re-inhabit.

## A10. PURPOSE STATEMENTS FROM REAL MEN

**The Creator** — "To turn silence into signal."

He writes. That's it. Essays, lyrics, journal pages — words that translate internal chaos into coherence. His measure of progress: fewer unsaid truths left rotting inside. The work is medicine.

**The Steward** — "To leave every space — physical, emotional, financial — stronger than I found it."

From marriage to investments to the local park he helps maintain, that one line directs everything. Purpose became a filter for consumption, waste, and integrity.

**The Friend** — "To stand beside men when everyone else steps back."

A firefighter who lost two mates to suicide. His mission now is simple: presence. No lectures, no rescue — just showing up. Purpose distilled to proximity.

**The Seeker** — "To live close to truth and bring others near it."

A teacher who traded curriculum for conversations. His students say he teaches subjects, but what he's teaching is awareness. The goal isn't grades — it's clarity.

You don't need to copy these lines. You need to write the one that makes your pulse quicken — the sentence that feels like a vow rather than a wish. When you can say it aloud and feel your shoulders drop, that's it. That's yours.

To find a purpose you can test under pressure and still choose again tomorrow. If your purpose doesn't cost you comfort, it's still a slogan. When it costs you and you stay — it's real.

# A10B. PURPOSE INTEGRATION WORKSHEET

Convert your purpose from words into rhythm. The only purpose that matters is the one you practice. This worksheet turns philosophy into pattern — a repeatable ritual for building a life that matches your line.

## STEP 1 — TRACE YOUR VALUES

List your top five values from Appendix A3. Write why each matter to you, where you're already living it, and where you're not. Circle the one that feels most like your North Star — the value that anchors every other. Let that be your compass for what follows.

## STEP 2 — WRITE YOUR LINE

Use this simple formula:

"To [verb] [what] — [why it matters]."

Write three to five versions. Read each one aloud. The line that hits your body hardest — the one that feels lived, not performed

## A10B. PURPOSE INTEGRATION WORKSHEET

— is the one that stays. Write that version cleanly beneath and sign it like a contract.

## STEP 3 — PRESSURE TEST

Ask yourself three questions:

1. Would I still do this if no one applauded?
2. Would I still do this if it didn't pay?
3. Would I still do this when I'm tired, broke, or unseen?

If you can answer *yes* to all three, it's purpose. If not, refine until you can.

## STEP 4 — BUILD PROOF

Purpose lives in pattern, not proclamation. Name three visible actions that will prove your line this week. Write how often you'll do them, and when you'll begin. You'll know it's working when you can point to real-world evidence instead of intention.

## STEP 5 — THE WITNESS TEST

Share your purpose line and your three proofs with one man you trust. Ask him directly: "Does this sound like me?" If he hesitates, refine it again. Purpose should sound like your blood speaking — not a résumé, not a brand.

## STEP 6 — REVIEW LOOP

At the end of each month, read your purpose line again. Cross-check it against your actual calendar. Ask: Does my schedule reflect my sentence? If not, change the week — not the words. Integration beats inspiration.

## A10B. PURPOSE INTEGRATION WORKSHEET

## STEP 7 — THE REWRITE RULE

Your purpose can evolve, but it must never drift. When it changes, write the new version by hand, date it, and sign again. Growth doesn't mean inconsistency — it means integration. Every rewrite is proof of evolution, not instability.

Move from clarity to consistency to contribution — a purpose that lives in your calendar, not just your head. If your daily pattern doesn't echo your purpose line, you're still in rehearsal. Start running the code.

# A11. THE OUTCOMES INDEX — MEASURE WHAT MATTERS

Healing doesn't post to social media; it shows up quietly — in tone, breath, and how fast you return to truth. That's why ManOS tracks movement, not perfection.

The *Outcomes Index* [i] [ii] [iii] is your coherence check — five measurable shifts:

1. *Silent* → *Seen*: How connected do you feel to others — in truth, not performance?
2. *Tired* → *Directed*: How clearly do you feel your life has direction or purpose?
3. *Ashamed* → *Accountable*: How often do you take ownership without self-attack?
4. *Numb* → *Aware*: How often can you name what you're feeling when it happens?
5. *Fragmented* → *Whole*: How aligned do your actions feel with your values and truth?

How these map to the BRIC framework:

## A11. THE OUTCOMES INDEX — MEASURE WHAT MATTERS

1. BARE — Silent → Seen ◇ connection, openness, honesty
2. REFORGE — Ashamed → Accountable ◇ integrity, responsibility
3. INSTALL — Tired → Directed ◇ purpose, discipline
4. COHERE — Numb → Aware & Fragmented → Whole ◇ emotional literacy, integration, congruence

You can complete it solo or within your Table.

If you're tracking this in brotherhood, compare your shifts out loud — coherence grows faster when witnessed.

Each domain marks a movement from fracture to function.

Score yourself, honestly, from **1 to 10** every 30 days.

(1 = you live mostly in the first state; 10 = you live mostly in the second.)

The aim isn't perfection — it's progress.

### SILENT → SEEN (Connection)

How connected do you feel to others — in truth, not performance?

☐ ☐ ☐ ☐ ☐ ☐ ☐ ☐ ☐

Write one moment this month where you felt genuinely seen.

### TIRED → DIRECTED (Purpose)

How clearly do you feel your life has direction or meaning?

☐ ☐ ☐ ☐ ☐ ☐ ☐ ☐ ☐

Name one decision that reflected purpose instead of fatigue.

## A11. THE OUTCOMES INDEX — MEASURE WHAT MATTERS

### ASHAMED → ACCOUNTABLE (Integrity)

How often do you take ownership without attacking yourself?

☐ ☐ ☐ ☐ ☐ ☐ ☐ ☐ ☐

Write one situation where you repaired instead of retreated.

### NUMB → AWARE (Emotional Literacy)

How often can you name what you're feeling when it happens?

☐ ☐ ☐ ☐ ☐ ☐ ☐ ☐ ☐

Write one emotion you noticed in real time this week.

### FRAGMENTED → WHOLE (Coherence)

How aligned do your actions feel with your values and truth?

☐ ☐ ☐ ☐ ☐ ☐ ☐ ☐ ☐

Write one example where you acted from alignment instead of fear.

Repeat the exercise at entry, 30 days, and 90 days.

Circle what changed — or what stayed steady under pressure.

ManOS doesn't grade men.

It graphs coherence.

*ManOS* isn't theory. It's a systematic response to well-documented conditions — isolation, emotional illiteracy, relational harm, and blocked help-seeking — identified across decades of global research. What's been missing is synthesis. The data existed, but it lived in silos: psychology measured it, sociology mapped it, medicine treated its symptoms. *ManOS* is the first framework to integrate those strands into one coherent system — turning evidence into embodiment, science into practice, and statistics into soul.

ManOS is the first integrated operating system for men that links isolation, economic destabilization, shame, emotional disconnection, and existential drift into a single, runnable model.

Progress isn't loud.

It's the quiet between relapses — the space where you notice you've come home to yourself.

# APPENDIX: A LEGACY BLUEPRINT — HOW TO GATE PORNOGRAPHY RESPONSIBLY

*For readers who want to move from awareness to action, the following appendix offers a simple framework for how our society could protect younger minds from premature sexual exposure. It's not activism. It's stewardship — a practical outline of what responsible technology and leadership can look like when guided by conscience rather than convenience.*

This isn't a crusade. It's civic maintenance. Before we can protect our children's innocence, we have to reclaim our own presence. The same way we install locks on doors and guardrails on highways, we can build boundaries around what the youngest eyes in our culture are exposed to. Technology already gives us the tools. What's missing is the alignment of will.

The fix doesn't require new technology — only new defaults. Responsibility can be coded into the infrastructure itself.

Each layer below shows how.

## 1. THE NETWORK LAYER — RAISING FRICTION

Every harmful economy begins with frictionless access. The first step is to make access *a little harder* for those who shouldn't have it.

<u>Default Filtering at the ISP Level:</u>

Internet service providers already categorize domains for malware, spam, and gambling. Adult content can be included by default.

Adults who wish to opt out simply verify age through a $0 credit-card authorization or a digital ID check.

Privacy stays intact, only the defaults shift.

<u>Accountability through Transparency:</u>

ISPs publish quarterly reports: number of filtered accounts, opt-out requests, and compliance audits. No individual data—just statistics.

When visibility rises, so does accountability.

This single step would cut exposure dramatically within months. The technology exists. The resistance is cultural.

## 2. THE PLATFORM LAYER — CLOSING THE GATEWAYS

The second layer isn't about policing; it's about **standards**.

When platforms adopt unified thresholds, the ecosystem shifts.

<u>App Stores:</u>

Apple and Google already vet for malware and payment compliance. Add one more rule: adult apps and web views must honor the device's verified age token. Non-compliant apps lose listing rights. Simple, immediate, effective.

<u>Ad and Payment Networks:</u>

No revenue flow to non-compliant sites. Ad networks and payment processors already perform risk assessments; this becomes one more field on the checklist. The incentive structure flips: compliance pays, exploitation costs. When money and distribution align with responsibility, behavior follows faster than any law.

## 3. THE HOME LAYER — DEFAULT SAFETY AT THE SOURCE

The safest system is the one that doesn't depend on technical knowledge. Protection should be built into the hardware, switched *on by default*, and handled during installation—not left for parents to configure later.

Router & Device Defaults:

Manufacturers can ship routers, modems, and mobile devices with adult-content filtering enabled from the factory. During installation, the technician or setup wizard presents a single option: *Keep protection on* or *disable after verified adulthood.*

Verification uses the same $0 credit-card or digital-ID check as the network layer. No menus, no manual DNS changes, no extra software. One binary choice at activation.

Automatic Updates:

Firmware updates keep blocklists current and self-maintaining. Parents never need to log in or manage settings—the device stays compliant by design.

Legal Mandate:

Governments can mandate default protection in all new consumer devices. Certification could mirror existing electrical or safety standards, ensuring that ISPs and retailers distribute only compliant equipment.

This isn't about restricting freedom. It's about intelligent design—building responsibility into the system itself so that safety isn't optional or dependent on technical skill.

When the connection is installed, the protection is already there. That's the simplest fix, and the one most likely to last.

## APPENDIX: A LEGACY BLUEPRINT — HOW TO GATE PORN…

These three layers don't restrict freedom; they restore order. They make care the default.

## FROM AWARENESS TO STEWARDSHIP

Implementing these layers would not censor adults or sanitize reality. It would *buy children time*—to grow nervous systems that can handle what they see, and to form ideas of intimacy that involve more than pixels.

Governments can coordinate.

ISPs can default to safety.

Platforms can enforce consistency.

Parents can reclaim authority.

Men can lead the call—not through outrage, but through example.

## HOW TO ADVANCE IT WHERE YOU ARE

If this section moves you, here's how to begin:

- Write to your local representative or regulator requesting mandatory default filtering with opt-out verification.
- Contact your ISP—ask if adult filtering is enabled by default. If not, request it.
- Share this blueprint with fathers, teachers, and community leaders.
- Model presence—show what grounded masculinity looks like in a digital age.

You don't need a campaign. You need a conversation. One household at a time. One provider at a time. One law at a time. That's how stewardship spreads.

APPENDIX: A LEGACY BLUEPRINT — HOW TO GATE PORN...

## CLOSING NOTE

Future generations will judge us by what we normalized —

not by our slogans, but by our silences. If we can build an internet that knows what we want to buy before we do, we can build one that protects our children's minds while they're still forming.

But this isn't just about children. It's about what kind of species we become. Connection is the defining trait of humanity.

For two hundred thousand years, survival has depended on it — our ability to bond, cooperate, and form trust-based groups is what allowed culture to exist at all.

And that drive to connect isn't only social — it's chemical.

When we touch, make love, share truth, or even meet another's eyes, the body releases oxytocin, dopamine, serotonin, vasopressin, and endogenous opioids — the ancient neurotransmitters of safety and belonging. [1] They're the biological glue that

---

1. Uvnäs-Moberg, K. (1998). *Oxytocin may mediate the benefits of positive social interaction and emotions.* Psychoneuroendocrinology, 23(8), 819–835.
   Carter, C. S. (2014). *Oxytocin pathways and the evolution of human behavior.* Annual Review of Psychology, 65, 17–39.
   Porges, S. W. (2011). *The Polyvagal Theory: Neurophysiological foundations of emotions, attachment, communication, and self-regulation.* W. W. Norton & Company.
   Insel, T. R., & Young, L. J. (2001). *The neurobiology of attachment.* Nature Reviews Neuroscience, 2(2), 129–136.
   Machin, A. J., & Dunbar, R. I. M. (2011). *The brain opioid theory of social attachment: a review of the evidence.* Behaviour, 148(9–10), 985–1025.
   Berridge, K. C., & Robinson, T. E. (1998). *What is the role of dopamine in reward: hedonic impact, reward learning, or incentive salience?* Brain Research Reviews, 28(3), 309–369.
   Young, S. N., & Leyton, M. (2002). *The role of serotonin in human mood*

binds us to one another, the molecules that make care feel worth it.

When intimacy becomes transactional and attention becomes a commodity, we begin dismantling that chemistry — rewiring our reward systems away from people toward pixels.

Unchecked, that erosion doesn't just weaken families — it weakens civilization itself. Because a culture that forgets how to connect eventually forgets how to care.

The question isn't *can we build better systems?*

It's *will we choose to protect the parts of ourselves that machines can't replace?*

---

*and social interaction: Insight from altered tryptophan levels.* Pharmacology Biochemistry and Behavior, 71(4), 857–865.

# ACKNOWLEDGMENTS

For the men I've mentored, and the men who have mentored me back — your wounds and wisdom gave this book its spine.

For Elliott — the youngest, at 25, for being brave enough to take on the *ManOS* work. Respect.

For David and Susan — for decades of encouragement and support.

For Caroline, whose art therapy heals in color and canvas (https://cata.org.au/). And for Elena, whose foundation taught me that gratitude and intention create all good things. You remind me that service itself is a form of art (https://thefredliuzzifoundation.org.au/).

And for the teachers who shaped me from afar: John L. Fitzgerald, Carl Jung, Gabor Maté, Wim Hof, David Brooks, Ken Wilber, John Lennox, Gary Brecka, Chris Bale , Dan Martell, David D. Burns, Dr. Ramani, Richard Grannon, and so many others — each gave me a tool, a language, or a lens I could not have found alone.

# TESTIMONIES

"ManOS isn't another self-help book—it's scar tissue transformed into an operating system that works."

"Finally, a book that shows men how to be both strong and soft, both warrior and gardener, without apologizing for either."

"This is the book I needed twenty years ago. It would have saved me a marriage, a fortune, and a decade of drift."

"This is the first book to successfully blend: Literary memoir quality, practical system architecture, masculine vulnerability without weakness and both spiritual depth and secular accessibility."

## ABOUT THE AUTHOR

Lee Powell didn't set out to write a book on masculinity. He set out to survive collapse.

On paper, his life worked: Oxford-educated, MSc. in engineering, founder of global software platforms. He built companies, sold companies, raised a family. By thirty, he had every measure of success — and still found himself empty, asking, *Is this it?*

The breakdown wasn't optional. It was lived. And it forced him into a rebuild. Out of that scar tissue came *ManOS* — not as theory, but as the operating system he wished he'd had twenty years earlier.

Lee blends engineering precision with the human mess of recovery. His work resonates with men who know the grind: the years of building something from scratch, answering every email, juggling jobs just to make ends meet — only to find themselves running on fumes. He knows what it's like to look successful on the outside while coming apart inside.

This book isn't a résumé line. It's a field report. If it helps you avoid even one of the crashes he lived through, then the scars weren't wasted.

For resources, tools, and the ManOS network, visit getmanos.com.

instagram.com/getmanos

# NOTES

## 1. THE LIE OF THE LINE

i. Jung, C. G. (1951). *Aion: Researches into the Phenomenology of the Self*. Collected Works, Vol. 9, Part II, ¶126. Princeton University Press.
ii. Jack, D. C., & Dill, D. (1992). "The Silencing the Self Scale: Schemas of Intimacy Associated With Depression in Women." *Psychology of Women Quarterly*.
iii. Impett, E. A., et al. (2012). "Sacrificing for Approach and Avoidance Goals: A Daily Diary Study of Married Couples." *Journal of Personality and Social Psychology*.

## 2. WHEN THE LIFE YOU BUILT STOPS WORKING

i. Hopper, G. M. (1981). Quoted in Philip C. Brooks (Ed.), *The Wit and Wisdom of Grace Hopper*. Washington, DC: U.S. Navy Archives.
ii. Centers for Disease Control and Prevention. (2023). *Suicide mortality in the United States, 2000–2021*. National Vital Statistics Reports, 72(15).
iii. Raley, R. K., & Sweeney, M. M. (2020). Divorce, repartnering, and stepfamilies: A decade in review. *Journal of Marriage and Family*, 82(1), 81–99.
iv. Schlegel, R. J., Hicks, J. A., King, L. A., & Arndt, J. (2009). Feeling like you know who you are: Meaning in life as a function of authenticity. *Journal of Personality and Social Psychology*, 96(2), 457–482.
v. Addis, M. E., & Mahalik, J. R. (2003). Men, masculinity, and the contexts of help seeking. *American Psychologist*, 58(1), 5–14.
vi. Williams, K., & Umberson, D. (2004). "Marital Status, Marital Transitions, and Health: A Gendered Life Course Perspective." *Journal of Health and Social Behavior*.

## 4. RUNNING DAD'S CODE

i. Widely attributed to Carl Jung. Closest discussion of the unconscious as "fate" appears in Jung, C. G. (1951). *Aion: Researches

into the Phenomenology of the Self*. Collected Works Vol. 9, Part II. Princeton University Press.
ii. CDC National Center for Health Statistics. (2023). *Suicide Mortality in the United States, 2001–2021*. NCHS Data Brief No. 464. Hyattsville, MD: National Center for Health Statistics.
iii. National Center for Health Statistics. (2020). *Mental Health Treatment Among Adults: United States, 2019*. NCHS Data Brief No. 380. Centers for Disease Control and Prevention.
iv. Levant, R. F., Hall, R. J., & Rankin, T. J. (2013). Male alexithymia: Gender differences in emotional expression and regulation. *Psychology of Men & Masculinity, 14*(4), 373–384.
v. Mahalik, J. R., Burns, S. M., & Syzdek, M. (2007). Masculinity and perceived normative health behaviors as predictors of men's health behaviors. *Social Science & Medicine, 64*(11), 2201–2209.

## 5. THE DASHBOARD YOU NEVER HAD

i. Mipham, Sakyong. (2012). *Running with the Mind of Meditation: Lessons for Training Body and Mind.* New York: Harmony Books.
ii. Mattila, A. K., Salminen, J. K., Nummi, T., & Joukamaa, M. (2006). Age is strongly associated with alexithymia in the general population. *Journal of Psychosomatic Research, 61*(5), 629-635.
iii. Li, S., Zhang, B., Guo, Y., & Zhang, J. (2015). The association between alexithymia as assessed by the 20-item Toronto Alexithymia Scale and depression: A meta-analysis. Psychiatry Research, 227(1), 1-9.
iv. National Center for Health Statistics (NCHS). (2020). *Mental Health Treatment Among Adults: United States, 2019.* NCHS Data Brief No. 380. Centers for Disease Control and Prevention.
v. Greenberg, L. S., & Watson, J. C. (2006). *Emotion-Focused Therapy for Depression.* Washington, DC: American Psychological Association.
vi. Alberts B et al. *Molecular Biology of the Cell.* 7th ed. Garland Science, 2022.
vii. Manolio T A, Collins F S. "The Missing Heritability of Complex Diseases." *Nat Rev Genet.* 2009;10: 574–582.
viii. International Human Genome Sequencing Consortium. *Nature.* 2001;409: 860–921.
ix. National Human Genome Research Institute. "Comparative Genomics Fact Sheet." 2023.

## 6. LIVING BY THE VALUES YOU ACTUALLY CHOOSE

i. Jung, C. G. (1963). *Memories, Dreams, Reflections*. New York: Pantheon Books.
ii. Schwartz, S. H. (1992). *Universals in the Content and Structure of Values: Theoretical Advances and Empirical Tests in 20 Countries. Advances in Experimental Social Psychology*, 25, 1–65. (Foundational model of human value structures across cultures). See also Rokeach, M. (1973). *The Nature of Human Values*. Free Press. (Classic study of intergenerational value transmission and conflict).
iii. Mattila, A. K., Salminen, J. K., Nummi, T., & Joukamaa, M. (2006). *Age is strongly associated with alexithymia in the general population.* Journal of Psychosomatic Research, 61(5), 629–635.
iv. National Center for Health Statistics. (2020). *Mental Health Treatment Among Adults: United States, 2019*. NCHS Data Brief No. 380. Centers for Disease Control and Prevention.
v. Waldinger, R. J., & Schulz, M. (2023). *The Good Life: Lessons from the World's Longest Scientific Study of Happiness*. New York: Simon & Schuster.

## 7. WHEN YOUR WOUNDS REWRITE REALITY

i. This is my own adaptation of "name it to tame it" from Daniel Siegel, *The Whole-Brain Child*, 2011
ii. Levant, R. F., Hall, R. J., Williams, C. M., & Hasan, N. T. (2009). Gender differences in alexithymia. Psychology of Men & Masculinity, 10(3), 190–203.
iii. Haviland, M. G., Warren, W. L., & Riggs, M. L. (2000). An observer scale to measure alexithymia. Psychosomatics, 41(5), 385–392.
iv. Beck, A. T. (1976). Cognitive therapy and the emotional disorders. International Universities Press.
v. McCrory, E., Gerin, M. I., & Viding, E. (2017). Childhood maltreatment, latent vulnerability, and biased threat processing. Journal of Child Psychology and Psychiatry, 58(4), 338–357.
vi. Sweet, P. L. (2019). The sociology of gaslighting: how interpersonal invalidation distorts perception. American Sociological Review, 84(5), 851–875.
vii. **Australian Institute of Family Studies (AIFS).** (2025). *Male Isolation, Depression, and Intimate Partner Violence: Longitudinal Findings from the Ten to Men Study*. Canberra: Australian Government Department of Social Services.
viii. **Flood, M., & Pease, B.** (2009). Factors Influencing Attitudes to

## NOTES

      *Violence Against Women*. Melbourne: Victorian Health Promotion Foundation.

ix. **Langhinrichsen-Rohling, J., McCullars, A., & Misra, T. A.** (2012). Motivations for Men and Women's Intimate Partner Violence Perpetration: A Comprehensive Review. *Partner Abuse*, 3(4), 429–468.

x. Australian Institute of Family Studies. (2025). *Ten to Men: The Australian Longitudinal Study on Male Health — Wave 5 Summary Report.

xi. **Ogrodniczuk, J. S., Oliffe, J. L., Beharry, J., & Goldenberg, S. L.** (2021). Men's Mental Health: Social Determinants and Implications for Policy and Practice. *The Lancet Psychiatry*, 8(9), 795–807.

xii. **Addis, M. E., & Mahalik, J. R.** (2003). Men, Masculinity, and the Contexts of Help Seeking. *American Psychologist*, 58(1), 5–14.

## 8. DECODING THE DATA OF EMOTION

i. *ManOS: The Operating System for Men*. Resonates with psychological research on emotional literacy and alexithymia (see Bagby, Parker & Taylor, *Journal of Personality Disorders*, 1994).

ii. Movember Foundation. (2023). Social connections and men's health: A global report. Retrieved from https://movember.com/reports/social-connections

iii. Levant, R. F., Hall, R. J., Williams, C. M., & Hasan, N. T. (2009). Gender differences in alexithymia. *Psychology of Men & Masculinity*, 10(3), 190-203.

iv. Rosenfeld, M. J., & Roesler, K. (2019). Who wants the breakup? Gender and breakup in heterosexual couples. *Social Forces*, 97(3), 1091-1114.

v. World Health Organization. (2023). Suicide worldwide in 2019: Global health estimates. Geneva: World Health Organization.

## 9. HOW TO ACTUALLY CONNECT

i. *ManOS: The Operating System for Men*. Rooted in long traditions of stoic thought emphasizing self-knowledge as the basis for freedom and stability.

ii. Lance Secretan, *Inspire! What Great Leaders Do* (Hoboken: John Wiley & Sons, 2004), 33.

iii. Institute for Family Studies. (2023). "The State of Our Unions 2023: Marriage and Relationship Satisfaction Trends." National Marriage Project, University of Virginia.

# NOTES

iv. Levant, R. F., et al. (2023). "Alexithymia and normative male alexithymia as predictors of relationship satisfaction." Psychology of Men & Masculinities, 24(2), 156-167.

v. Rosenfeld, M. J. (2023). "Who wants the breakup? Gender and breakup in heterosexual couples." Demographic Research, 48, 891-914.

vi. Cox, D. A. (2021). "The state of male friendship in America." Survey Center on American Life, American Enterprise Institute.

vii. Ambady, N., & Rosenthal, R. (1992). *Thin slices of expressive behavior as predictors of interpersonal consequences: A meta-analysis.* Psychological Bulletin, 111(2), 256–274. (People make surprisingly accurate judgments of others within seconds, based on microexpressions, posture, tone, and other cues.)

viii. de Groot, J. H. B., & Smeets, M. A. M. (2017). *Human chemosignals of emotion: A review.* Current Opinion in Psychology, 17, 67–73. See also Lundström, J. N., et al. (2003). *Androstadienone, a putative human pheromone, affects mood and cortisol responses.* Biological Psychology, 63(3), 283–291. (Certain chemical signals—sometimes subconscious—have been shown to influence mood, attention, and social perception.)

ix. **Carvalheira A et al., 2021** – "Problematic pornography consumption and erectile dysfunction among men," *Journal of Sexual Medicine*, 18(10). PubMed 34534092

x. **Covenant Eyes Report**, "Porn-Induced ED: Science, Stats & Stories," 2024. Link

xi. **Wéry A et al., 2021** – "Problematic pornography use and mental health in men," *Frontiers in Psychology*. PMC8569536

xii. **Kraus S W et al., 2016** – "The impact of pornography on sexual satisfaction: A review," *Clinical Psychology Review*, 45. PMC5039517

## 10. BROTHERHOOD OR BUST

i. *ManOS: The Operating System for Men.* Supported by research on male social bonds and resilience (see Vaillant, *The Natural History of Male Psychological Health*, 2002).

ii. Centers for Disease Control and Prevention. (2023). *Suicide mortality in the United States, 2000–2021*. National Vital Statistics Reports, 72(15). Hyattsville, MD: National Center for Health Statistics.

iii. National Center for Health Statistics. (2023). *National Health Interview Survey, Early Release Program: Mental Health Indicators by Age and Sex*. Hyattsville, MD: CDC.

iv. Survey Center on American Life. (2021). *The State of American Friendship: Change, Challenges, and Loss*. Washington, DC: American Enterprise Institute.

## 11. GETTING YOUR MONEY RIGHT

i. Commonly attributed to John D. Rockefeller; original authorship uncertain. Phrase appears in early 20th-century business collections as an anonymous maxim.
ii. Helen Keller, *The Open Door* (Garden City, NY: Doubleday, 1957), p. 46.
iii. Pew Research Center, *Financial Resilience in America* (2023). Nearly half of households reported income volatility in the prior 12 months.
iv. Federal Reserve Bank of New York, *Quarterly Report on Household Debt and Credit* (2023). Total household debt rose over 30% between 2019 and 2023.
v. Gallup, *State of the Global Workplace* (2022). Only about one-third of employees report being engaged or seeing their work as connected to purpose.
vi. Board of Governors of the Federal Reserve System, *Report on the Economic Well-Being of U.S. Households* (2023). More than half of Americans report having less than $10,000 in retirement savings.
vii. Organization for Economic Co-operation and Development (OECD). (2024).

## 12. TAKING CARE OF THE MACHINE

i. Rohn, J. **The Treasury of Quotes**. Southlake, TX: Jim Rohn International; 1994. (Commonly quoted as: "Take care of your body. It's the only place you have to live.")
ii. Travison TG, et al. *A population-level decline in serum testosterone levels in American men.* J Clin Endocrinol Metab. 2007;92(1):196-202.
iii. Fantus RJ, et al. *Decline in serum testosterone levels among adolescent and young adult men in the U.S., 1999–2016.* Eur Urol Focus. 2020.
iv. Wheaton AG, et al. *Short sleep duration among U.S. adults, 2020* (BRFSS). Prev Chronic Dis. 2023;20:220400. (~33% <7 h).
v. Gallup Poll. *Sleep in America survey,* 2023. (~20% report ≤5 h/night).
vi. Fryar CD, Carroll MD, Afful J. *Prevalence of overweight, obesity,*

*and severe obesity among adults: U.S. 2017–2018.* NCHS Health E-Stats. (~77% of men overweight+obese).

vii. Ford ES, et al. *Trends in mean waist circumference among U.S. adults, 1999–2012.* JAMA. 2014. (95.5 → 98.5 cm).

viii. USDA Food and Nutrition Service. *SNAP Product Purchase Data 2022 Report.* (Soda/beverages consistently rank as top expenditure).

ix. Ludwig, D. S., & Ebbeling, C. B. (2018). "The Carbohydrate-Insulin Model of Obesity: Beyond 'Calories In, Calories Out.'" *JAMA Internal Medicine,* 178(8):1098-1103.

x. Hall, K. D. et al. (2021). "Ultra-Processed Diets Cause Excess Calorie Intake and Weight Gain." *Cell Metabolism,* 32(1):69-83.

xi. Zeevi, D. et al. (2015). "Personalized Nutrition by Prediction of Glycemic Responses." *Cell,* 163(5):1079-1094.

xii. Cacioppo, J. T., & Cacioppo, S. (2018). *The Neuroendocrinology of Social Isolation.* Annual Review of Psychology, 69:733–758.

xiii. Young, S. N. (2007). "How to Increase Serotonin in the Human Brain Without Drugs." *Journal of Psychiatry & Neuroscience,* 32(6):394–399.

xiv. Richard, D. M. et al. (2009). "L-Tryptophan: Basic Metabolic Functions, Behavioral Research and Therapeutic Indications." *International Journal of Tryptophan Research,* 2:45–60.

xv. Kennedy, D. O. (2016). "B Vitamins and the Brain: Mechanisms, Dose and Efficacy." *Nutrients,* 8(2):68.

xvi. Carter, C. S. (2014). "Oxytocin Pathways and the Evolution of Human Behavior." *Annual Review of Psychology,* 65:17–39.

xvii. Heinrichs, M. & Domes, G. (2008). "Neurobiology of Trust." *Nature Reviews Neuroscience,* 9(8):593–602.

xviii. Miller, A. H., & Raison, C. L. (2016). "The Role of Inflammation in Depression." *Nature Reviews Immunology,* 16(1):22–34.

xix. Sapolsky, R. M. (2004). *Why Zebras Don't Get Ulcers.* Holt Paperbacks.

xx. Humphrey LL, Fu R, Rogers K, Freeman M, Helfand M. Homocysteine level and coronary heart disease incidence: a systematic review and meta-analysis. *Mayo Clin Proc.* 2008;83(11):1203–1212.

xxi. Holick MF. Vitamin D deficiency. *N Engl J Med.* 2007;357(3):266–281.

xxii. Bhasin S, Brito JP, Cunningham GR, Hayes FJ, et al. Testosterone therapy in men with hypogonadism: Endocrine Society clinical practice guideline. *J Clin Endocrinol Metab.* 2018;103(5):1715–1744.

xxiii. Bahn RS, Burch HB, Cooper DS, et al. Hyperthyroidism and other causes of thyrotoxicosis: management guidelines. *Thyroid.* 2011;21(6):593–646.

xxiv. Bailey LB, Ayling JE. The MTHFR polymorphism: effects on folate metabolism and disease risk. *Am J Clin Nutr.* 2009;89(1):17–25.

# NOTES

xxv. Ridker PM. High-sensitivity C-reactive protein and cardiovascular risk. *Circulation*. 2003;107(3):363–369.

xxvi. EFSA Panel on Contaminants in the Food Chain. Scientific opinion on lead in food. *EFSA Journal*. 2010;8(4):1570.

xxvii. Shapiro, F. (1996). "Eye Movement Desensitization and Reprocessing (EMDR): Evaluation of Controlled PTSD Research." *Journal of Behavior Therapy and Experimental Psychiatry*.

xxviii. Koenig, H. G., McCullough, M. E., & Larson, D. B. (2001). *Handbook of Religion and Health*.

xxix. Pargament, K. I. (1997). *The Psychology of Religion and Coping*. New York: Guilford Press.

xxx. Simard, S. W. (1997). "Net transfer of carbon between tree species with shared mycorrhizal fungi." *Nature*.

xxxi. Narango, D. L., et al. (2018). "Native Plants Improve Bird Populations and Ecosystem Health." *Proceedings of the National Academy of Sciences*.

xxxii. Janzen, D. H. (1977). "Why Fruits Rot, Seeds Mold, and Meat Spoils." *American Naturalist*.

xxxiii. Uvnäs-Moberg, K. (1998). "Oxytocin May Mediate the Benefits of Positive Social Interaction and Emotions." *Psychoneuroendocrinology*, 23(8):819–835.

## 13. QUICK WINS THAT STICK

i. Zig Ziglar, *See You at the Top* (Gretna, LA: Pelican Publishing, 1975). Ziglar frequently used this phrase in his talks and writings to illustrate how small daily actions lead to major life changes.

## 14. THE 30-DAY REBOOT

i. Joseph Campbell, *The Power of Myth* with Bill Moyers (New York: Doubleday, 1988), p. 23.

ii. Behavioral Science Institute, "Goal-Setting and Action-Taking Gender Study," 2024.

iii. Stanford Habit Lab, "Procrastination and Perfectionism in Habit Formation," 2024.

iv. Nature Neuroscience, "Neural Pathway Formation in Micro-Habit Development," 2024.

## 15. INSTALLING PURPOSE

i. Quote Investigator (2014). "The purpose of life is not to be happy..." — credit to Leo Rosten.

ii. Hill, P. L., & Turiano, N. A. (2014). *Purpose in life as a predictor of mortality across adulthood*. Psychological Science, 25(7), 1482–1486.
iii. Li, Y. I., et al. (2023). *Purpose in life and stress: an individual-participant meta-analysis*. Journal of Affective Disorders. See also Disabato, D. J., et al. (2023). *The relationship between purpose in life and depression and anxiety: A meta-analysis*.
iv. Steptoe, A., & Fancourt, D. (2019). *Leading a meaningful life at older ages and its relationship with subsequent health and wellbeing*. PNAS, 116(4), 1207–1212.
v. Gallup (2024). *State of the Global Workplace 2024*.
vi. Hatfield, E., Cacioppo, J. T., & Rapson, R. L. (1994). *Emotional Contagion*. Cambridge University Press.
vii. Vicaria, I. M., & Dickens, L. (2025). *Multimodal interpersonal synchrony: Systematic review and meta-analysis*. Neuroscience & Biobehavioral Reviews.
viii. Friston, K. (2010). Attention, uncertainty, and free-energy. *Frontiers in Human Neuroscience*.
ix. Seth, A. K., Suzuki, K., & Critchley, H. D. (2012). Predictions, perception, and a sense of self. *Philosophical Transactions of the Royal Society B*.
x. Buonomano, D. V., & Merzenich, M. M. (1998). Cortical plasticity: From synapses to maps. *Annual Review of Neuroscience*.
xi. Anderson, B. A. (2013). Persistence of value-driven attentional capture. *Journal of Experimental Psychology: Human Perception & Performance*.
xii. Xia, H.-S., et al. (2023). Attention bias modification for depression: Meta-analysis. *Frontiers in Psychiatry*.

## 16. LEADING BY EXAMPLE, NOT TITLE

i. Schweitzer, Albert. *Out of My Life and Thought: An Autobiography* (1933).
ii. Freud, S. (1920). *Beyond the Pleasure Principle*. Standard Edition, Vol. 18. (Introduced the concept of repetition compulsion — the unconscious drive to repeat traumatic experiences). See also van der Kolk, B. (2014). *The Body Keeps the Score*. New York: Viking. (Modern trauma research confirming how unresolved trauma leads people to unconsciously recreate familiar harmful patterns until they become conscious and interrupted).
iii. labor for Creative Leadership (2023). "Leadership Transitions and Imposter Syndrome." Greensboro, NC. (Survey of global managers reporting widespread imposter feelings in leadership roles).
iv. Pew Research Center (2024). "America's Missing Mentors: Young Men and Role Model Crisis." Washington, DC. (National survey

showing 2/3 of young men lack a positive male role model they would willingly follow).
v. Gallup (2023). *State of the Global Workplace: Male Leadership Confidence Gap*. Gallup, Washington, DC. (Study showing disconnect between managerial authority and genuine developmental leadership).

## 17. WHAT YOUR KIDS WILL REMEMBER

i. Australian Bureau of Statistics, *Causes of Death*, 2022.
ii. National Survey of Mental Health and Wellbeing, Australian Institute of Health and Welfare, 2022.
iii. merican Perspectives Survey, Survey Center on American Life, 2021.
iv. U.S. Bureau of Labor Statistics, *Labor Force Participation Rate of Men, 1950–2020*.
v. U.S. Department of Health and Human Services, Office of the Surgeon General. (2023). *Our Epidemic of Loneliness and Isolation: The U.S. Surgeon General's Advisory on the Healing Effects of Social Connection and Community*.
vi. Jesse Jackson, *Speech at the Democratic National Convention*, 1984.
vii. *Parenting Styles and Psychological Resilience: The Mediating Role of Error-Related Negativity (ERN)*, Journal of Neuroscience & Behavioral Research (2023).
viii. Vrij, A., Granhag, P. A., & Mann, S. (2010). "Good liars." *Journal of Psychiatry & Law*, 38(1-2), 77–98.
ix. Grusec, J. E., & Goodnow, J. J. (1994). "Impact of parental discipline methods on the child's internalization of values: A reconceptualization of current points of view." *Developmental Psychology*, 30(1), 4–19.
x. Burke, C. S., Sims, D. E., Lazzara, E. H., & Salas, E. (2007). "Trust in leadership: A multi-level review and integration." *The Leadership Quarterly*, 18(6), 606–632.
xi. Przybylski, A. K., & Weinstein, N. (2013). "Can you connect with me now? How the presence of mobile communication technology influences face-to-face conversation quality." *Journal of Social and Personal Relationships*, 30(3), 237–246.
xii. Kushlev, K., Dunn, E. W., & Davidson, B. I. (2016). "The effects of mobile phone use on parent-child interaction." *Developmental Psychology*, 52(9), 1369–1378.
xiii. Miller-Ott, A. E., & Kelly, L. (2017). "Phubbing and relationship satisfaction: Examining the roles of relational quality and communication satisfaction." *Communication Studies*, 68(5), 472–488.

# NOTES

## 18. THIS IS THE MOMENT

i. Fischer, A. H., et al. (2018). "Gender differences in emotion perception and self-reported emotional intelligence: A test of the emotion sensitivity hypothesis." PLOS ONE, 13(1).
ii. Pew Research Center. (2024). "More Young Women Than Men Have College Degrees."
iii. FRED / U.S. Bureau of Labor Statistics. (2024). "Women Make Up Majority of College-Educated Labor Force."
iv. Australian Bureau of Statistics, "Education and Work, Australia, 2024," Table on non-school qualifications and domestic higher education enrollments. (https://www.abs.gov.au/statistics/people/education/education-and-work-australia/latest-release?utm_source=chatgpt.com)
v. UK Office for National Statistics & FTSE Women Leaders Review, 2024, "Gender Pay Gap" and FTSE Board Representation Reports. (https://www.ons.gov.uk/employmentandlabourmarket/peopleinwork/earningsandworkinghours/bulletins/genderpaygapintheuk/2024?utm_source=chatgpt.com)

## A7. WHEN YOU'RE BEING PLAYED — TOXIC PATTERNS TO RECOGNIZE

i. Dr John L. Lund, *How to Hug a Porcupine: Dealing with Toxic & Difficult to Love Personalities* (Deseret Book, 2008).
ii. Dr John L. Lund, "Am I a Toxic Person?" YouTube video, published July 2017. Lund is a communications psychologist with over 40 years of experience teaching interpersonal accountability and emotional literacy. His 21-question self-assessment is used in communication workshops and counseling curricula for identifying maladaptive relational behaviors.

## A9C. FIAT AND PROGRAMMABLE MONEY OVERVIEW

i. Ferguson, Niall. *The Ascent of Money: A Financial History of the World*. Penguin Press, 2008.
ii. Bernholz, Peter. *Monetary Regimes and Inflation: History, Economic and Political Relationships*. Edward Elgar Publishing, 2003.
iii. Reinhart, Carmen M., and Rogoff, Kenneth S. *This Time Is Different: Eight Centuries of Financial Folly*. Princeton University Press, 2009.
iv. Graeber, David. *Debt: The First 5,000 Years*. Melville House, 2011.

## NOTES

v. Bank of England. "The Value of the Pound Over Time." Historical Inflation Data, 2023.
vi. U.S. Bureau of Labor Statistics. Consumer Price Index Data, 1913–2023 (showing cumulative dollar purchasing power decline).
vii. Greenspan, Alan. *The Age of Turbulence: Adventures in a New World.* Penguin Press, 2007.
viii. Bonner, Bill & Wiggin, Addison. *Empire of Debt: The Rise of an Epic Financial Crisis.* John Wiley & Sons, 2006. (Describes the U.S. credit system as "a grand Ponzi" sustained by confidence and debt growth.)
ix. Grant, James. *The Trouble with Prosperity.* Times Books, 1996. (Analyzes Federal Reserve policy under Greenspan and the self-reinforcing nature of debt-fueled markets.)
x. Rothbard, Murray N. *The Mystery of Banking.* Ludwig von Mises Institute, 2008 [original 1983]. (Explains fractional-reserve banking as inherently expansionary and unstable.)
xi. Zuboff, Shoshana. *The Age of Surveillance Capitalism.* PublicAffairs, 2019.
xii. Cato Institute, *The Risks of CBDCs: Financial Privacy at Risk.* 2024.
xiii. IMF Working Paper 2023/058, *Central Bank Digital Currencies: Opportunities, Risks, and Policy Considerations.*
xiv. Bank for International Settlements (BIS) Annual Report 2023, *CBDCs and the Future of the Monetary System.*
xv. Nakamoto, Satoshi. *Bitcoin: A Peer-to-Peer Electronic Cash System.* 2008. (Original whitepaper outlining a decentralized, trustless network designed to prevent double-spending without central authority.)

## A11. THE OUTCOMES INDEX – MEASURE WHAT MATTERS

i. *UCLA Loneliness Scale, Version 3* (Russell, 1996)
ii. Ryff, C. D. (1989). *Scales of Psychological Well-Being. Journal of Personality and Social Psychology*
iii. Greenberg, L. & Watson, J. (2006). *Emotion-Focused Therapy for Depression.* APA Press

# INDEX

Symbols

75 Hard, 28, 30, 237, 385

A

Abandonment, 310, 317, 320, 385

Accountability, 19, 67, 132, 135, 186, 275, 281, 301–302, 304, 321, 346, 360, 383, 385

Adaptability, 50, 275, 279, 385

Addiction, 16, 19–20, 94, 123, 193, 233, 306, 385

Alert, 54, 95, 179, 287, 385

Alexithymia, 46, 53, 58–59, 93, 374–377, 385

Amino Acids, 162, 385

Anger, 37, 47, 64, 89, 93, 95, 99–100, 128–129, 239, 245, 269, 286–287, 294, 385–386

# INDEX

Anger Unspent, 287, 386

Anxious, 100, 111, 286, 292, 386

Authenticity, 18, 101, 276, 279, 281, 373, 386

Awareness, 7, 54, 59–61, 81, 97, 113, 115, 117, 120–121, 238, 255, 276, 278, 281, 292, 333, 338, 346, 349, 359, 364, 386, 396

## B

Balance, 146, 148, 163, 178, 194, 275–276, 278, 295, 337, 340, 386

Bandwidth, 58, 386

Beauty, 23–24, 276, 278, 291, 348, 386

Betrayal, 40, 42, 70, 77, 107, 178, 229, 293, 295, 306, 386

Blood Pressure, 346, 386

Boundaries, 20, 74, 212, 278, 281, 299, 311, 359, 386

BRIC, 5, 248, 256, 262, 355, 386

Brotherhood, 19, 67, 89, 119, 122, 125, 128, 130, 132–134, 136, 140, 210, 240, 244, 246–248, 256–258, 261–262, 297–307, 356, 377, 386

Burdened, 286–287, 386

Business, 17, 19, 27, 32, 34, 47–48, 54–57, 60, 70, 73–74, 84, 95, 97, 121, 130–132, 146–148, 151–152, 158, 165, 176, 194, 211–212, 216, 223, 226, 236, 246, 267, 270, 335, 347, 378, 386–387

Business Mentor, 57, 386

# INDEX

Business Partner, 55, 270, 387

## C

Calisthenics, 169, 387

Career, 56, 69, 143, 197, 387

Children, 114, 169, 219, 226, 228, 232, 246, 254, 359, 364–365, 387

Citizenship, 276, 387

Clarity, 20, 24, 48, 61, 78, 84, 111, 125, 151–152, 156–157, 171, 200, 203, 213, 236, 261, 276, 281–283, 289, 291, 306, 333–334, 347, 349, 353, 387

Collapse, 25, 30, 41, 70, 76, 86, 144, 146, 157, 168, 176, 183–184, 196, 200, 202, 206, 238, 244, 246, 282, 303, 317, 339, 343, 371, 387

Compassion, 24, 50, 259, 276, 278, 280, 293, 387

Competition, 177, 287, 290, 328, 387

Compounding, 56, 165, 335, 344, 387

Conflict, 328

Confused, 105, 215, 286, 291, 319, 323, 331, 387

Connection, 5, 8, 48, 50, 59, 67, 83, 100–102, 104–106, 109–112, 115–117, 120–121, 123, 139, 146, 162, 244–246, 256–257, 270, 280, 282, 288, 356, 362, 365, 376, 382, 387

Contracts, 19, 56, 73, 84, 86, 147, 236, 387

Contribution, 204, 261, 276–277, 282, 304, 334, 338, 353, 387

INDEX

Control, 63–64, 72–73, 85, 88–90, 94, 116–117, 120–122, 164, 177, 184, 208, 211, 221, 225, 229, 239, 259, 280–281, 286, 288, 291–292, 295, 305, 320–321, 324, 334, 344–346, 373–375, 377, 388

Cooperation, 277, 388

Cortisol, 161–162, 377, 388

Counsellor, 58, 129, 388

Courage, 135, 178, 203, 242, 277, 279, 290, 292, 304, 330, 348, 388

Creativity, 277, 388

Crisis, 82, 113, 138, 156, 195–196, 239, 241, 243, 248, 300, 306, 311, 330, 381, 384, 388

Curiosity, 116, 227, 276–277, 279, 291, 294, 330, 388

D

Deep Seat, 301, 306, 388

Defensive, 82, 120, 207, 270, 286, 388

Depleted, 271, 287, 388

Depressed, 40, 287, 388

Depression, 17, 28, 50, 53, 89, 125, 168, 196, 204, 373–375, 379, 381, 384, 388

Devil's Advocate, 48, 69, 209, 388

Diet, 29, 160, 379, 388

Discipline, 5, 9, 30, 50, 52, 120–121, 139, 141, 187–188, 231, 238, 242, 256, 276–277, 280–281, 304, 333, 336, 339, 341,

344, 356, 382, 388, 401

Disconnection, 28, 53, 101, 113, 244, 287, 358, 389

Disgust, 286, 293, 389

Doctor, 55, 63, 158–160, 165, 172, 183, 257, 263–265, 389

Dopamine, 110, 115, 149, 164, 365–366, 389

Drift, 7, 45, 52, 126, 234–237, 239, 241, 243–244, 246–248, 253, 260, 298, 353, 358, 369, 389

Drive, 22, 41–42, 122, 149, 159, 162, 164, 178, 208, 212, 281, 287–295, 365, 381, 389

E

Embarrassed, 287, 290, 389

Empowerment, 277, 282, 389

Equality, 277–279, 389

Equanimity, 278, 280, 389

Evolution, 51, 62, 231, 279, 353, 365–366, 379, 389

Excited, 286–287, 294, 389

Exercise, 24, 38, 43, 64–65, 87, 90, 100, 111, 136, 139, 155, 171, 183, 189, 205, 217, 232–233, 236, 253, 318, 357, 389

F

Failure, 17, 40, 46–47, 50, 59, 67, 84, 114, 129, 131, 138, 158, 165, 167, 182, 187, 202, 210, 228, 237, 247, 255, 288–289, 329, 345, 389

Faith, 70, 73, 168, 184, 278–280, 282, 389

# INDEX

Father, 19, 29, 34, 45, 47–50, 52, 64, 69, 78, 83, 121, 132, 144–145, 157, 159, 194, 208–210, 225–226, 228–230, 234, 236, 243, 245–246, 255, 273, 297, 310, 320, 347, 364, 367, 390

Father-Son, 390

Fatherhood, 222, 390

Fatigued, 286–287, 390

Fear, 36, 61, 64, 66, 83–85, 88–90, 99, 105, 119, 121–122, 124, 130, 147, 152, 156, 177–178, 181, 183–185, 203, 225, 277–278, 281, 286–287, 292–294, 339, 357, 390

Fear of Direction, 287, 390

Fearful, 286, 390

Feedback Loop, 63, 106, 161, 390

Fieldkit, 255–262, 390

Financial Freedom, 150, 260, 337–341, 346, 390

Financial Stress, 286, 390

Five Fires, 150, 260, 337–341, 346, 390

FORGE, 150, 155, 260, 297–299, 337–341, 346, 348, 390

Forgiveness, 276, 278, 390

Freedom, 83, 118, 150–154, 197, 200, 209–210, 226, 231, 234, 247, 260, 277–278, 281, 330, 333, 336–341, 344, 346–347, 362–363, 376, 390

Friend, 3, 19, 29, 37, 56–57, 93, 96, 101, 104, 106, 111, 119–120, 123, 147, 149, 217, 219, 235, 269, 318, 321, 349, 390

Frustrated, 271, 286, 328, 390

# INDEX

## G

Gaslighting, 18, 213, 375, 391

Genetics, 160, 391

Gratitude, 24–25, 52, 66, 79, 87, 100, 111, 151, 155, 217, 232, 260, 276–280, 291–292, 338–340, 367, 391

Grief, 21–22, 24, 64, 99–100, 125, 186, 216, 240, 286, 288, 391

Grieving, 268, 286, 288, 391

Grounding, 205, 287, 391, 393

Growth, 24–25, 70, 105, 155, 160, 169, 260, 275, 279–280, 289, 292, 317, 330–331, 334, 338, 341, 353, 384, 391

Guilt, 21, 47, 88, 90, 161, 232, 286, 289–290, 315, 339, 341, 391

## H

Healing, 22, 33, 89, 165, 197, 237, 320, 355, 382, 391

Health Debt, 172, 391

Heart Rate, 241, 391

Honesty, 67, 70–71, 79, 84, 90, 96, 100, 102, 118, 131, 134, 203, 277, 279, 304, 346, 356, 391

Hope, 24, 56, 94, 170, 247, 278–280, 288–289, 391

Humility, 42, 71, 121, 247, 276–277, 279, 282, 290–292, 391

## I

# INDEX

Identity, 8, 42–43, 70, 78, 125, 138, 144, 187, 196, 234, 241, 336, 339, 341, 392

Impatience, 287, 294, 392

Inclusivity, 279, 282, 392

Inherited Code, 46, 49, 245, 392

Insecurity, 286, 392

Integration, 6, 19, 25, 50, 206, 244, 260, 304, 333, 351–353, 356, 382, 392

Integrity, 17, 33, 59, 70, 147, 177, 179, 252, 276–279, 281–282, 288, 293, 315, 333, 335, 344–345, 349, 356–357, 392

Intimacy, 8, 75, 90, 102, 105–111, 113, 271, 328, 364, 366, 373, 392

Intuition Ignored, 286, 392

Investment, 146, 335, 349, 392

Isolation, 8, 50, 67, 89, 94, 135–136, 162, 288, 317, 357–358, 375, 379, 382, 392

## J

Joy, 23, 48, 69, 71, 99–100, 107, 151, 154, 236, 247, 279–280, 282, 329, 392

Justice, 278, 280–281, 288, 294, 392

## L

Lack of Support, 286, 392

Leadership, 120, 157, 208–210, 215, 217, 245, 247, 258, 359, 381–382, 392

# INDEX

Legacy, 11, 51–52, 70, 79, 114–115, 149, 230, 246, 251, 254, 359–366, 393

Loneliness, 88, 120, 124–125, 128, 182, 244, 288, 382, 384, 393

Lonely, 169, 182, 286, 288, 393

Loss of Grounding, 287, 393

Love, 3, 50, 71, 74, 85, 89–90, 93, 100, 118, 120–122, 128, 146, 161–162, 169, 184, 194, 209, 213–216, 224, 226, 232, 236, 247, 250–251, 258–259, 270–273, 278, 280, 282, 288, 294, 309–314, 316, 324–325, 327, 329–331, 344, 365, 383, 393

Loyalty, 74–76, 124, 133, 280, 282, 393

## M

Marriage, 16–17, 21, 27, 47, 55–56, 71, 82–83, 88, 94, 102–103, 106, 123–125, 135, 144, 194, 197, 209, 228, 267–268, 349, 369, 373, 376, 393

Masculinity, 120–121, 364, 371, 373–377, 393

Mechanic, 42, 129, 222–223, 393

Mentor, 57, 133, 151, 256, 304, 348, 381, 386, 393

Metabolism, 379, 393

Methylation, 163, 264, 393

Mirror, 17, 38, 65, 115, 155, 170, 177, 195, 362, 393

Mission, 77, 79, 170, 200, 260, 348–349, 393

Mitochondria, 160, 393

# INDEX

Money, 9, 23, 27, 49, 74, 79, 87, 105, 111, 124–125, 141, 143–148, 150–152, 155–156, 177, 184, 194–195, 197, 201, 211, 217, 226, 240, 250–252, 256, 259–260, 271–272, 322, 328, 333–337, 339, 341, 343–346, 361, 378, 383, 394

## N

Narcissistic, 315, 394

Nervous System, 7, 40–41, 86, 95–96, 98–99, 104, 161, 212, 237, 250, 259–260, 272, 324, 327, 331, 335–336, 339–340, 364, 394

North Star, 10, 351, 394

## O

Obligation, 147, 286, 394

Operating System, 46, 50, 56, 61–62, 79, 102, 110, 159, 182, 186, 197, 206, 243, 247, 256, 261–262, 297, 310, 358, 369, 371, 376–377, 394, 401

Optimism, 236, 280, 288, 338, 394

Organization, 246, 376, 378, 394

Overwhelmed, 96, 105, 286–287, 292, 330, 394

Oxytocin, 110, 161–162, 172, 365–366, 379–380, 394

## P

Parenting, 225, 382, 394

Partner, 55, 72–73, 94, 100, 104, 111, 116, 118, 194, 203, 240, 247, 250, 256–258, 267, 270–271, 309–314, 318, 321, 327–328, 330, 375–376, 387, 394

# INDEX

Partnership, 82, 87, 270, 394

Partnerships, 267, 395

Patience, 209, 214, 275, 280, 294, 395

Peace, 17, 58, 71, 73–76, 102, 122–123, 147, 152–153, 155, 169, 177, 208–209, 215, 243, 276, 278, 280–283, 289, 291–292, 315, 334–335, 395

People-Pleasing, 48, 50, 56–57, 75, 186, 292, 395

Performance, 17, 34, 36, 40–41, 49, 55, 106–111, 113, 115–116, 118, 120–123, 126, 128, 135, 138–140, 164, 196, 198, 209–210, 213, 216–217, 244, 246, 261, 273, 288, 290, 292, 298–299, 303, 341, 348, 355–356, 381, 395

Perseverance, 277, 280, 395

Powerlessness, 286, 295, 395

Presence, 10, 18–22, 25, 50, 59, 76–77, 79, 105–106, 109–111, 115–116, 118, 120, 123, 127–128, 132–133, 138, 152, 159, 177–178, 180, 194, 203–206, 208, 213, 216–217, 219, 227–229, 231–232, 239, 243–244, 246, 248, 251–253, 261, 273, 275, 277, 280–281, 288, 291, 295, 299–301, 303, 305, 331, 348–349, 359, 364, 382, 395, 401

Pressure, 29, 41, 55, 57–58, 64, 66, 88–91, 94, 114, 127, 132, 159, 163, 228, 245, 252–253, 278, 280, 286, 290, 300, 305, 346–347, 349, 352, 357, 386, 395, 401

Projection, 31, 124, 395

Purpose, 5, 28, 34, 50, 115–116, 121–122, 145, 151, 158, 172, 184, 191, 193, 195–197, 199–206, 231, 256, 260–261, 278, 280–282, 304, 334, 341, 347–353, 355–356, 378, 380–381, 395

# INDEX

## R

Readiness to Act, 287, 396

Recovery, 99, 165–166, 229, 371, 396

Regret, 18, 130, 182, 211, 230, 241, 286, 289, 396

Relapse, 9, 239–240, 348, 358, 396

Relationships, 50, 53, 101, 105–106, 112, 137, 143, 157, 205, 228, 259–260, 267, 382–383, 396

Relief, 29–30, 60, 109, 131, 183, 221, 279, 291, 323, 396

Resentful, 286, 294, 396

Resigned, 287, 396

Resilience, 33, 50, 52, 168, 204, 225, 245, 279, 377–378, 382, 396

Resistance to Change, 286, 396

Respect, 27, 42, 74, 196, 213, 215, 263, 277–278, 281, 301–302, 304, 306, 318, 346, 367, 396

Responsible, 286, 317, 359, 396

Restlessness, 287, 396

Revenue, 60, 361, 396

Rigidity, 275–276, 286, 293, 396

## S

S.A.L.T., 300, 396

Scar Tissue, 17, 30, 33, 105, 369, 371, 396

Self-Awareness, 120, 276, 281, 396

# INDEX

Self-Betrayal, 42

Self-Mastery, 277, 281, 396

Self-Reliance, 203, 281, 397

Separation, 17, 29–30, 175, 186, 212, 397

Serotonin, 110, 161–162, 164, 365–366, 379, 397

Service, 53, 60, 71, 161, 173, 204, 260, 263, 265, 276–277, 281–282, 303, 360, 367, 375, 379, 382, 397

Shame, 16, 19, 21, 41, 83–84, 90, 93, 96, 98–100, 103, 113, 116, 122, 129, 132, 147–148, 182–183, 185–186, 236, 241, 247, 259, 286–287, 289–290, 293, 340, 358, 397

Simplicity, 42, 78, 178, 282, 397

Sleep, 47, 54, 56, 60–61, 128–129, 144, 150, 157, 161–162, 165, 170–171, 183, 193, 234, 237, 378, 397

Son, 3, 19, 35–36, 50, 60, 69–73, 77–78, 83–84, 86, 97, 121, 159, 186, 194, 200–201, 203, 207–210, 214–216, 219, 221–222, 224, 226–227, 230, 236, 242, 246–247, 250–251, 253, 269, 376, 384, 390, 397

Sovereignty, 61, 123, 154, 339, 344–345, 397

Spirituality, 105, 282, 397

Standards, 98, 263, 278, 293, 361–362, 397

Stewardship, 151–152, 184, 275, 281–282, 334, 359, 364, 397

Streaks, 38, 397

Strength, 16, 24, 50, 52, 54, 60, 73–74, 79, 94, 100–102, 104–105, 120–121, 123, 129–130, 167, 170, 179–180, 184, 208,

INDEX

210, 239, 244, 247, 276–277, 279, 282, 303, 305, 312, 315, 397

Stress, 29–30, 53, 81, 105, 144, 151, 159–162, 164, 169, 204, 228, 241, 259, 286, 331, 338–339, 381, 390, 397

Success, 10, 20, 70, 73, 145, 191, 194–197, 206, 243, 247, 290, 348, 371, 398

Surrender, 105, 209, 268, 287, 398

System Architecture, 369, 398

System Crash, 55, 398

System Reboot, 206, 398

T

Table, 49, 56, 71, 82, 85, 126, 128–129, 132, 134–135, 138–139, 146, 149, 160, 166, 207, 211, 214, 216–217, 228, 230, 245, 248, 252, 258, 279, 297–298, 300–307, 356, 383, 398

Tasmania, 20, 250, 398

Teenager, 270, 398

Testosterone, 157, 159, 162–163, 171, 233, 264, 378–379, 398

Thyroid, 163, 171, 264, 379, 398

Toxic, 71, 120–121, 150, 246, 259, 315–325, 327, 331, 383, 398

Training, 30, 73, 97, 103, 165, 202, 234, 240, 374, 398, 401

Transformation, 177, 187, 198, 234, 398

Transparency, 345–346, 360, 398

# INDEX

Trauma, 104, 129, 209, 331, 381, 398

Trevor, 168–169, 398

Truth, 5, 7–10, 15–18, 21–23, 25, 28–29, 34–36, 55–56, 58–60, 62, 65, 67, 70–73, 75, 79, 82–86, 89–90, 95–97, 102, 104, 106–109, 111, 113, 116–117, 121–122, 124–127, 130–135, 138–141, 144, 146, 148, 151, 155, 160, 167, 179, 187, 191, 203, 209–210, 212, 214–217, 223–224, 228, 238–242, 245–246, 248, 252–253, 256, 258–259, 261, 271–272, 276–277, 279, 282, 286, 289, 292–295, 297–302, 304, 310–311, 313, 319, 321, 323, 328, 334, 349, 355–357, 365, 398–399

Truth Delayed, 399

Truth Suppressed, 286, 399

## U

Unheard, 286, 399

Unity, 277, 279–280, 282, 399

Unsupported, 286, 399

## V

Valuation, 19, 399

Values, 8, 58, 67, 69–70, 73–75, 77–79, 143, 155, 178, 201–203, 205, 242–243, 245–247, 252–253, 257, 260, 275–283, 295, 334, 341, 351, 355, 357, 375, 382, 399

Vitality, 158, 277, 279, 282, 339, 399

Vitamin D, 159, 164, 171, 264, 379, 399

Vulnerability, 50, 111, 131, 136, 215, 287, 369, 375, 399

Vulnerable, 286, 399

W

Warning Lights, 7, 54, 66, 164, 399

Wife, 3, 47, 54, 58–61, 81–82, 94, 105, 107, 150, 158, 170, 240–241, 321, 400

Wisdom, 24, 49, 74, 124, 133, 151, 210, 276–277, 279, 281–283, 367, 373, 400

Wounds, 8, 22, 24, 67, 81, 83, 86–87, 130, 212, 215, 245–247, 329, 367, 375, 400

# ALSO BY LEE POWELL

**ManOS: Rebuild the Man Beneath the Mask** The complete operating system for modern men.

**ManOS: Quick Start Guide** The core framework in 30 minutes. For men who need traction now.

**The Tactical Field Manual** Field-tested protocols for the moments that matter most — conflict, decision, pressure, repair.

**ManOS Emergency Protocol** When everything's falling apart. What to do first, second, third.

**ManOS: The 28 Meditations** An audio training series for building presence, discipline, emotional regulation, and personal coherence across every ManOS domain.

Learn more at: **getManOS.com**

**The Art** The paintings referenced throughout this book — and the wider body of work that came from the rebuild — can be found at: **leepowell.com** (keny)

www.ingramcontent.com/pod-product-compliance
Lightning Source LLC
Chambersburg PA
CBHW022025290426
44109CB00014B/751